New Concepts of Hypnosis

As an Adjunct to Psychotherapy and Medicine

Bernard C. Gindes, M.D.

Introduction by Dr. Robert M. Lindner
Foreword by Melvin Powers

D0963718

Melvin Powers
Wilshire Book Company

12015 Sherman Road, No. Hollywood, CA 91605

*Wilshire Book Company edition
is published by special arrangement
with Julian Press, Inc., N.Y.*

*Library of Congress Catalog Card Number 64-20848
Printed in the United States of America*

ISBN 0-87980-108-5

To Hanna Elizabeth
Wife—Companion—Critic

Oh magic sleep! O comfortable bird,
That broodest o'er the troubled sea of the mind
Till it is hush'd and smooth!

KEATS: *Endymion*

Contents

Contents

Contents

Contents

FOREWORD

Although the current resurgence of hypnosis has been in progress for more than a decade, misconceptions about the nature and use of this potent therapeutic modality are still so prevalent that its existence is continually threatened by misguided medical alarmists. These alarmists have discarded the early superstitions surrounding hypnosis but profess to see new dangers in its use—dangers which can be avoided only by psychiatrists oriented in "psychodynamics," a term so misused that the most prominent neuropsychiatrist in America has called it meaningless. The obvious purpose is to limit hypnosis to psychiatrists by creating fear in general practice physicians and non-psychiatric specialists. Fear is also being created in the public by "scarehead" stories released by these alarmists to mass media publications.

No other hypnotherapist, perhaps, is better able to refute the nonsense stories of those who would limit or destroy hypnosis than Dr. Bernard C. Gindes, author of *New Concepts of Hypnosis,* a pioneer in the field, who knows the true role of hypnosis and uses it as part of a multi-faceted approach to psychosomatic problems. Dr. Gindes would be the last one to say that hypnosis alone is a cure for anything, but he utilizes its proved ability to alleviate symptoms while causes are being sought. He considers it a valuable adjunctive procedure, and it was on that basis that the American Medical Association accepted it as a valid medical tool to be used electively by *all* physicians within the area of their own proficiency. It was felt, in particular, that many time-consuming methods could be speeded up by the judicious use of hypnosis, and it is to this role that Dr. Gindes devotes a large portion of his book.

It would astonish the late Dr. Robert M. Lindner, who wrote the perceptive introduction to this book a dozen years ago, to discover that many laymen still think the hypnotic state itself is a cure for a variety of emotional, behavioral and organic disorders. The writer, however, can attest to the fact that this is true. Scarcely a day passes during which he is not asked if hypnosis is a *permanent* cure for obesity, insomnia, alcoholism and other unpleasant problems. The answer, of course, is that hypnosis can be extremely helpful in these cases if combined with more orthodox techniques directed to root causes of the symptoms.

In a way, hypnosis is its own worst enemy. Some of the phenomena it produces are so dramatic that it seems logical to search for answers in the realm of the occult or supernatural. Failing to find answers outside the human sphere, many individuals attribute hypnotic results to extraordinary powers possessed by the hypnotist.

Fortunately, none of these explanations is true. If there is anything remarkable about hypnosis, it is the ability of the hypnotized person to translate suggestions into constructive actions when all other forms of therapy have failed.

The real truth about hypnosis is, as Dr. Gindes points out, that subjects hypnotize themselves. It is they who must generate the belief, expectation and imagination which results in a state which makes them receptive to whatever therapy is necessary to ameliorate symptoms and uncover causes. Inappropriate suggestions are invariably rejected and the "dangers" of hypnosis per se are simply nonexistent.

Dr. Gindes is a firm advocate of the premise that a patient with a functional malady will get well when he is convinced that he will get well, and that he will be cured at the exact moment he convinces himself that he will be cured. Dr. William S. Kroger, another pioneer hypnotherapist, puts it this way: Conviction of hypnosis is hypnosis, conviction of cure is cure.

Neither conviction of hypnosis nor conviction of cure results from one suggestion. A spiral of conviction results when the proper reaction to one suggestion increases belief and expectation to the point where further suggestions are acted upon, and it is this compounding of suggestions that leads to the ultimate conviction that cure is not only possible but certain.

Although Dr. Gindes has his own theories about hypnosis, he is extremely generous in not passing judgment on the theories of others. He ranges through all the theories about how hypnosis works, according them all a respectful hearing, but it is plain he thinks hypnosis is a psychological rather than a physiological process. A great deal of knowledge about the physiology of the brain has been uncovered in recent years, but the writer feels, as Dr. Gindes does, that the mechanics of hypnosis are psychological even though physiological phenomena result.

All in all, it is my feeling that *New Concepts of Hypnosis* can be read with profit by both professional hypnotherapists and those who seek its therapeutic aid. Dr. Gindes has used hypnosis with such conspicuous success that this book should give pause to those who would do damage to this powerful medical and psychological ally.

Melvin Powers

12015 Sherman Road
No. Hollywood, California 91605

Introduction

The late Abraham Myerson has recorded a remark of an old teacher of his who, observing that hypnosis is older by far than anesthesia, older than asepsis and antisepsis, than the bacterial theory of disease, knowledge of vitamins and psychoanalysis, said of it: "Hypnosis is like the proverbial woman of the streets . . . every so often she becomes respectable, but soon relapses into her old status."

We are now, it seems, in the midst of one of the periods when this therapeutic coquette has put away her lace panties and rouge. And while it may be regretted by a few that her allure has suffered somewhat from this, most of us hope fervently that she continues to walk with the virtuous and to shun forever those dark alleys and narrow streets where, until lately, she has plied a trade that barely kept her alive.

This book of Dr. Gindes' represents a valiant effort to insure the rehabilitation of hypnosis. One of the few such books likely to succeed, its aim is to incorporate the instrument within the respectable corpus of psychotherapeutics, there to be used as a medico-psychological adjuvant of tested and proven stability. More than a handbook for practitioners or a translation and illustration to the laity of technique, it is a sober and balanced survey of the uses and range of a powerful instrument—one of the pitifully few weapons available to men in their eternal struggle against the troubles that plague them. Unique among the many volumes that have tumbled without pause from the presses in this third great wave of concern with hypnosis as a therapeutic agent, it achieves its aim not by the exploitation of the startling and the sensational, but by an accurate rendering of the facts in the matter, and by a conscientious devotion to the two elements that mark the scientific spirit; observation and skepticism. These, indeed, make the difference. Without doubt they are the qualities which will go far toward salvaging hypnosis, toward insuring that never again will such a powerful therapeutic tool fall into discard and disuse—or, worse, pass once more into the hands of charlatans therein to be abused, misused, and maltreated.

Of the many outstanding features of this volume, one deserves special comment and emphasis. It is a feature representative of the modern orientation in hypnotherapy, a product of laborious research and thought, and, perhaps, in itself a guarantee that a permanent absorption of hypnosis into conservative psychotherapeutics will eventuate. I refer to the important implicit distinction our author makes throughout between hypnosis as a *method* and hypnosis as a *condition*. This implied differentiation is, to my mind, the theme of the book, as well as the hinge upon which the door to therapeutic success swings wide. I believe it calls for comment precisely because nowhere else, to my knowledge, has it been made so apparent.

Until the beginning of the decade just past, hypnosis was employed almost exclusively as a *suggestive method*. This is to say that the phenomenon or state was induced and then exploited for treatment purposes in the tacit expectation that the state itself would be the therapeutically effective factor. Because of this, not only were the accomplishments of hypnotherapists transient, but much that is now deplored was tolerated—from the subversion of the patient's dignity to the open employment of the most fantastic tricks and devices to promote the trance state. With the increased awareness among the psychiatric fraternity of the dynamic nature of all therapeutic processes, however, came an understanding of the necessity to abandon hypnosis as method, and to sharpen and develop the tool for use as a condition—a condition under which therapy transpires with increased chances for success. Latter-day use of hypnosis, therefore, except in certain instances of which the reader will be made aware in due time, is founded upon this insight: that the trance state should be, in essence, a carefully arranged and sensitively controlled psychological condition or "climate" allowing for those processes to become operative which are necessary for the restoration of integration to the personality. How significant this insight is, how effective it can be in the hands of the expert hypnotherapist, and what amazing vistas and possibilities it opens for treatment; these the reader will discover for himself as the following chapters unfold. But what may not be so apparent to him unless he possesses a historical grasp of the subject, is the major change this insight has wrought in the hypnotherapeutic situation as a consequence of the altered status this grants to the patient. No longer a pliant pawn to be tricked out of his complaint or perplexity, no longer a meek robot to be conjured out of his pain or distress, the patient retains his identity, his human dignity, and his self-respect. That he does so is surely a major reason why the successes of the modern hypnotherapist are long-lasting and stable.

Apart from the adeptness with which this all-important distinction between hypnosis as method and hypnosis as condition is drawn by Dr. Gindes, the volume you are about to read renders another signal service by relating hypnotherapy directly to psychoanalysis. I am particularly glad to see this done at last, and done with such forthrightness. For it is, I think, a matter of cardinal significance that the referential frame for this branch of psychotherapy be defined with clarity, and the well-spring for its evident potency in the warfare we are conducting against individual and social disorder be identified. My own view, stated many times, in print, is that there could be no hypnotherapy—in the modern sense as I have indicated in the foregoing—without psychoanalysis; that, in short, the valid utilization of hypnosis for medico-psychological purposes beyond the suggestive, temporizing level, had to await the development to maturity of psychoanalysis. This thesis is sustained, I believe, by the curious history of hypnotherapy. It will be recalled, in this connection, that the initial formulations of psychoanalysis were obtained with the aid of hypnosis, that Sigmund Freud then abandoned hypnosis in favor of free-association, and that hypnosis was recalled from limbo chiefly by psychoanalysts after their discipline had come of age.

In subsequent pages Dr. Gindes provides dramatic confirmation of psychoanalytic theory as it relates to the psychogenesis of the neuroses and psychosomatic illnesses. This, as I have inferred, should surprise none of us. To my knowledge, wherever hypnotherapy has been used with the aim of relatively permanent "cure" and not merely of transient relief, it provides continuous affirmation of psychoanalytic formulations and regularly testifies to the genuine worth of psychoanalytic theory. In the more than 10 years of my own research, reading, and practice with all varieties of hypnotherapy, I have never come across a single instance where findings ran counter to existing basic knowledge of pathogenic mechanisms or pathological processes as these appear in the clinical literature of psychoanalysis; nor, what is more, have I ever observed that the dynamics of therapy departed in any respect (save that of foreshortening) from those described by psychoanalysis. Now it can be—and has been—claimed that such observations proceed from a bias in favor of a particular theory and the subtle effects this has upon methodology and the interpretation of results. But here I would enter the serious reminder that until hypnotherapy was conducted within the framework of psychoanalysis, its results were evanescent and inconclusive.

Little remains to be said about Dr. Gindes' book that the reader will not discover for himself. It is a volume that will repay serious study by both professionals and laymen. An admirably concise and unpretentious introduction to a newly-consolidated branch of psychotherapy, it presents novel horizons to the open-minded, exploring an adjunct to medical psychology that is daily proving its effectiveness.

Dr. Robert M. Lindner

Baltimore, Maryland
August, 1951

I

Why Hypnosis?

Few fields of science have suffered as much from the encumbrances of poor definition as hypnosis. We have been much too prone to lump hypnosis in the same category in which we file our ideas on witches, warlocks and wizards; even orthodox science is inclined to approach the subject with very much the attitude of an average man investigating a haunted house; he doesn't believe in ghosts, but he definitely hopes he won't meet one!

Hypnotism, stripped of its occult raiment, is a method of therapy which seeks to dramatize thought into specific action for a definite end. Together with psychoanalysis, it is a means for acquiring information in areas that are not easily accessible by other methods. By this means we are in a position to release the negative effects of past traumatic experiences. When hypnosis is utilized for the animation of thought, we call this activation *suggestion*. It is the means by which a thought may be placed in the mind of a subject for directed or controlled reaction.

4

How powerful are these thoughts? Let us examine the potential of one thought—any given thought.

Thought, basically, is the mainspring of all human existence. It is the foundation of every idea. Bridges are built, canvases painted, books written—all as a result of thought. It is the stimulus of every aggression, of every submission. Millions of years ago it was a thought which started primitive man on the long pathway to civilization.

A thought can cause a man to give or to steal, to kill or to heal. Culprit or saint, man must be motivated by one thought or by a cluster of thoughts. We are all too familiar with the thoughts that kill. From Hamilcar to Hitler, from hatchets to Hari-Kari, the pages of history are splattered by the bloody results of destructive thoughts.

We have learned, too, that thoughts may control the functions of the human body. They can cause changes in temperature, make us perspire or break out into goose-flesh. They can alter the regularity of a heart-beat, or the rate of blood-pressure and respiration. A fear thought compels the blood to leave the brain; if severe enough, the victim faints. Psychosomatics, a branch of medical science that recognizes a mental basis for physical ailments, makes the bold assertion that eighty-five percent of illnesses, hitherto regarded as organic, are actually functional in origin; i.e., they result directly from the impact upon the body of a thought charged with emotion. This claim would seem fantastic were it not backed up by incontrovertible clinical data.

"Some People Have All the Accidents," a recent publication by an Accident Analyst, states that some people appear to be accident prone; they continually meet with disaster. He analyzed hard-luck cases, and reached the conclusion that the unlucky chap who seems to attract accidents as flowers attract bees is always one who is "emotionally disturbed;" that is, the victim of conscious or unconscious emotional conflicts who feels insecure in one way or another.

Mrs. J. and her daughter occupy a house with steep cellar steps. Mrs. J., obscurely worried because Janie is growing away from her maternal solicitude, has an argument with the girl—and shortly thereafter falls down the steps, breaking a leg. Emotional upset during her convalescence leads to a tooth infection that requires total extraction and dentures. While waiting for the dentures, her mingled rage and frustration produce glandular imbalance, and "gall trouble" results. Worry over the "gall trouble" intensifies *it* to the point where an operation is necessary. This is an actual case history of one singularly "unlucky" woman.

Jane—who was just as angry—batted balls around the tennis court, got the "rage" out of her system—and "luckily" escaped the dire consequences of the argument.

By the way, according to Cannon, anger can cause the adrenal glands to flow actively, preparing the victim for fight or flight. Suppressed, this poison can flow into the system as surely as though a "shot" of the drug were introduced hypodermically into an otherwise healthy organism. The woman who cleans house when she is irked may work some of the excess adrenalin out of her system and thus escape the effect of the "poison." The business man who constantly "stews in his own juice" (a peculiarly apt and singularly accurate phrase, incidentally!) develops ulcers!

Repressed anger, painful experiences, forgotten fears, drop into the unconscious mind—which never forgets anything—and set up conflicts there which result in functional disturbances of the system. Psychosomatic medicine recognizes this fact, and while not ignoring physical treatment of symptoms, also seeks to penetrate that unconscious mind through the study of dreams, word-associations and hypnosis to discover the traumatic cause of the disturbance. Of these methods, hypnosis is by far the most direct route to the understanding and re-education of the unconscious.

If, for instance, Mrs. J.—through hypnosis—had been induced to accept the fact that Jane was growing up, to face it and consciously come to terms with the situation, rather than attempting to ignore, repress and struggle futilely against all the signs, her medical history for that "unlucky" year might have been totally different.

Why hypnosis? If the psychosomatic surveys are correct, if it be true that suppressed fears and anxieties account directly for the functional disorders of mankind (and the proof of this fact is a matter of record!) then hypnosis easily becomes one of the most useful instruments in the hands of any physician, for these reasons:

1. It is possible, with hypnosis, to penetrate the blockade that separates man from his painful experiences. The proper guidance to conscious awareness of traumatic incidents and thoughts of the past can utterly disintegrate a neurosis.

2. Hypnotism as a suggestive technique has been known to overcome such habits as alcoholism, drug-addiction, etc., with only a modicum of distress to the patient and his family in a minimum number of treatments.

3. Its power of control over the senses can block an impulse of a nerve along its path, creating complete anaesthesia of any given part of the body so entirely that pain can be controlled for surgery.

4. Hypnotism is a direct route to the unconscious. It is a scientific telescope that can penetrate the deepest crevices of the functioning mind, dissolve the nightmare of jumbled fears, provide a key to the causes of damaging emotions, and, above all else, CURE!

The war aftermath has shown the value of this direct and hitherto improperly evaluated method, because in addition to its effectiveness, it shortens the time element in the treatment of war neuroses.

John B. was brought back from overseas dumb and blind. We could find no physical cause for his difficulty. He had been picked up from the battlefield in that state, and in that state he remained, impervious to psychoanalysis, unresponsive to any other treatment.

Hypnosis was attempted as a last resort. Under Medium Sleep (see Chapter VIII) his speech returned, and a distressing story was disclosed. He and two close friends had been hiding in a shell-hole, slightly though not seriously wounded. Jim was unable to walk, and John and Joe tossed a coin to see who would climb out to get help. John lost, was boosted out, and scouted around for a stretcher-bearer. When they returned to the hole, only fragments of men remained; it had suffered a direct hit. He blamed himself for Joe's death because he had tossed the coin; he blamed himself for Jim's death because had he located the bearers sooner, both men might have escaped.

Unconscious mechanisms appear to be punishing him for these "murders" by denying him sight and speech. (The question of why sight and speech were affected rather than hearing or walking is one that complete psychoanalysis might have answered. In this case the point was unimportant, as it had no relevance to his full recovery nor caused later trouble.)

While he was under hypnosis, the suggestion was given him that the fortunes of war were responsible for the death of his buddies, not he; that his conscience was clear, and that upon waking he would have no recollection of the event or of his illness other than the mere fact that he had been sick from his wound, and that, above all, *he had nothing for which to reproach himself.*

One session did it. He woke, well on the road to recovery, and as soon as his flesh wounds healed, was able to rejoin his outfit.

Without hypnosis, this chap would probably be an unhappy case in a mental ward today, an expense to his government and a heartache to his family. Through hypnosis, properly administered, he is a useful member of society, a happy husband and proud father!

In the routine of office practice, we find the case of Mrs. B., age 64, who had suffered the torment of alcoholism for a number of years. She was a grandmother; had had sanitarium care so many times that she had lost count. I placed her in hypnotic trance; when she proved sufficiently accessible to suggestion, I facilitated her "mental return" to her first experience with alcohol, which had occurred seventeen years prior to this office visit. With careful prompting she recalled an experience, the understanding of which, in time, led to the alleviation of her illness. On this occasion she had returned home from a rather gay party where liquor had been plentiful. She did not particularly relish her imbibing, nor did she enjoy its consequent effect. Her husband, who had abstained from drinking, expressed loud annoyance with her behavior. It was the first time that she had succeeded in upsetting him, and the fact that he was emotionally overcome gave her no end of gratification, for previously he seemed unaffected by her antics. Thereafter, whenever she wished to "get his dander up," she would resort to alcohol. In time, the original motivation disappeared from consciousness, only to be used by the unconscious mechanism to satisfy the same ends. When finally she did awaken to the realization that there was no further cause for her drinking, as her husband had passed away a few years before, she accepted the situation and had no further use for alcohol.

Another patient, typical of many in his class, was Mr. L., a grown-up "blue baby." He had been born with a defective heart and survived only by exercising the greatest of care. The condition was serious enough to bar him from all games, sports, excitement, and even from climbing stairs or a steep hill. His doctor contacted me; the man's appendix was bad and an operation necessary. His heart condition precluded the use of anaesthesia, yet without it he was almost certain to die of shock.

Again we resorted to the Medium Sleep, telling the patient that on Wednesday, the sixth, his right side would become entirely devoid of feeling; at three o'clock he would go into a deep sleep (Depth Hypnosis) for seventy-two hours; that whatever happened to his body during that sleep would be beneficial and need not in the least concern him; that when he wakened he would feel rested, without pain, and well on the way to complete recovery. With Mr. L., we gave daily conditioning sessions for two weeks before the operation. It was successful, and today, he is going about his quiet business, as well as his cardiac trouble will ever let him be!

An interesting case was Mrs. H., whose obstetrician feared that she would "break down" in anticipation of labor. His fears were not unfounded, for when she presented herself for examination she was at the point of hysteria. In the course of conversation we learned that her mother had died during labor, and she was certain that she would be similarly affected. To add to her difficulties she manifested poor tolerance for ether, and displayed an intense dread of hypodermic needles. Our experience with her and many others led me to conclude that scientific hypnosis has a very definite place in any childbirth.

We conditioned her with weekly hypnotic sessions throughout pregnancy. By means of post-hypnotic suggestion she was able to react favorably to the usual pains of labor without anaesthesia! When the time came, she experienced no pain; assisted her doctor by "bearing down" with each contraction of the uterine muscle, laughing and chatting the while. She found the experience thoroughly enjoyable, rose from bed the same day, and resumed her household routine shortly thereafter.

Later experiments, without the complications her emotional condition presented, show that routine may be resumed the fourth day after delivery at the very latest. Through hypnosis, fear is eliminated, and in the normal birth, the hypnotist can so pre-condition the patient for loss of the sense of pain but retention of full consciousness that he need not even be present at the childbirth. This factor is particularly appreciated by the sensitive woman who is embarrassed by the presence of strangers at that time.

It is regrettable that in these examples, as in most cases referred to the practitioner, hypnosis is appealed to only as a "last resort." Its use early in the matter, either alone or in conjunction with other therapeutic methods, can provide an effective means of recovery, sparing both the patient and his family many hours of suffering and worry.

As the findings of study, research and experiment accumulate, scientific hypnotism will take its place as an invaluable tool for both medicine and psychotherapy.

2

The History of Hypnotism

A. EARLY BEGINNINGS

The question arises at this point: why, if hypnosis is such a valuable tool, has it been neglected by the medical profession for so long?

The answer is available: we know that in the evolution of all scientific learning one factor remains constant: *superstition precedes knowledge.*

Magical alchemy preceded modern chemistry; the "occult science" of astrology was the forerunner of astronomy; the evolution from "witch-doctor" to physician required centuries for its accomplishment. Actually, it seems that any idea passes through three phases before it is accepted. First it is "impossible"; then it becomes either "sacrilegious" or "preposterous"; and finally it becomes so axiomatic that "everybody knew it all the time."

Hypnosis stalled in the second stage, largely due to the antics of its early experimenters. Whether lust for power, inordinate exhibitionism or greed for money motivated the charlatan tactics of these men, the fact remains that their practices relegated the science of hypnotism to the category of an orgiastic rite, practiced only by wizards who had entered into the traditional satanic pact. Scholarly investigators who dared honest examination of its undoubted phenomena were excoriated instantly by both church and science.

At the moment, hypnosis is having its third renascence. In the beginning it was a religious rite. From the temples of Isis, Nature Goddess of the Nile, Egyptologists have copied numerous engravings showing worshippers in poses unmistakably characteristic of hypnotic trance. Priest-kings of the Two Lands used entranced virgins as message-bearers from the gods, and as late as Biblical times, the High Priests of Khem utilized mass hypnotism to still the mutterings of the people.

A Greek engraving (928 B.C.) shows Chiron, most renowned physician of his time, placing his pupil Aesculapius under hypnosis. The Delphic Oracle and other contemporary oracles all operated under hypnosis, either self-induced or assisted by drugs or volcanic fumes.

From every country, from every period of man's history, we find documents, paintings, sculptures and bas-reliefs attesting to the universality of the practice. In fact, there is adequate reason to believe that hypnosis in some form has appeared spontaneously and almost concurrently wherever human beings have congregated.

Western civilization saw the practice fall completely into disuse, save for demon worshippers and heretics, until, in the eighteenth century, it blossomed forth as a "new science" and enjoyed again a temporary respectability. Medicine was failing miserably to meet the challenge of the new industrial age with its accompanying diseases. When medicine kills more patients than it cures, the hopeless multitude turns from the orthodox practitioner to the charlatan for relief. A few doctors drifted away from orthodox therapies in a wild search for a new cure-all that would lure their missing patients back again. Some went so far as to invent fantastic gadgets designed to accomplish equally fantastic cures. The dawning of the eighteenth century found medicine still largely a matter of superstition, but the masses were less credulous than they once were, and "cures" that had worked earlier failed to serve.

B. MESMER

Frederick Anton Mesmer could not have come upon the scene at a more opportune time. In 1773 he presented the Faculty of Medicine of the University of Vienna with his thesis on "The Influence of the Stars and Planets as Curative Powers." In this peculiar manuscript, Mesmer claimed that the moon, sun and stars affected the human organism through an invisible fluid which he termed "Animal Magnetism"; that this subtle substance could be derived from a magnet or lodestone, and that all cellular structures had an affinity for the magnet. Shortly after he presented his theory, young Dr. Mesmer experimented with Father Hell, a Jesuit priest, who claimed to perform marvelous cures by means of magnetized objects. At once Mesmer recognized the similarity of contentions, and he himself attempted the use of the magnet. Soon the journals published stirring accounts of Mesmer's success with apparently hopeless cases.

Why Mesmer left Vienna at the height of his glory remains a mystery. Perhaps the Church intervened or the Emperor objected. However, free-thinking Paris offered a haven where he might continue his experiments, free from interference of Church, State or jealous colleagues. His success was boundless; thousands of invalids wore the proverbial pathway to his door. Mesmerism became the topic of every *salon* conversation; one was simply *no-one,* until he had been mesmerized.

As Mesmer's popularity grew, he was forced to devise a

form of mass-production in order to treat the hordes who sought his aid. He built a tremendous *baquet,* into which he poured "magnetized" water. The scene is graphically depicted by Deleuze, Librarian of the Royal Botanical and Zoological Gardens, who wrote:

> "In one room, under the influence of rods issuing from tubs filled with large bottles—the said rods applied upon different parts of the subjects' bodies—the most extraordinary scenes took place daily. Sardonic laughter, piteous moans and torrents of tears burst forth on all sides. The subjects were thrown back in spasmodic jerks, the respirations sounded like death rattles, and terrifying symptoms were exhibited. Suddenly, the actors of these strange performances would frantically or rapturously rush towards each other, either rejoicing and embracing, or thrusting away their neighbors with every appearance of horror.
>
> "Another room was padded, and presented a different spectacle. There, women beat their heads against the padded walls or rolled on the cushion-covered floor in fits of suffocation. In the midst of the panting, quivering throng, Mesmer, dressed in a lilac coat, moved about, halting in front of the most violently excited, and gazing steadily into their eyes, while he held both their hands in his, bringing the middle fingers into immediate contact to establish the communication. At another moment he would, by a motion of open hands and extended fingers, operate with the great current, crossing and uncrossing his arms with wonderful rapidity to make the final passes." *

(*En passant,* is it surprising that the world of the nineteenth and twentieth centuries has been disposed to dismiss Mesmer and all his works as "stuff and nonsense"?)

As his popularity grew, the original mission—that of extending relief to the unfortunate—perished in his very success, for Mesmer's Haven became a showplace for those in-

---

* Deleuze, F., *Histoire Critique du Magnétisme Animal,* Hippolyte Baillière, Paris, 1819, Vol. II, p. 34.

toxicated with his sensationalism. Magnetism was no longer associated with curing the ills of the afflicted; it became an extravaganza, a three-ring circus. All that was lacking was the Barnum to exploit it! It is no wonder that to this day, Mesmerism is associated with quackery in the eyes of science!

Mesmer's downfall is a pathetic story with serious consequences, for his unorthodox practices resulted not only in ostracism for the man, but in complete rejection of the work which he had introduced. In desperation, he begged for a hearing before the Academy of Science in Paris that a proper evaluation might be made of his experiments. The Academy, with much reservation, decided that the "Charlatan" should have one more chance. In 1784, they appointed an official committee consisting of three renowned scientists, Lavoisier, Bailly, and our own Benjamin Franklin. These learned gentlemen dipped their hands in Mesmer's magnetic bath, but, not expecting such, they naturally did not react with convulsions, hysterics or fits. Finally, they recorded their bitter conclusions: Mesmer was a fraud, the hysterical outbursts had been occasioned by the imaginations of the patients; and all others had been so affected because of conscious imitation and a desire to be "in the swim."

Mesmer had lost the faith of the country which had adopted him. He returned to Vienna to die a discredited pauper, with only an amazing past to keep his memory alive.

C. THE MARQUIS DE PUYSÉGUR

For a number of years the science which suffered so much at Mesmer's hands was forgotten. The afflicted returned to orthodox treatment, and hypnotism became a lost art. However, the influential Marquis de Puységur, a former student of Mesmer's, revived some of the ideas which had sunk into oblivion. While the Marquis was living in luxurious retirement on his estates near Soissons, he amused himself by magnetizing peasants from surrounding villages after much the same fashion as his master.

During his haphazard experiments, he observed a curious phenomenon unknown during his association with Mesmer. A young peasant named Victor had become afflicted with a serious lung condition, accompanied by excruciating pains in the thorax and lumbar regions. Upon magnetization, the young man fell into light, restful sleep, marked by a lack of demoniacal convulsions. While in this peculiar state, his lips parted, and he spoke. De Puységur at once recognized the magnitude of this new phenomenon, and proceeded to experiment with it. He easily converted his patient's thoughts to peace and relaxation, and suggested the abolition of pain, and "peace. . . . peace. . . . peace. . . ." Victor responded instantly; his pain left him, and in its place he imagined that he was floating in the "arms of Magna Mater. . . . Great Mother. . . . cool waves lapping against him. . . . white arms of sea nymphs embracing him. . . . as in a dream, he was one with the Mighty Ones. . . ."

However, de Puységur was impressed by a much more remarkable feat. Victor, in his normal state anything but brilliant, exhibited astounding intellect during trance. He seemed to have the power to step into other people's minds and tell their thoughts. He even outlined the treatment necessary for his own cure. . . . and, more astounding, upon administration of this treatment, he effected complete recovery!

News of this miracle spread rapidly, and the demanding throng clamored for de Puységur's attention. His château became a mecca for the afflicted, and he repeated his experiments again and again, always with the same success. Naturally he was elated, and wrote to the Academy of Medicine, "My head is turned with joy, when I see the good I am doing."

The science of hypnotism owes a tremendous debt to de

Puységur, for he was the first to demonstrate "artificial som-nambulism" as opposed to the hysterical outbursts occasioned by Mesmer. While the latter's methods caused storms of weeping, convulsions and fainting, de Puységur induced calm, peaceful sleep, which left the patient placid, content, and in a previously unexperienced state of relaxation upon awakening. Mesmer sought the spectacular; de Puységur shunned it. Whether Mesmer even knew of this induction of light sleep is uncertain, but if he was aware of this state, he certainly made no use of it himself, nor did he impart the knowledge to his students.

"Artificial somnambulism," de Puységur's discovery, demonstrated the first contention of hypnotism; namely, that a state analogous to sleep can be produced artificially in an entirely awake individual. Further, it showed that during this state the thoughts and actions of the patient are to a great degree subservient to the direction of the practitioner. Although his original contributions are of the utmost importance to the world of science, de Puységur weakened his work by mingling his accepted facts with phenomena he claimed to have witnessed but was unable to prove—phenomena such as thought transference and clairvoyance.

D. FATHER GASSNER

Simultaneously with the acclaim de Puységur was winning with his experiments, Father Gassner, a Jesuit priest, was creating a furor in Southern Germany with spectacular methods and even more spectacular cures. Accounts of his achievements wear the coloring and glory of the old Arabian Nights.

Picture a room, black-draped, with one feeble light flickering. The patient is ushered in and seated. Within a few minutes the curtain draws back of its own accord, and the imposing Father Gassner enters, arms outstretched, bearing aloft a diamond-studded crucifix. He peers searchingly into the eyes of the sufferer. . . . Suddenly, his thunderous voice echoes and re-echoes about the room:

"Detur mihi evidens signum praestigae praeter naturalis, praecipio hoc in nomine Jesu!" his deep voice intones. Soon the patient falls into a deep sleep, and with a mighty crescendo, the Father's voice banishes the "evil spirits" from the victim's body.

One of his recorded séances relates of his fantastic methods employed to transfix a young girl. She reacted instantly, and he commanded, "Agitetur bracium sinistrum." Her left arm began to move slowly in answer, and soon it gained impetus, faster and faster, when Father Gassner boomed, "Cesset!" The arm lost motion and dropped limply to her side. Then it was suggested that she was going mad; her face contorted horribly and she leaped around the room on all fours, displaying all the symptoms of mania. "Pacet!" thundered the voice, and she stood quiescent, as though nothing had happened. Father Gassner commanded her to speak Latin, and she replied, *in that language,* that she could not.

Finally came the climax of all his experiments. He told her that her pulse was becoming very slow. A physician of the town who witnessed this performance felt the girl's wrist and confirmed the fact that the pulse was truly beating more slowly. Satisfied that his visitors were impressed, Father Gassner suggested that the pulse leap and beat more quickly. In a few minutes, upon examination, it was found that the pulse rate had risen fifty beats per minute beyond normal.

Then the priest made a strange test. He told his patient to lie quietly; her pulse would beat slower and slower, and finally cease. Her muscles would relax completely and she would die for a short time. He informed her that she need not fear; his powers would restore life to her body. Beads of perspiration appeared on the physician's forehead as he knelt to take her pulse. His face was ashen as he pronounced her—

DEAD! With this, Gassner smiled confidently and commenced to utter the words which would restore her to consciousness. Her pulse began to beat; muscles jerked spasmodically and she sat up happily, rejoicing that she had been blessed by a miracle. She was reborn; her pains had left and she was cured of all her ills.

Father Gassner was not merely a clever hypnotist; he knew how to capitalize on the superstitions of his ignorant flock to command respect for himself and adoration of his Church as the true vehicle of miracles.

E. BRAID

Doctor James Braid, a prominent Manchester surgeon, is the father of the scientific evaluation of hypnotism. In 1841, he was the first doctor to challenge the mystic claims of Mesmer and his followers. A thorough sceptic, his very scepticism led him astray, for at first, after watching a public demonstration by a M. Lafontaine, he dismissed the phenomenon as an insult to scientific intelligence. However, his curiosity had been aroused and he attended another demonstration. This time the magnetizer proved to his entire satisfaction that the subject was completely under control. Braid pondered the problem. He dismissed all the "magic fluid" theories as old wives' tales. . . . but, having eliminated the explanation, he found the phenomenon present. After much meditation, he concluded there must be a physical cause—that a continued tiring of the sense of sight could paralyze optic nerve centers, causing a condition not unlike sleep. Returning home, he asked a friend to fix his gaze upon the neck of an ornamental vase. To Doctor Braid's delight, the subject responded, and fell into sound slumber. Next he experimented upon his wife, with similar findings.

In these meager tests lies the indisputable origin of scientific hypnotism. First and foremost, Braid was a scientist and experimentalist; there was nothing of the charlatan in his makeup. He was the first to stipulate that hypnotic sleep could be induced by physical agents, and gave us the term "hypnotism," a word he himself coined from the Greek *hypnos,* meaning "sleep."

He won little recognition from his conservative English colleagues, but his articles stirred the interest of French investigators. A Professor Azam of Bordeaux was particularly impressed. He duplicated the experiments and published his findings, stressing the claim that it was possible to produce anaesthesia during hypnotic sleep, under which surgery could be performed with a minimum of pain and shock.

Curiously enough, Braid's work, ignored in England, was recognized in France . . . while Azam, his French disciple, found himself disparaged in France and widely acclaimed in England! In that country, several distinguished scientists not only accepted Azam's findings, but utilized them as a basis for further experimentation.

The physiological concept of hypnosis was formulated during these experiments; namely, that the excess nervous energy not consumed by processes of thought during the sleeping state had an accumulative action; therefore, hypnotic sleep resulted from an overabundance of unused nerve-force. The contention was that an excited or stimulated sense caused an inhibition of the actions of a special portion of the brain, and by so doing, a mental impression could be produced by suggestion, of equal intensity to that of one perceived by the five senses under real circumstances.

It would be unfair to credit only Braid and Azam with those principles of hypnotism that are scientifically tenable today. By doing so, we would detract from the experimenters who followed them. Each one offered his professional reputation in sacrifice to an attempt to spread a doctrine which a backward world was not yet ready to accept. Each suffered charges of quackery and charlatanism from his contemporaries. Nevertheless, hypnotism has survived to boast of the famous scientists who carried its banners.

F. BURCQ

In 1876, a French physician, Doctor Burcq, was critically ill. Suspecting that death was near, he summoned a servant and dictated a curious letter to his friend and teacher, the eminent physiologist, Claude Bernard.

He wrote that before dying he wished to ascertain the validity of certain conclusions drawn from the observations of twenty-five years of medical practice. Bernard, who was also the President of the French Biological Society, quickly responded by appointing a commission to investigate his friend's findings. Outstanding on the list of investigators were the celebrated Doctor Luys, who later invented the revolving mirror for the production of somnambulistic sleep, and Doctor Charcot, of neurological fame. After several years of experimentation and research in the clinic, the commission published a favorable report and consequent acceptance of Burcq's theory, which concerned the treating of the sick with metals.

The way he evolved this curiously twisted idea must not be overlooked; no history of hypnotism could be complete without it:

While treating a hysterical woman in his office, Burcq was called out on an emergency case. Realizing that he dared not release his patient to roam the streets in her emotional state, he locked her in the office. On his return, he heard a sudden thump, as though a body had fallen to the floor. He dashed up the stairs and into his office, to find the patient crumpled on the floor in a cataleptic state. Contemplating this reaction in the light of his knowledge of magnetism, his eyes lit upon a highly polished brass doorknob. Was this the answer? Could it be?

The following day, he repeated the conditions, except for covering the shiny knob with a strip of cloth, and again left the office, locking the girl in. Allowing a similar length of time to elapse, he returned. . . . to find no reaction. His patient offered no explanation; yesterday she had gone to sleep; today she had not.

Pondering the situation, Doctor Burcq decided that further experiment along these lines was indicated. At the Salpêtrière Hospital, which was the center for neurological experimentation, Burcq submitted a great many patients to his knob of polished brass, with unquestionable response. Using brass and other metals, each with its own distinguishable action, he was able to bring relief to many strange cases. In one notable case, he returned sensitivity to a portion of the body which had become anaesthetic. From these experiments, he developed a supposedly effective therapy which he named "metaloscopy"—a science dealing with the supposed therapeutic action of metal surfaces upon the nervous system.

Burcq's experiments were later modified to include the direct application of metals to diseased parts. Iron became the metal of choice for drawing out pustular lesions; lead placed over the heart was the specific metal in anemia and in morbid cardiac function. When these substances were applied directly to the site of lesion and allowed to remain with moderate pressure for periods ranging from a few days to several weeks, depending upon the severity of the pathological process, spectacular functional changes were presumably manifested. The question of whether identical changes might have been effected in time, without the application of metals, due primarily to the body's own curative powers, is controversial.

To this very day, Burcq's theory is perpetuated by itinerant magnetizers who acquire notoriety with shining pendulums which they use for locating the "centers" of illness and effecting cures.

G. CHARCOT

During the investigation of Burcq's theories, Charcot, the neurologist, became enthralled by the findings. The professor was positive that metalotherapy was the answer to a physician's prayer; the fate of the patient rested on the correct use of metals in treatment. Upon completion of the formal inquiry on Burcq's behalf, he embarked upon experiments of his own.

In 1878, Charcot and his pupils at the Academy succeeded in proving that there are several stages of hypnotic sleep; that the hypnotized subject is capable of manifesting varying symptoms in each stage. This was the first attempt at scientific classification of hypnotic phenomena, and it is fortunate for the later history of the science that Charcot adopted it, for he was a man who was eminently sound in his own line. His treatise, presented for the French Academy of Sciences exactly four years after his introductory experiments, was entitled, "On the Distinct Nosography of the Different Phases Comprised Under the Name of Hypnotism," and is still regarded as an academic classic in the field.

Although the majority of Charcot's conclusions have been verified, his metallic theory has been ignored by investigators of this century because of their inability to duplicate his experiments.

The origin of his preoccupation with the possibilities of metalotherapy makes an interesting story. One day, while practicing at the Salpêtrière, a group of English doctors paid him a visit. While Charcot showed them through the hospital, they became engaged in a lively discussion concerning the differences in nervous symptoms as they exist in peoples in various parts of the world. The professor took issue, arguing that loss of sensation of a part of the body is the same, whether it occurs in England, France or Timbuctu, and, to prove his point, he pierced the arm of a patient afflicted with this type of insensibility. To Charcot's astonishment and to the amusement of the visitors, the patient screamed wildly. It seems that during Charcot's absence, Burcq had attached a gold plate to the patient's arm, and the power of sensation had reappeared! That experience convinced Charcot, once and for all, of the value of metalotherapy.

Other hypnotists gained notoriety by exploitation of Charcot's fame. Curious crowds mobbed the lecture halls for a glimpse of hypnotism in action. Notable among these public exhibitors were a Belgian, Donato, and a Dane, Hanson, both of whom stimulated close government supervision by their antics with voluntary subjects. Although the authorities attempted to intervene by prohibiting such exhibitions, public feeling ran too high to permit enforcement of the new laws.

A complete historical presentation of hypnotism would require many volumes and must needs cover all the experiments that caused these researchers to arrive at their conclusions. We would have to trace the work of Liébault and Bernheim in their Nancy School, Janet and his experiments at the Salpêtrière; yet to tell of these and to omit the names of others whose work has been overlooked or forgotten would be unfair to all of these scientific adventurers.

Suffice it to say that Professor Charcot found hypnosis at a crucial period in its history and rescued it from an almost certain grave. His essays and lectures at the French Academy of Sciences received world attention, for he was too much of an authority in his own field to be ignored by even the greatest sceptics. He blazed a trail which gave impetus to many explorers of the mind. They followed in his footsteps a little way, only to branch off into their own pioneering.

REFERENCES

BERNHEIM, H., *Suggestive Therapeutics,* translated by C. A. Herter, G. P. Putnam's Sons, New York, 1899.

BINET, A. AND FÉRÉ, C., *Animal Magnetism,* D. Appleton & Co., New York, 1888.

BRAID, J., *Neurypnology,* George Redway, London, 1899.

BRAMWELL, J. M., *Hypnotism,* Wm. Rider & Sons, London, 1913.

CHARCOT, J. M., *Oeuvres Complètes, Metallotherapie et Hypnotisme,* Bourneville et E. Brissaud, Paris, 1890.

CHARCOT, J. M., *Lectures on the Diseases of the Nervous System,* The New Sydenham Society, London, 1877.

FAHNESTOCK, W. B., *Statuvolism or Artificial Somnambulism,* Religio-Philosophical Publishing House, Chicago, 1871.

FISHBOUGH, W., *Library of Mesmerism and Psychology,* Fowler & Wells, New York, 1852.

TESTE, A., *A Practical Manual of Animal Magnetism,* translated by D. Spillan, Hippolyte Baillière, London, 1843.

TOWNSHEND, C. H., *Facts in Mesmerism,* Hippolyte Baillière, London, 1844.

3

Theoretical Aspects

No one can claim complete immunity to suggestion. That fact is the cornerstone of modern advertising. The typical radio program demonstrates a trick of disguised elementary hypnotism specifically designed to lure us into buying an advertised product.

Upon analysis, this is the procedure. Tired from a busy day, we relax into easy chairs, click the knob of our radios, and wait for our favorite comedian. Soft or stimulating music comes through the loudspeaker; the favorite comedian comes on, and soon has us chuckling heartily. In the very middle of that relaxing chuckle, we hear a jingle praising—for example —a soap. Quickly, before we can build up a healthy resistance to the suggestion, our comedian is back and we are laughing again. The chances are largely in favor of our buying that soap. . . . not tomorrow. . . . not necessarily next week. . . . but, eventually, we shall all *try* that soap! Were it not so, our comedian would soon lose his sponsor and go off the air entirely!

If humanity's imagination did not react favorably to suggestion in advertising, we should have few radio programs, fewer magazines, and fewer, if any, newspapers!

Just such favorable reaction to suggestion is what the therapist strives to accomplish with his subject. He recognizes that he cannot expect a subject to carry out a suggestion while in full command of his reasoning faculty. A suggestion might easily be ignored because of argumentative resistance on the part of the subject. For instance, if a man fully awake is told that he cannot close his eyes no matter how hard he may try, he will consciously rebel at the absurdity and promptly shut his eyelids to prove you wrong! Thus, the therapist must partially inactivate, temporarily, the center of conscious reason in the individual so that he will be more prone to accept a suggestion of this sort without resistance.

What is this mind and what particular functions are relegated to it?

Every organism must adapt itself to changing conditions. When protoplasm—even in its lowly protozoan form—is stimulated, a response must occur. This response is the organism's reaction to alterations in its environment. We can only speculate that the higher functions of man are evolutionary modifications of characteristics that prevail in all living substances. Man's environment with its myriad of stimuli is infinitely more complex than the media which surround the protozoan form of life. As a product of zoological evolution he was caused to expand to a level of consciousness by the necessities promulgated by an ever-changing environment, for only in this way could he become integrated in the continuity of nature. In the light of present day knowledge one can only surmise that awareness is the product of human growth—that the organic has been superimposed upon the inorganic, the biological upon the organic, and the psychobiological upon the biological, with consciousness as its probable outcome. Mind, therefore, is a complex function through which man adjusts and responds to stimuli of a changing environment.*

It would seem evident that inhibition of conscious reason plays a role in the induction of hypnosis, and is one important factor desired in this state. Experimentation at the Nancy School in France postulated the theory that acuity of reason is the greatest hindrance to the accomplishment of deep hypnosis. This led to a belief which appears logical on the surface, and yet which, upon closer examination, presents a curious twist of error.

The theory was accepted that if the senses could be blocked off, the conscious mind would no longer draw external perceptions, and its function would be inhibited. This conclusion was reached after controlled surveillance of a patient in a French hospital who had been deprived of all his senses by an unfortunate accident. He lay in constant coma because there were no sensory stimuli powerful enough to arouse him. The Nancy experimenters concluded that because the sensory supply was cut off, the conscious mechanism could offer no resistance. Later Heidenhain, whose propositions are widely accepted today for lack of something better, phrased the theory more technically. He claimed that hypnosis is caused by a "monotonous gentle stimulation of a sense, causing inhibition of the cortical cells, with consequent suspension of the higher cerebral function."

As evidence is presented, I believe that we shall discover that hypnosis depends upon no such physical device; that hypnosis cannot be produced merely by the stimulation of a sense.

* Noyes, A. P., in his *Modern Clinical Psychiatry,* W. B. Saunders Co., Philadelphia, 1948, p. 6, has written an interesting evaluation of the development of consciousness. There is much in the literature of psychology in all its branches which offers definitions of conscious and unconscious processes. I refrain here from discussion of this complex subject except as it relates to the application of hypnosis.

In the light of our definition of consciousness it would be difficult to reconcile a suspension of higher cerebral function.

A. HYPNOSIS IS NOT SLEEP

First of all, let us eliminate the commonest fallacy held by doctor and layman alike. Hypnotism is *not* the induction of a state of sleep. Hypnosis and sleep actually bear slight resemblance to each other, and an attempt to confine hypnotic phenomena within the limits of the sleep state would prove not only impossible but absurd.

Broadly defined, hypnotism is an induced condition, in some few respects similar to normal sleep, in which the suggestibility of an individual is increased.

No definition can be complete that does not mention the motivational and behavior factors of this phenomenon.

Warren's *Dictionary of Psychology* provides a workable description, although its precision leaves much to be desired. Here hypnosis is defined as follows: "An artificially induced state, usually (though not always) resembling sleep, but physiologically distinct from it, which is characterized by heightened suggestibility, as a result of which certain sensory, motor, and memory abnormalities may be induced more readily than in the normal state." *

De Puységur seems to have been the first hypnotist to associate the hypnotic state with sleep as a result of his experiments with his subject, Victor. During these "séances," he observed that this boy presented all of the characteristics of a sleep-walker. He could open his eyes in this state, talk, although the speech was slurred, and carry out the normal actions of a waking state. De Puységur regarded this state of "magnetism" as an artificially induced somnambulism.

* Warren, H. C. (Ed.), *Dictionary of Psychology*, Houghton Mifflin, Boston, 1934.

While opinion varies among authorities on the question of whether or not hypnosis may be regarded as a sleep state, Braid's classical description offers an expression to the contrary:

"The most striking proofs that it is different from common sleep are the extraordinary effects produced by it." Here he goes on to describe the symptoms of common sleep and their comparison with symptoms paramount in the hypnotic state: in common sleep, "the limbs become flaccid from cessation of muscular tone and action. . . . In the hypnotic state, induced with the view to exhibiting what I call hypnotic phenomena . . . [the arms and legs] are maintained in a state of tonic *rigidity* for any length of time I have thought it prudent to try."

In another instance, he claims:

"Of the circumstances connected with the artificial sleep which I induce, nothing so strongly marks the difference between it and *natural* sleep as the wonderful power the former evinces in curing many diseases of long standing, and which had resisted *natural* sleep."*

The research psychologists, Wible and Jenness, concluded after exhaustive experiments with electrocardiographic and respiratory studies that the heart and lung action during hypnosis was more similar to that of the waking state than to that of normal physiological sleep. Nygard, measuring cerebral circulation during waking, sleeping, and hypnotic states, surmised that blood circulation during hypnosis resembled that of the waking state rather than that of sleep. Bass found that the patellar reflex was decreased during actual sleep, but was very much the same in both the hypnotic and the wide-awake states.

The electroencephalographic findings in my own psy-

* Braid, J., *Neurypnology*, George Redway, London, 1899, p. 126.

chological laboratory show that the recordings of brain waves during the hypnotic and waking states are noticeably similar, but evidence a remarkable difference in the physiological sleep state.

B. PHYSIOLOGICAL CHANGES NOTED IN HYPNOSIS

There is a plethora of evidence to the effect that the sleep-like state of hypnosis bears close proximity to real physiological depression; that in many instances it resembles the states brought on by the use of large amounts of alcohol, narcotics or anaesthetics, and that it contains many of the symptoms noticed in conditions of general fatigue. Observation of the hypnotized subject reveals signs of complete lethargy. We note an abnormal relaxation with slower, somewhat heavier, breathing. From outward indications he appears to be in actual sleep. He responds listlessly, his arms drop limply by his sides, the head falls on his chest as though its weight had become unbearable. His features show complete lack of expression, and soon this stolidity deprives him of aggression. His usual activity becomes passivity.

Of special interest are the physiological changes which ensue during these manifestations. Shaffer and Dorcus reported that there is a slowing of the pulse at the advent of the hypnotic state, together with a decrease in blood pressure. Waldon found a sudden short constriction of the peripheral blood vessels at the first signs of hypnosis, which was followed by a progressive dilation until waking, when the subject's vessels underwent sudden constriction. He also noted a slight rise in surface temperature with a concomitant drop in the rectal temperature. The findings of others attempt to bear out these and similar physiological changes.

These observations seem to sustain the theories which purport that suggestibility has greater endurance when the higher nerve-centers have been inhibited. It is difficult to confirm these findings, as the evidence has been too scanty to warrant acceptance without further experimentation. Unfortunately, the results have varied with each investigator because of the diversity of the subjects chosen. Minds are uniquely different and responses in some individuals will not conform with responses of others. Each subject develops habit patterns throughout his life-time which differ extraordinarily from those developed in others. Physiological changes occur simultaneously with a shift in state of mind or a change in emotion. It has been known for a long time that a subject could react in a certain fashion because he had seen others respond similarly. Few experimentalists have ventured to question the moods of their subjects and to compare them with those expressed by other subjects. To know why an individual acts in a given way, it is necessary to consider the myriad of factors that have occurred in his life which are responsible for the present act. No such observation could really be extensive except with a thorough psychoanalysis. A single word from a hypnotist can give rise to the manifestations of a painful trauma which has been repressed in the deeper levels of the unconscious mind. This alone would be sufficient to cause a sudden anxiety, resulting in a change in physiological processes. A patient in hypnotic trance may rebel against the hypnotist's suggestion if he construes it as an order which he *must* follow. In this instance, he might unconsciously associate the operator's demeanor with his employer's domination over him. The result would be that he would obey the suggestion because he could not help himself, but his obedience would also be marked by feelings of rebellion. This type of behavior resistance must necessarily be marked by physiological change. Thus, the various schools of psychology have faltered in their entire experimental approach by ignoring the over-all personality integration of the subject.

C. PHENOMENA PRODUCED DURING HYPNOSIS

1. *Amnesia*

Subjects who have proceeded beyond the light stages of the hypnotic trance will, in most instances, forget everything that occurred during the state upon awakening. I have found that only sixty per cent of my subjects have complete amnesia of this sort without a suggestion to the effect that they will forget. The phenomenon of amnesia is one of the conclusive tests for evaluating the height of suggestive susceptibility of the subject. The patient in hypnosis can rise from his chair, walk in the streets for two hours, carry on lengthy conversations with people he meets, even see a movie, but upon return to normal waking, will remember nothing that occurred during the state of hypnosis. He has no way of accounting for the lapse of time. This has led many investigators to believe that the subject loses consciousness during hypnosis. Such assumptions are erroneous, for the subject still manifests an ample degree of consciousness; hypnosis merely played a peculiar trick on his memory. If he were replaced in a deep trance, he would be able to recall every incident that happened in his previous trance. Most patients can remember word for word the suggestions given to them in previous séances.

I experimented with this phenomenon during an Army research project. A soldier with only grade school education was able to memorize an entire page of Shakespeare's "Hamlet" after listening to the passages seven times. Upon awakening, he could not recall any of the lines, and even more startling was the fact that he had no remembrance of the hypnotic experience. A week later he was hypnotized again. In this state, he was able to repeat the entire page without a single error. In another experiment, to test the validity of increased memory retention, five soldiers were hypnotized *en masse* and given a jumbled "code" consisting of twenty-five words without phonetic consistency. They were allowed sixty seconds to commit the list to memory. In the waking state, each man was asked to repeat the code; this none of them could do. One man hazily remembered having had some association with a code but could not remember more than that. The other four soldiers were allowed to study the code consciously for another sixty seconds, but all denied previous acquaintance with it. During re-hypnotization, they were individually able to recall the exact content of the code message.

Amnesia by post-hypnotic suggestion is evident in a still greater percentage of cases, even in states of lighter trance. With suggestion we have magnificent control over the amnesiac condition, for even partial forgetting is possible. For example, we are able to cause a subject to forget one hypnotic incident and recall another upon awakening. An example follows:

Subject B is placed in a state of Medium Hypnosis. The therapist suggests that he is unable to open his eyes; B tries uselessly to defy the suggestion. It is then suggested to him that certain muscles have become rigid and paralyzed. He attempts to move these parts, again unsuccessfully. In like fashion, he follows other orders suggested to him. Before B is awakened, a pencil is placed in the palm of his hand. He holds the pencil tightly. He is told that he will not be able to open his hand to release the pencil until he is given a certain signal by the therapist. He is also told that he will remember everything that happened during the hypnotic state except the final suggestion. He will not know why he is unable to open his hand, why he continues to hold the pencil, or the little matter of the signal. At this point, B is roused. Upon questioning, he hastens to assure us that he remembers everything, and he gives an accurate account of the entire hypnotic procedure, omitting only the suggestion that the operator caused him to forget. When the fact is mentioned to him that he cannot release the pencil from his hand, he makes a futile effort to break his grasp of the object and his face assumes an expression of awe and bewilderment. At the given signal, B opens his hand and the pencil falls to the floor. He grins sheepishly, but even this clue fails to restore memory of the now obliterated post-hypnotic suggestion. If B were re-hypnotized, he could immediately recall what he had been ordered to forget.

This is a very simple phenomenon of hypnosis that can be duplicated with almost every subject.

Hypnotic amnesia may be compared with traumatic amnesia, where an individual may lose all recognition of personal identity or forget an experience or situation that has been painful for him to remember—a common symptom of neurosis. This and other factors of hypnosis led the neurologist, Charcot, to classify the hypnotic state as a condition of induced hysteria.

In rare instances, a subject will emerge from the hypnotic state with remembrance of everything that he has experienced despite the therapist's suggestion of amnesia. In these cases, the suggestion has a delayed reaction, for within a short time these reminiscences are completely lost from memory. To illustrate, let us consider the case of Miss H.:

She was hypnotized for purposes of post-hypnotic anaesthesia relative to a tonsillectomy, for use within the week. Complete amnesia was suggested. Upon her return to consciousness, she recalled every suggestion that I had given her. She went through surgery with no need for chemical anaesthesia and experienced no sensation of pain. The day after the operation she informed me that she remembered being hypnotized the week before but was unable to recall any of the hypnotic events.

Although amnesia is of therapeutic importance in most patients, therapy can still be effectively facilitated even if the details of the trance be recalled. Later we shall discuss the advantages of amnesia in suggestive healing.

2. *Control of the Senses*

One of the most interesting phenomena noticed in hypnosis is the control of the therapist over the sensorium of his subject. He can persuade the subject that he is perceiving an object that is not actually there, and can produce many other illusions and hallucinations. Experiments along these lines have enabled psychiatrists to gain greater insight into various symptoms seen in psychosis.

A common trick from the magician's hand, guaranteed to amuse the coldest audience, is the one where a gullible gentleman is chosen from the theatre and asked to step to the stage. The magician hypnotizes him, and when he has reached the proper state for suggestion, he is given an umbrella and told that the fishing is excellent. The subject extends the pole before him. Pretty soon he is sure that the fish are biting, and he pulls frantically on the umbrella, seemingly delighted with the imaginary fish he has caught.

The illusion created by the magician is what psychologists call a "visual hallucination," the same type of hallucination evident in schizophrenic cases, where those afflicted see objects that are not perceptible to normal people. No amount of reason can penetrate these "logic-tight compartments," as Hart called them. By the same token, if another person were to tell this victim of hypnotic exhibitionism that he is in reality sitting on a stage before an audience of a thousand people, and that the object which he holds is not a fishing pole but an umbrella, the subject would look bewildered, and then accuse his enlightener of vicious deception!

Perhaps we can further understand this mental process if it be illustrated in the light of a common experience. A man returns to his apartment after dark. He opens the door and fumbles for the light switch on the wall, but fails to find it. The moonlight penetrates the sash, casting weird and ominous reflections upon the curtain. Panic-stricken for the moment, his mind distorts the shape of the curtain, convincing him that a sinister figure lurks behind the drapery. His imagination promptly runs wild, embellishing his mental picture of the "prowler" with such vivid detail that any other explanation becomes practically impossible for him to accept.

Bentivegni, a hypnotist of the nineteenth century, related a case pertinent to imaginative sense-perception. In connection with some judicial dispute, it became necessary to exhume a body from the grave. When the hole was dug, as the coffin was about to be lifted from the ground, an official, unaccustomed to such procedure, swore roundly that he already detected the odor of putrefaction. When the casket was opened, it was discovered to be empty!

Taste-buds and salivary glands are dominated by suggestion to a great extent. When unfamiliar foods are tantalizingly described to us, they are anticipated with great relish; should we ever eat them, the chances are that they will live up to our expectations. So in hypnosis; we can feed our subject a cake of soap and convince him that he is eating a delicious pie. Similarly, it is possible to make the hypnotic subject accept chili-peppers as sweet milk chocolates and ice-cubes as burning hot coals.

Induced auditory hallucinations are likewise produced by suggestion. To illustrate, we shall return to our vaudeville magician. Not only could he conjure his illusion for the fisherman; he was also able to create all of the effects which accompany such an experience. For instance, he could shut out the laughter of the audience from the mind of his subject and replace it with the lulling sounds of a rippling brook.

As a sense may be confused, so can its function be inhibited. This hypnotic device serves a very practical purpose in the production of general and local anaesthesias for surgery. This phenomenon may also provide a clue to inhibition of function as manifested in psychosomatic disorders.

It has long been known that hysterical conditions can

bring with them total loss of tactile sensation. Innumerable cases of fear and shock during battle have been created as a result of war, where soldiers have lost feeling in some portion of the body to the extent that it could be stuck with pins or burned with cigarettes without any sensation of pain.

We know of experiences in daily life, commonly aligned with suggestion, which demonstrate the effect of the latter upon actual body sensations. For instance, the surgeon with a working knowledge of anaesthetics knows the psychological reactions of these drugs on his patients and is also aware of their responses to minimum doses that are hardly sufficient to render them partially unconscious. Consequently, when the surgeon himself undergoes surgery, he is found to be immune to the usual dosage, and must have enormous amounts of the drug before he can succumb to its effects. On the other hand, every doctor is familiar with the patient who takes an aspirin and loses his headache long before his system has had an adequate opportunity to absorb the drug. The dentist realizes that if his patient's attention can be distracted from the zone where he is working, it will only hurt half as much. Two people earnestly engaged in fisticuffs are generally so engrossed in their encounter that they scarcely become aware of their bruises until after the fight.

In deep trance, pain can be quickly alleviated by suggestion. The Heidelberg Clinic in Germany has reported thousands of childbirths by the utilization of hypnotic methods. In Soviet Russia, it is reported that suggestion has been used almost exclusively in obstetrical cases. Zkravosmislov, of the First Moscow University, reported his findings in ninety cases extending over the period from November, 1935 to April, 1936 as follows:

"Fifty-five percent were entirely without pain, thirty-three percent were partially successful, and eleven percent showed very little result."

Other workers in the field have claimed greater success.

Esdaile in 1852 reported an amazing number of surgical cases, including visceral surgeries, amputations, etc., where hypnosis served successfully as the only anaesthesia. Every hypnotic therapist has experienced favorable results with suggestion as an analgesic in pains of both functional and organic origin.

Before the discoveries of ether and chloroform many doctors employed hypnosis to relieve the distress of painful conditions. Some even claimed that they were able to transplant pain from one person to another by suggestion. This was probably done merely by creating a tactile sensation in one body, dispelling a like sensation in another.

In England, where hypnotism was commonly practiced during the nineteenth century, newspapers carried announcements of recent births, and frequently at the bottom of the notices would be found the statement: "Painlessly, during mesmeric trance."

The various senses respond to hypnotic control even after the subject has been roused, provided, of course, that post-hypnotic suggestions have been instituted during trance. For instance, it is suggested to Subject A in the hypnotic state that, upon awakening from the trance, he will find himself in a garden, surrounded by exotic flowers. He will hear the chirping of the birds and the sound of crickets in the distance. He will pick a berry from a nearby bush and eat it. Then he will pluck a flower and smell its fragrance. Suddenly, a bee will light on his arm and sting him. He will feel the pain momentarily, and he will find himself in his usual surroundings.

Here we have demonstrated control over every sense, and the subject follows the entire suggestion in the waking state. It is truly remarkable how long such post-hypnotic control can last. In one of my experimental cases, a college student was told under hypnosis that she would see her brother (who had been dead for two years!) six months later, at 11:00

a.m. on a specified date. At precisely the appointed time, she was astounded to "meet" her brother on a street in Los Angeles. These are her words:

"I was so happy to see him, but I was astonished because I knew he was dead. However, in a way, his presence seemed perfectly natural at the time. He accompanied me to my apartment, and there we talked about different things, but in all that time, nothing was ever mentioned about his leaving. Soon he rose from his chair with the excuse that he had to keep an appointment, and left. I did not become fully aware of the impossibility of the situation until after he was gone, and then I felt dazed. This feeling of bewilderment stayed with me until it was explained that my illusion was part of an hypnotic experiment."

O. H. Estabrook, Professor of Psychology at Colgate University, commented upon this type of experience:

"Every phenomenon that we can obtain in hypnotism, we can get by means of the so-called post-hypnotic suggestion. For example, I suggest to my subject that he sees his brother standing in a corner of the room. He does so. But I can also suggest to him that, tomorrow afternoon at three, or two months from today, or next Christmas Eve, he will see his brother in that same corner. Strange to say, he will do so. At the time specified, his brother will appear before his eyes and he will act in every way as if this person were actually in the room." *

Bernheim has spoken of many cases which bear out this phenomenon:

"I wish to speak of the possibility of inducing in somnambulists, by means of suggestion, acts, illusions of the senses, and hallucinations which shall not be manifested during the sleeping condition, but upon waking. The patient hears what I tell him in his sleep, but no memory of what I said

* Estabrook, O. H., "Hypnotism is Akin to Sleep Walking and Insanity," *Scientific American*, March, 1936.

remains. He no longer knows that I spoke to him. The idea suggested arises in his mind when he wakes, but he has forgotten its origin, and believes it is spontaneous. Facts of this kind have been recorded by A. Bertrand, Gen. Noiset, Dr. Liébault, and Charles Richet." *

Several of my own patients have responded to post-hypnotic suggestions for the alleviation of pains of childbirth, even though these suggestions were given a few months prior to the process of labor. Others, who have been given suggestions that dental work would bring with it no discomfort, still continue to react favorably to the initial suggestion, although in some instances, several years have elapsed.

3. Release of Inhibitions

Inhibitions which are normally present in the waking states are partially lifted in conditions of trance. However, it has been stated by the majority of observers that the most important inhibitions—those which have been ingrained in the personality of the individual by earlier training—are permanent, and remain active despite contrary suggestions. It is their belief that a person will not ordinarily follow any order under hypnosis which he would not carry out in his normal waking state. This precludes the possibility of criminal acts caused by suggestion from the therapist, and obviates any immoral intentions from the latter toward his subject.

Whether or not crimes can be committed as a result of suggestion is an issue of great controversy. While most experimenters are of the opinion that subjects awaken immediately when presented with a suggestion counter to their morals, a great body of evidence contradicting this contention is available.

I witnessed a private exhibition of hypnotism several years ago during which the hypnotist attempted to prove that

* Bernheim, H., *Suggestive Therapeutics*, transl. by C. A. Herter, G. P. Putnam's Sons, New York, 1899, p. 31.

it is impossible to make a subject do anything contrary to his moral sense. He used an age-old demonstration, which presumably has always worked successfully. A girl who had been conditioned to hypnotism was placed in a deep somnambulism. After subjecting her to the usual routine tests, the operator told her to open her eyes and to take the knife he proffered. She accepted it without comment. Then he suggested that she stab him. She brought the knife back, preparing to drive the weapon through his body, when suddenly she hesitated, looked very much confused, dropped the knife and laughed nervously as if the suggestion had been part of a rather silly game. The hypnotist, content with his subject's responses so far, substituted a rubber knife for the real one and repeated his suggestion that she kill him with the knife. This time she offered no resistance to the hypnotist's command; without hesitation, she stabbed him with the rubber knife.

In one of my own experiments, I gave a girl the post-hypnotic suggestion that, upon awakening, she would turn on the radio, but that she would not know why. Upon return to the waking state, she became quite nervous. Several times she arose from her chair and walked toward the radio, only to return to the chair without reacting entirely to the suggestion. When I asked what made her so jittery, she answered that she had an almost irresistible compulsion to get some music on her radio, but she realized that it quite late and it might waken the baby next door.

It was apparent that the suggestion she had received violated a certain moral propriety which was a part of her nature; therefore, she was unable to follow it.

Now the question arose; could she be conditioned to accept a thought to which she would not respond normally? I re-hypnotized her and impressed her mind with the fact that a baby no longer lived next door, thus she would be able to follow through with the original suggestion without a qualm.

She awoke from hypnosis and obeyed the suggestion instantly. (N.b., I *did* respect her wishes and shut off the music before it could disturb that baby!)

The stage hypnotist at the county fair uses a similar conditioning device. It would be impossible to cause a man to remove his clothes before an audience, but by telling him that he is alone, that he feels very dirty and should take a shower, he will begin to undress and take off every garment unless the hypnotist intervenes at a crucial moment. Many unethical exhibitionists, whose skill surpasses their good taste, have delighted audiences by waiting until the subject is almost stripped before rousing him to a state of utter consternation and embarrassment!

Bramwell surveyed the experiences of other hypnotists, covering observation of over 50,000 patients, to conclude that, under hypnosis, the subject is more scrupulous in his moral standards than he would ordinarily be. He reported that he had "never seen a single instance in which mental or physical harm had been caused by hypnotism." De Jong, Liébeault, Moll, Wetterstrand and many others have written similarly.

Janet of the Salpêtrière illustrated this issue with a noteworthy experiment in the traditional fashion. A hypnotized woman was given a paper sword and directed to stab people. She followed the command with emotions of violence, as if she were actually venting her rage upon the persons she stabbed. Then she was ordered to poison others with a concoction which suggested real poison. She reacted in the same way as before, but with added vehemence. Next, she was offered a pistol containing blank cartridges. She aimed it at certain people and blazed away unhesitatingly until the gun was empty. From her expression in all three demonstrations, little doubt was left that she would enjoy using the actual weapons in this state if opportunity offered. To climax the experiment, Janet ordered her to accept the delusion that she was alone in the hall, and would now remove her clothes and bathe. At first, she became angry; this indignation turned into uncontrollable rage during which she awoke and burst out in a "violent fit of hysterics."

It is difficult to comprehend why Janet concluded from this experiment that there is an apparent distinction between a subject engaging in crimes of a fictitious character and the same subject carrying out *real* immoral acts under hypnosis. From the account of his experiment, one might gather that the subject, by her display of violence, was intent upon committing homicide under the induced delusion. Janet had created in the woman's mind an actual paranoid process, and there would be no reason to suspect that any paranoic is "just foolin'."

Society, of necessity, places certain restrictions upon all of us. If we could behave as our emotions dictate without fear of social rebuke (a privilege limited to paranoics), we should be more apt to follow our urges, although those urges might strongly resemble the ones exhibited by our primitive ancestors. The entire argument hinges on the controversy over the potential control exerted by hypnosis over the inhibitory factor which serves as our social restrictor.

Janet also overlooked his subject's normal capacity for murder as well as her inner recoil from body exposure. There are many murderers who think little of taking life who would object strenuously to disrobing in public.

It is possible, too, that at the time of the homicidal suggestions the subject was in deep trance and could accept the delusion because of inhibition-release, but had deflected to a lighter stage by the time Janet attempted to induce the "immoral" suggestion.

Björnström mentions an instance in which a person was induced first to steal under hypnosis, then, later, to accuse someone else! Forel wrote of the fact that subjects in somnambulism could commit hideous crimes and remember nothing of them upon waking. Binet and Féré were convinced that subjects could receive suggestions of crime which would be executed in the waking state. Schilder and Kauders voice the contention that the "man or woman hypnotized may be more readily induced to perform sexual acts than other 'crimes.'"

Wells, an experimenter versed in the art of hypnosis, as evidenced by his thoroughness of investigation, blamed upon faulty techniques the inability of certain hypnotists to induce successfully executed suggestions of crime. He points out that "numerous failures do not invalidate one single success when the latter comes!"*

Obviously, any testimony, however convincing, must be based on hypothesis only, for to the present time, we have no recorded case in the annals of criminology of hypnotically-instigated crime.

It is true that ample conditioning by an experienced hypnotist will alter behavior patterns which have been developed in a subject through early training. As he has been taught to conceive the difference between "right" and "wrong," so can he be conditioned to reject previous ideation in favor of a newly instilled concept. In this instance, one concept will overshadow another. At the same time, it must be considered that under powerful enough stress, confusion or intense emotion, most of us will consciously ignore earlier training and temporarily resort to acts of moral turpitude—even to murder, given a strong enough stimulus (viz: the transition from a peaceful civilian to a competent soldier).

4. *Incapacity for Volitional Activity*

The subject under hypnotic control loses his ability to initiate actions arising from his own will. His expression seems to evince an "I don't give a damn" feeling, and he doesn't. He

* Wells, W. R., "Experiments in the Hypnotic Production of Crime," *Journal of Psychology*, 11, 63–102, 1941, p. 88.

sits stolidly with a dreamy and almost blank demeanor, as if he had thrown his mind, soul and body upon the mercy of the therapist. Even when suggestions are thrust upon him, he will respond slowly, as if with great effort, and will finally obey the order given. He is like a robot, inactive, incapable, without initiative, waiting a command to spur him to action. If he is told to walk around the room and shake hands with an on-looker, he does so. If his arm is raised overhead in catalepsy, he offers no objection, keeping his arm outstretched until released by the therapist. It is as though the subject and the therapist have tested their strength against each other, with the hypnotist emerging victor from the battle and demanding the spoils; the loser, beaten and resigned, yields apathetically to each request.

The Salpêtrière School contended that the subject's docility and puppetlike submission were occasioned by a change in the physio-chemical function of the nervous system; that inaction arises from the retardation of certain neurological processes caused by the blocking of the nerve-paths.

Seeking to justify hypnotism on a physiological plane, its adherents were convinced that the trance state was induced by physical methods alone and that suggestion played only an incidental part in this induction. The school of Nancy, on the other hand, adopted an opposite position, claiming that the doctrine of the "physical power theory"—formulated and taught by Charcot, its leading exponent, was founded on an unworthy premise, i.e., the theory that sensory fatigue and its consequent nerve inhibition were the chief factors in producing hypnotic states. It was natural for Charcot to prefer the physical explanation to the Nancy theory because of his neurological background. Each school condemned the findings of the other. The issue still persists, despite the fact that the greatest scientific body of its time, the *Institut de France*, accepted Charcot and his school.

For a clearer picture of the vanquished volitional phenomenon, it is necessary to examine the subject's motivation. First, we notice that he has voiced his consent to hypnosis, meaning that he has consciously agreed to surrender his will temporarily. Why should he place himself at the mercy of the therapist? There are many possible answers to this question. He might be merely curious. He might wish to return to a state which he previously discovered to be pleasant. Whatever the reason, we must assume that the subject first willed the transfer of his conscious control to that of the therapist. First of all, his confidence must have been thoroughly won. As a patient awaiting surgery responds to the drugs of the anaesthetist although he knows that he is forsaking the presence of his consciousness, so does the hypnotized subject surrender to the commands of another will.

To understand the psychological mechanism here, it may be well to observe the child as he accepts orders from a parent, although the order may not be entirely to his liking. Accordingly, efficacy of hypnosis depends upon the child-like submission to adult will, transferred to the therapist. (Freud) No such transference could exist without faith and confidence on the part of the subject.

The *en-rapport* spoken of by hypnotists resembles psychoanalytic *transference* in many respects, that transference where the patient identifies the psychotherapist with some mentor of his past to whom he could come with his problems —father, brother, etc.

Psychoanalysis would point to motivation (masochism, death-wish, escape mechanisms and the like) as possible sources for the response to hypnosis. So little has been propounded along these lines that research investigation conducted with psychoanalytical procedures should offer a fertile field for exploration.

Voluntary submission of a subject provides a temporary transference and in no case constitutes a permanent abolition of will. The hypnotist merely causes the subject to place his will momentarily in abeyance for replacement by the will of the therapist. Lack of initiative depends upon the subject's voluntary intention to forego conscious thinking and action in favor of submission to the thoughts suggested to him by another.

5. *Hypermnesia*

This implies an increase of the power of memory consequent to the hypnotic process to an extent not ordinarily apparent in waking states. Events which have long been dropped from conscious memory can be recalled by subjects in the hypnotic state. Experimenters have furnished sufficient proof to bear out this phenomenon. Freud's psychoanalytic theory was founded upon observations of hypnotized patients, although most orthodox analysts following Freud's procedure have shown reluctance to accept the established validity of hypnotic hypermnesia.

During somnambulism, I have been able to bring a twenty-four-year-old patient back to the memory of his first birthday. While under hypnosis he recalled the happenings of that day and described the clothes he wore to the minutest detail. His mother confirmed everything the boy recalled, albeit with unbelieving astonishment.

In another case I regressed a thirty-two-year-old patient to the age of eight. By regressing, she remembered hearing screams emanate from the basement of her house. Opening the door of the basement, she found her mother dangling from a rope attached to the shaft of the ceiling, while her drunken father stood by, laughing wildly. The child shrieked, and when her screams became uncontrollable her father sobered enough to release his wife from the grasp of the noose. Shortly after, when the mother regained consciousness and all danger had passed, the father made the patient promise that she would forget what she had seen and never tell anyone.

The experience had been so painful she tried to erase it from her mind and succeeded in repressing it.

A logical reason for this repression is that her father commanded her to "forget" while the patient was in a state of emotional confusion. Confusion also acts as an inhibitor of reason, thus, heightened suggestibility is a probable consequence of it. For this reason terror and pain produce a state analogous to hypnosis, and the command to forget might be likened to a post-hypnotic suggestion. This could well serve as an explanation of the exclusion from consciousness of painful or unacceptable psychic material which is thus compelled to manifest itself through the unconscious. This repression was so complete that all memory of it was gone until she was regressed to the age at which the event occurred. Under hypnosis, she recalled the whole thing vividly and exhibited the same hysteria evoked by the original experience.

Before a post-graduate class of physicians, a young doctor volunteered for my demonstration of regression. He sank into deep trance and by regression was returned to the age of six. I suggested that he was in his classroom, and asked him to tell me the name of each student, row by row. He promptly named thirty-one students. Then I suggested that he write his name on the blackboard. After each letter, which he printed in a child-like hand, he hesitated, as if groping for the next letter. It took five minutes for him to complete this task. Next he was told to write his name on a sheet of paper, and in both cases similar mistakes appeared. A few weeks later he brought me his first-grade notebook, which his mother had affectionately preserved in the attic and dug out upon hearing of his regression. His name, with its child-like block letters, compared in every detail with the name he had scrawled on the sheet of paper while in trance.

I have repeated this experiment before many professional groups, usually with subjects chosen from the audience, with amazingly few failures.

Moll in his book, *Hypnotism,* states:

"Events of the normal life can also be remembered in hypnosis, even when they have apparently been long forgotten."*

The psychologist, McDougall, also commented on the authenticity of this phenomenon: "It is true that in hypnosis, especially in its deeper stages, the power of recall of seemingly forgotten incidents, especially those of childhood, is greatly increased. . . ."†

Freud and Breuer might have continued with their experimental analysis of this remarkable power of recall had it not been for their difficulty in achieving consistent results with hypnosis. Freud visited the Salpêtrière school, where his interest became so absorbed with the findings that he spent a year with Janet and others, trying to master their techniques. Finally, possibly because he himself was an inferior hypnotist, he observed certain limitations. The recall of lost memories could not be evoked in every patient. Despite this, the origin of the Freudian concept did begin with his trial and error hypnotic experiments. An earlier article written in collaboration with Breuer—before he discarded hypnosis as a therapeutic device—states:

> "Instigated by a number of accidental observations, we have
> investigated for a number of years the different forms and
> symptoms of hysteria in order to find the cause and the
> process which provoked the phenomena in question for the
> first time, in a great many cases, years back. In the great
> majority of cases we did not succeed in elucidating this
> starting point from the mere history, no matter how de-

* Moll, A., *Hypnotism,* transl. by A. F. Hopkirk, Charles Scribner's Sons, New York, 1913, p. 124.

† McDougall, W., *Outline of Abnormal Psychology,* Charles Scribner's Sons, New York, 1913, p. 94.

tailed it might have been, partly because we had to deal with experiences about which discussion was disagreeable to the patients, but mainly because they could not recall them; often they had no inkling as to the causal connection between the occasioning process and the pathological phenomenon. It was generally necessary to hypnotize the patients and reawaken the memory of that time in which the symptom first appeared, and we thus succeeded in exposing that connection in a most precise and convincing manner." *

Again in the same work they write:

". . . . we had to emphasize the fact that the recollection of the effective psychic trauma is not to be found in the normal memory of the patient, but in the hypnotized memory. . . ."

Soon, with the aid of conscious free-association and dream interpretation, Freud broke away from the hypnotic process which had first served him so well. Perhaps if he had experienced the success with hypnotism reported by others, the present psychoanalytical techniques might be totally different.

Bramwell's views are in accord with those of most investigators. He writes:

"The improvement of memory as to remote events is still more interesting; and this I have frequently demonstrated in the following manner:

Certain subjects were first questioned in the normal state as to the earliest events they could remember, when it was generally found that they could recall nothing which had happened before the age of five or six. They were then hypnotized, and, starting from the first event in their lives they could recall, it was suggested that they should revive the memory of earlier and earlier incidents. Some of

* Freud, S., *Selected Papers on Hysteria and Other Psychoneurosis,* transl. by A. A. Brill, Nervous and Mental Disease Publishing Co., New York, 1912, p. 1.

> the subjects related what they stated had happened at the age of two, and one described a children's party given on the first anniversary of her birthday."*

Nothing is ever obliterated from the unconscious storehouse of memory. Every incident, however trivial, leaves its impressions, only to be revived by associations and called back to consciousness. Painful events which we are advised to "forget" are never actually cast off by the mind; they are buried in the caverns of memory, whence they reappear as ghosts in disguised form in distorted dreams, or show themselves in indistinguishable symptoms which harass the neurotic personality. The mechanism of repression is, as Freud so ably pointed out, the cause of most mental disease and psychosomatic illness.

We can see the gratifying possibilities of this power of recall, if it is employed in our inquiry into the neurotic, for it provides a powerful potential in the elimination of psychic disorders.

Several observers have raised the question that this phenomenon may be limited to subjects who are capable of fabrication for the benefit of the analyst's ego. However, the preponderance of evidence to the contrary tends to relegate negative results to the limbo of inadequate hypnotic techniques. The competent operator has little trouble regressing any subject in whom he is able to produce the hypnotic state.

There is no doubt that memory recall and retention are heightened through the use of hypnosis. In one experiment with fifteen average college students about to take their final examinations, I hypnotized them and gave these suggestions for post-hypnotic effect:

"Everything you learned during classes you have committed to your memory; you retain all this knowledge. When-

* Bramwell, J. M., *Hypnotism,* Wm. Rider and Sons, London, 1913, p. 102.

ever you are required to bring this information forth, you will be able to do it without the slightest hesitation. You will have full confidence during your examination, for you will be able to recall immediately all that you have learned."

This speech was repeated twice, and the subjects awakened and dismissed. The examination took place a week later, and all but one received amazingly higher grades than others of similar intellectual calibre in the class.

For a later experiment, to test the power of recall in hypnotized subjects, three students in the waking state were given the following jumbled words to memorize, being allowed fifteen minutes to study the list:

1. ordinary—sqlcnrbc
2. tendency—tmslnfsk
3. black—nfkdsnp
4. center—cfpnges
5. curtain—krptbal
6. table—pfysktea
7. woman—nepqadf
8. walk—lpfqrtzh
9. paper—ppslgrpt
10. stone—nrsftplr

The papers were taken from them, and they stepped to the blackboard. As each English word was spoken, they were to write that word's alien equivalent. Each made a futile effort to respond. Two of the three were able to provide the equivalent for the first word, but there it ended.

All three responded to deep hypnotic states, during which I repeated the experiment. While their responses, as indicated below, are not completely accurate, they conform sufficiently to indicate that hypnosis causes greater recall of facts committed to memory than would be possible in the normal state. The following are the results of the test under hypnosis (the errors are italicized):

54

SUBJECT A
1. ordinary—sqlcnrbc
2. tendency—tm*c*lnfsk
3. black—nfkdsn*fr*
4. center—cfpnges
5. curtain—krptbsl
6. table—pfyskt*ch*
7. woman—ncpgadf
8. walk—lp*r*grtzh
9. paper—*ff*sl*f*rpt
10. stone—nrs*p*tplr*h*

SUBJECT B
1. ordinary—sqlcnrbc
2. tendency—tm*c*lnfsk
3. black—nfkdsn*f*
4. center—cfpnges
5. curtain—kr*bt*p*sl
6. table—pfyskt*ch*
7. woman—n*sf*gadf
8. walk—lp*f*grtzh
9. paper—*p*ff*lgrpt
10. stone—nr*ff*tpl*h*

SUBJECT C
1. ordinary—*s*glcnrbc
2. tendency—t*n*slnfsk
3. black—nfkdsnp
4. center—cfpng*ocf*
5. curtain—krptbal
6. table—pfyskt*co*
7. woman—n*sf*gad*p*
8. walk—l*fp*grtzh
9. paper—p*fc*lgrp*f*
10. stone—nrsftplr

The elevation of forgotten material to consciousness provides valid reason for the use of hypnosis. To quote Freud, "The hysteric suffers mostly from reminiscences." * His symptoms are memory symbols for traumatic events. The memory is filled with painful experiences which, because of their emotional overtones, cannot be openly accepted by the consciousness. Disagreeable impressions, shameful impulses and experiences are forcibly ejected from consciousness together with the emotions originally attending them. These emotions are repressed, for at the time of their presentation they could not be worked off. The process of repression is an es-

* Freud, S., *Selected Papers on Hysteria and Other Psychoneurosis,* trans. by A. A. Brill, Nervous and Mental Disease Publishing Co., New York, p. 5.

cape mechanism which prevents the individual's perpetual re-view of life's traumatic experiences.

Freud's treatment called "catharsis" has as its basis the reconduction of the sum of excitement to the repressed idea, which was originally conscious. When the patient is made to re-live the experience by intellectual effort the idea is rescued from its false path, the emotions are no longer strangulated and the symptoms disappear.

When one attempts to evoke the idea from the memory, he encounters a strong force of resistance, for the patient has no wish to re-experience an idea that might provoke mental anguish. An idea cannot live discordant with the ego, and as such, it is refused re-entrance into consciousness. A compromise must be affected because, 1. the idea is at variance with the ego; but, 2. the idea cannot be wholly evicted from consciousness. Disguising itself with adequate symbolism the idea, no longer recognizable behind its mask, is allowed entrance into the realm of consciousness. The dreams of the patient, his mental associations as key words are presented to him, his psychosomatic symptoms—all bear evidence of the idea's distortion.

Attempts at penetration of the mask by the usual methods of psychoanalysis can frequently lead to failure, for the patient's resistance must be overcome. His unyielding ego creates a stronger defensive wall as it desires the idea to remain safely interred.

Hypnosis provides an efficacious method, for when consciousness is inhibited the ego is, likewise, caused to be inhibited. Restraint of the ego provides a relatively unobstructed pathway to the memory. The ego, now somewhat relaxed, offers less resistance to the disinterment of the idea and therefore its rise to consciousness is facilitated. The patient, enjoying the calm that hypnosis usually brings, is less reluctant to relate occurrences which originally prompted his condition.

Drawing from my own experiences with patients under-going this method of therapy, it is my impression that the patient finds in hypnosis an opportunity to open up without fearing reproach or penalization. He expresses himself freely and in his state of well-being he feels that he cannot be held accountable for his statements or actions during hypnosis. This can be likened to the criminal's agreement to tell every-thing upon the assurance that the judge will "go easy on him." In this way the pathogenic idea emerges to consciousness with less obstruction by the censor of the ego.

The revivification of the material by itself offers relief to the patient, but not necessarily cure. The idea must be integrated in the light of present day understanding. The mechanism of integration can be observed in the hypno-analysis of one of our patients:

Mr. A., age 37, an electrician by occupation, develops states of panic when confronted by men with bright red hair.* Women and children with like characteristics exert no effect upon him; objects of similar color do not arouse these emo-tions. Through regression with hypnosis (that is, he is "re-turned" to infantile levels of reaction) he recalls very vividly an experience that took place in his home town in the Middle West at the age of five. His mother had gone to Wichita for surgery, being joined later by his father. Not wishing to be burdened with his care the child was put into the hands of a "kindly" neighbor. This man, who, incidentally, had red

* Our present day likes and dislikes are frequently rooted in past experiences of which we have no conscious recollection; thus, we can harbor various emotions without apparent reasonable con-sistency:

> "I do not like thee, Dr. Fell;
> The reason why I cannot tell;
> But this I know, and know full well,
> I do not like thee, Doctor Fell!"
>
> *Mother Goose*

hair, proved not so kindly, taking delight in teasing the boy and "playfully" pinching him until he cried. Those few days brought with them terror which he had not heretofore experienced. When his father returned, the child told him of the tortures inflicted upon him by the red-haired man, but his father dismissed the tale as the product of an active imagination and in return lectured the boy about appreciation of kindliness. In time, the experience went the way of all painful events—repression to lower levels.

Excavation of the experience to consciousness might have been adequate for the temporary relief of the patient, as any confessional would be, but no permanent effect could be elicited without the patient's integration of the material in the light of present day understanding. The mere travelling to the surface of an idea and its sequela of catharsis cannot be sufficient for the *dénouement* of the pathogenic idea. The patient had to be made to realize: first, that his tormentor was an individual of sadistic qualities; second, that not all men with red hair have these inclinations; and third, that it would be inopportune for him to base his likes and dislikes upon an experience which should have no effect upon him today.

Upon acceptance of these tenets the pathological process and its consequent symptom had no further effect upon the patient.

The reader is asked to consult the chapter devoted to hypno-analysis for a continuation of the application of hypnosis to deep therapy.

REFERENCES

Bass, M. J., "Differentiation of the Hypnotic Trance from Normal Sleep," *Journal of Experimental Psychology*, 14, 382–399, 1931.

Baudouin, C., *Suggestion and Autosuggestion*, translated by Eden and Cedar Paul, Allen & Unwin, London, 1920.

BERNHEIM, H., *Suggestive Therapeutics,* translated by C. A. Herter, G. P. Putnam's Sons, New York, 1899.

BERGSON, H., *Creative Evolution,* translated by A. Mitchell, Henry Holt, New York, 1926.

BJÖRNSTRÖM, F., *Hypnotism,* translated by Baron Nils Posse, Humboldt Publishing Co., New York, 1887.

BRAMWELL, J. M., *Hypnotism,* Wm. Rider & Sons, London, 1913.

BREUER, J. AND FREUD, S., *Studies in Hysteria,* Nervous and Mental Disease Publishing Co., New York, 1936.

ESDAILE, J., *Natural and Mesmeric Clairvoyance,* Hippolyte Baillière, London, 1852.

FERENCZI, S., *Further Contributions to the Theory and Technique of Psychoanalysis,* compiled by J. Rickman, translated by J. I. Suttie, Hogarth, London, 1926.

FOREL, A., *Hypnotism,* translated by H. W. Armit, Rebman, New York, 1907.

HEIDENHAIN, R., *Hypnotism or Animal Magnetism,* translated by L. C. Wooldridge, K. Paul, Trench, Trubner, London, 1906.

JANET, P., *Psychological Healing,* Macmillan Co., New York, 1925.

JANET, P., *Principles of Psychotherapy,* Macmillan Co., New York, 1924.

MOLL, A., *Hypnotism,* translated by A. F. Hopkirk, Charles Scribner's Sons, New York, 1913.

McDOUGALL, W., *Outline of Abnormal Psychology,* Charles Scribner's Sons, New York, 1913.

NYGARD, J. W., "Cerebral Circulation Prevailing During Sleep and Hypnosis," *Journal of Experimental Psychology,* 24, 1–20, 1939.

SCHILDER, P. AND KAUDERS, O., *Hypnosis,* translated by S. Rothenberg, Nervous and Mental Disease Publishing Co., New York, 1927.

SHAFFER, G. W. AND DORCUS, R. M., *Textbook of Abnormal Psychology,* Williams & Wilkins, Baltimore, 1939.

WELLS, W. R., "Experiments in Waking Hypnosis for Instructional Purposes," *Journal of Abnormal Psychology,* 18, 389–404, 1924.

WELLS, W. R., "Experiments in the Hypnotic Production of Crime," *Journal of Psychology,* 11, 63–102, 1941.

WIBLE, C. L. AND JENNESS, A., "Electrocardiograms During Sleep and Hypnosis," *Journal of Psychology,* 1, 235–245, 1936.

4

Mechanisms of Hypnosis

We have already seen that the most important phenomenon of the hypnotic state is the heightened ability of the subject to receive and follow instituted suggestions. Its very definition firmly implies heightened suggestibility as the chief characteristic of the trance.

At this point, we must adopt the stand that hypnotism is a normal phenomenon and that the power to hypnotize or to be hypnotized is latent in every individual. Every action elicited by suggestion may be observed in people during the normal waking state; to produce those actions at will would be difficult. Perhaps we can more easily recognize the universality of hypnosis by examining the phenomena common in every-day experience.

First, we notice that the subject is completely attentive to the therapist's demands. Attention is a necessary requisite in hypnosis, but attention is of equal importance when one becomes engrossed in an interesting problem, a fascinating book or a prize-fight. When we deal with attention, we consider that it is a total response of the entire consciousness, focusing itself upon a certain thing. It is reasonable to expect that when the entire psyche is absorbed in a problem, irrelevant stimuli will not intrude. When the mind is occupied with a major interest, a minor interest may not occupy the psyche simultaneously. Less relevant simuli can of course be registered at the time, but the consciousness will take little cognizance of them.

Physical changes also occur in the absorbed individual. Given sufficient intensity of concentration, he may develop nervous tenseness, symptoms of motor excitability, or partial or complete amnesia.

For instance, a housewife, deep in thought as she washes or irons, may react with slight shock symptoms if spoken to unexpectedly. A music student, busily engaged with scales or arpeggios, may be addressed and may even answer intelligently without retaining the slightest recollection of the incident. A scientist in his laboratory enters a world of his own, becoming almost oblivious to outside events while working with his equipment.

We might suspect that these persons are in a state analogous to hypnotic trance, save for one interesting factor! They have not been observed taking suggestions. This presents an intriguing problem: can a subject accept suggestion in the waking state?

This question may be answered by a simple experiment of your own. Take a suggestible friend to an exciting movie. When his attention is entirely centered upon the screen, suddenly command, "Stand up!" He will get up from his seat, look bewildered and then sit down, no end irritated by your suggestion. *But he will have followed it!*

Every student of psychology is familiar with this trick. Perhaps if enough suggestions were executed in this state, deep hypnosis would ultimately result. Fortunately, we need not wait until we can accompany our patients to the theatre before we can use hypnosis upon them. There are other methods for commanding attention.

A. MISDIRECTED ATTENTION

The "fascination" methods in such popular use among hypnotists depend upon attention-attracting devices. The subject is requested to concentrate upon a given object, while the operator suggests sleep. Many observers believe this tires the sense in use; this is demonstrably fallacious. The driver of an automobile concentrates on the road ahead, even fixing his vision upon the white line in the center of the road, but he does not become hypnotized. Neither does the subject who stares at the shiny surface of the operator's watch or whatever mysterious object is dangling before him. The visual sense does tire, but the fatigue does not produce the hypnotic state; the object merely occupies the subject's attention while the hypnotist institutes his suggestions.

An almost parallel case is that of the baby during feeding. The mother captures the child's attention with a toy that she dangles with one hand before his eyes. When the youngster is sufficiently engrossed with the object, she shoves the spoon into his mouth with the other hand. This is the identical procedure in the production of hypnosis. First, we cause the subject to concentrate on an object; then, when he "isn't looking" (i.e., wondering whether or not hypnosis will work on him) we "shove" the sleep suggestion at him.

Should we wait for his senses to "tire" it might take hours, and then he would fall into natural sleep through sheer fatigue! The effective hypnotist never depends upon sensory stimulation. Instead, he bases his technique upon "surprise attack" and therefore has few failures.

A patient with whom I had made several futile attempts at hypnosis did not seem to respond to any of my usual methods. After each trial she would fold her arms upon her chest and announce that she "guessed" she was a "hopeless case." Her pleased expression showed her pride in being refractory. For the next few moments I made no further effort to hypnotize her, allowing the conversation to proceed to other matters. As she spoke I assumed a position behind her chair. Without making her aware of my intention, I suddenly clapped my hands, at the same time commanding "SLEEP!" in a loud voice. Instantly she shut her eyes, her chin fell upon her chest, and she was in deep trance.

The Chinese gong used by many does not fatigue the auditory sense. Instead, the sound presents itself so unexpectedly that the subject is taken by surprise; his attention is focused suddenly, and the hypnotist takes advantage of the moment by shouting "SLEEP!"

It is my personal contention that when a hypnotist succeeds with a method requiring more than one minute of his time, his success is a matter of luck. Hypnosis is dependent upon misdirected attention; success which results during the course of an attempt to tire the senses occurs despite the method in use, not because of it.

B. BELIEF

The effectiveness of any method of induction depends largely upon the strength of the subject's belief in the power of his therapist. First, he must accept the validity of hypnotic phenomena; last, he must have the utmost confidence in the integrity as well as the technique of the hypnotist.

While the physician depends upon his prestige of position to inspire belief and confidence in his patient, the stage hypnotist, devoting his talents to the entertainment of the public, uses the common credulity of his audience to manifest the hypnotic process. As he does not intend seeing his subject again, he does not interest himself in any future harm which might befall the subject after he leaves the theatre. The antics of the stage hypnotist may cause great damage to his subject; also, of course, such lack of scruple is detrimental to the advancement of hypnosis as a scientific procedure. The situation is comparable to one in which a paid performer demonstrates a surgical technique for the amusement of his audience. No matter how good the technique, his performance can do much to discredit a science which satisfies an important therapeutic need.

It is by no means suggested that the laboratory experimentalist or the physician practice the technique that follows. Its inclusion here is only for the purpose of demonstrating the use of belief as an action potential in the phenomenon of hypnosis.

We notice principally that the theatrical performer has little regard for the consequences of his acts; therefore, he can proceed freely without the complications normally met in office procedure. First, he gives his explanation of hypnotism, wittily and vividly describing the marvels of the state; he boasts of his ability, creating an element of mysticism. He tells how few have been chosen for endowment of the Power; few of those are given the mystic training, and of those few, he, alone, was selected to study with the Indian Master. With audience interest at its height, he calls for a "volunteer." However clever the magician, his first volunteer is always a "plant," a subject who has been trained through constant conditioning and whose susceptibility is constant and dependable. He instantly enters such deep trance that the hypnotist can pierce his arm with a needle without drawing blood.

Now the audience is convinced, but more than that, the next volunteer—this time authentic—is also convinced. The showman need no longer deceive his audience; their belief is established. The legitimate subject responds partly because he saw the first subject respond. . . . and here the magician relies upon a psychological mechanism closely allied to *belief*:

imitation. The first subject acted in a certain fashion; the new subject knows exactly how to react, and accordingly he "delivers the goods."

But the hypnotist makes even greater use of the subject's belief. Hypnosis becomes deeper and deeper with more and more belief; therefore, he holds a swinging pendulum before the subject's eyes, explaining that soon his eyelids will become so heavy that he will find it difficult to keep awake. The subject soon feels the suggested fatigue and is convinced that hypnosis is working on him. The hypnotist has kept his word; there is reason to believe that subsequent suggestions will also take effect. Now the operator deepens that belief. He announces that the subject's arm is so stiff and rigid that he cannot move it. After a desperate attempt to move that arm, the subject realizes that he can't; one more proof *to him* of the mystic "power."

In following this process, we must recognize that the reason the subject could not move his arm was that he could not keep his eyes open. . . . and his eyelids *did* get tired (a clever example of the use of muscular fatigue to enhance the value of a suggestion, the fatigue serving no other than a suggestive value). The second suggestion worked on the basis of the success of the first; the third suggestion will be effective because the first two succeeded, and so on.

When the hypnotist has achieved results with simple suggestions, he may venture into more complex ones. Now he can conjure an illusion, prevent the reception of sensory perception or regress the subject to the age of six. But the only reason such suggestions will take effect is that the subject has willingly relinquished his capacity for struggle, and has focused all of his attention upon the words of the hypnotist. As he is preoccupied with actions occurring around him, his consciousness provides little haven for doubt.

Dr. Luys coined the word "credivity" to indicate that peculiar blind belief in the therapist's statements which accompanies the stages of hypnotism. However, he overlooked the expression of belief which must be evinced by a subject before any method of hypnotic induction can be effective.

We all are credulous to some degree, even when the situation in question furnishes inadequate substantiation. Blind belief is apparently a natural attribute of human personality. Were this not true, religious teachings would never have appeared, let alone have been accepted as widely as they are. Every day we assume the validity of ideas presented without the slightest trace of proof. We accept "authority," gladly shifting the responsibility of weighing evidence and making decisions.

Some of us cover our personal enigmas with alcoholic stimulation; others resort to "escape fiction," identifying ourselves with the invincible hero, the lovely heroine or the infallible detective. Similarly, many are inclined to prefer the unproven, romantic supernatural to what appears to be the drabness of the material. And all of us occasionally "believe" advertisements, editorials, and our friends.

A student of the mind must be unusually wary. Not long ago I attended a Sunday night gathering of acquaintances. During the conversation one chap mentioned that he was glad the next day was Sunday; he was more than ready to sleep late. I challenged him; today was Sunday, hence tomorrow would be a working day. He took issue with my correction, and everyone present earnestly assured me I was quite, quite wrong. Needless to say, I was confused, for mentally I could retrace my week-end activities, and I was sure that my friends were all wrong. Ah, but how sure was I? Not sure enough to avoid wondering what trick my thoughts might be playing upon me, certainly. Later I learned that I had been the victim of a genial conspiracy, but not soon enough to escape some quite serious self-examination.

We all tend to allow ourselves to be influenced by the ideas of others, and especially permit ourselves to accept things without conscious logical deductions. We either credit unproven ideas because we respect the authority behind them, or we become convinced of the validity of an assumption through continued repetition.

For example, suppose our next door neighbor looks like a thug: low hairline, receding jaw, cauliflower ears, and so on. We suspect he is up to no good. He is socially reticent; definitely not a "good mixer"; we distrust him a little further. Then we learn that he keeps odd hours, frequently coming home in the wee hours of the morning. Aha! Our suspicions are almost confirmed. Let a series of burglaries be reported in the neighborhood, and we are about ready to call the police. The fact that the gentleman in question may be a highly estimable research scientist who is occasionally detained at the laboratory affects our emotional response not one whit! Our suggestibility has proved itself all powerful.

Most of us solve our problems emotionally rather than logically, and if we dared to analyze our various beliefs, we should be appalled to discover the number that have no basis in logic.

When we depend upon belief manifested by a subject, we must not think of it in terms of logic but rather in terms of emotion, for if we permit the subject to analyze his confidence, he may not respond. Only when he becomes aware of the fact that hypnosis is an actuality will it become possible for him to be hypnotized.

This poses another problem: if the subject does not have sufficient belief in the hypnotic effect, is it possible for him to respond? Here it is my contention that, however much he may profess to discount the validity of hypnosis, he does so only consciously. The most logical of beings carries enough credulity in the depths of his unconscious to bolster the essential "credivity" for successful treatment.

While many ridicule the scientific possibilities of hypnotism, the very vehemence of their denunciations would indicate a substratum of belief charged with emotion strongly enough to cause them to respond easily to the procedure.

Under the heading of "Belief" we must also include fear, which is closely entwined. People who fear the effects of hypnosis generally make excellent subjects on the very basis of their anticipations. If they did not expect that it could be accomplished, they would not fear it. While it is occasionally advantageous to allay such anxieties, the trained hypnotist makes use of the emotion to induce the hypnotic state. Fear throws an entire psychological process into play. As long as the subject's mind is filled with it, there is no room for doubt, and his belief and imagination become so acute that the operator is furnished with potent tools which facilitate the process.

C. EXPECTATION

Belief is always occasioned by expectation. Whenever we are convinced of the validity of a certain assumption, we may expect its consequences to occur.

Many insomniacs are put to sleep with pharmaceutical concoctions consisting of inert substances of little value. The knowing physicians who prescribe such sleeping elixirs depend upon the patient's belief in the "drug" and on his expectation that it will have the desired effect. If later he learns the true nature of his "medicine," he will become immune to its influence; he no longer believes in its efficacy and will not expect it to take effect.

All the "faith cures" which have gained publicity have been effected through the beliefs and expectations of the patients. In such cases, the "healers" work with the disciple's belief in the omnipotence of a Supreme Being, stringing it to an emotional pitch of fullest intensity. When that belief becomes hysterical enough to dissolve nervous or emotional blocks, the patient is "healed." Thousands of invalids have journeyed many miles to a mission where cripples have been known to discard their crutches and walk; thousands of those invalids have been "healed." The most sceptical observer cannot doubt these facts; proof walks around us.

The explanation appears to be simple; the cure is the effect of suggestion and high-pitched expectation upon the human imagination, followed by its resultant effect upon the physical organism. It has been said that "faith can move mountains"; whenever a person has sufficient strength of belief, the phenomenon he expects is quite likely to occur. This premise is especially true in effects of an emotional nature.

There is an ancient fable about a Deadly Disease journeying to Bagdad, who met a Traveller going in the opposite direction.

"Where are you going?" asked the Traveller.

"I travel to Bagdad, where it is my duty to kill five thousand people," replied the Disease. "A merry journey to you, sir, for you are safe."

And each continued along his own path. Some months later they met again. The Traveller's greeting was cold. "You deceived me, O Disease," he complained. "You told me you were going to Bagdad to kill five thousand people, but lo, one hundred thousand perished!"

"Nay, Traveller, I deceived you not. I kept my word and killed five thousand; ninety-five thousand died of fear and expectation."

Every physician becomes acquainted with patients who announce on their sick-beds that death will come quickly, and it does. Some people have been known to will themselves to death. Conversely, patients afflicted with paralysis of hysterical origin often predict the very time when they will be able to walk. Occasionally these people swear that they received such "divine" messages in dreams—and the exact hour specified is the time that they become free of symptoms. We might say here that expectation of cure causes its fulfillment.

We have already seen in the case related by Bentivegni concerning an empty casket the manner in which sensory perceptions may be produced by expectation. The official expected an odor, and it appeared to him in full intensity. The fact that it did not exist was a small matter.

Other senses may be similarly confused. The person in the dentist's chair feels pain before the instrument touches him; the patient about to undergo surgery responds to valueless doses of anaesthesia; the girl who is enthusiastic about a "date" answers non-existent bells several times before the lad shows up. Expectation can either create sensory stimuli or exaggerate their proportion.

Psychiatrists are familiar with the habit reactions of stutterers. The one constant factor always in evidence is that the afflicted one stutters because he expects to stutter. Menstrual pains are generally functional in origin; the girl "expects" cramps, and cramps she gets. Real ones, too.

The hypnotist makes use of expectation, because the subject who expects to respond, does so. However, here we must differentiate between "wishing" and "expecting." The subject may *wish* to be hypnotized, with his conscious mind; yet it is not necessarily certain that he will succumb to the state. Likewise, an insomniac "wishes" he could go to sleep, but remembering that he slept badly the night before, he fully *expects* to toss and turn throughout another sleepless night. Consequently, he cannot *expect* to go to sleep.

Similarly, the subject will never be hypnotized until he *expects* to be hypnotized. This is a law which cannot be broken if we *expect* satisfactory results.

Fortunately, many factors are conducive to the desired feeling of expectation. We need mention only a few.

1. Our patients have heard of hypnosis. Whether or not they express belief is of little concern, for unconsciously they

fear the effect of the unknown. Fear results from some degree of credulity, and *expectation* invariably follows hard on the heels of fear.

2. The hypnotist's positive attitude produces a state of expectation in the subject. When the therapist exudes confidence and competence, the subject is convinced of success.

3. The very reputation of the therapist lends itself to a high degree of expectancy. Imitation also lends a hand: "If all these others reacted properly, of course, I shall too."

Under the heading of "Belief," we have already explained how suggestions are obeyed on the basis of previous suggestions which were likewise obeyed. Each executed suggestion further convinced the subject that he could not negate the hypnotist's commands. Each submission further impressed him with his lessening power of volition, until he became resigned to his state, placing his entire faculty of expectation under the control of the therapist.

The process is not complicated. To begin with, he *believed,* consciously or unconsciously, in hypnosis. When an inductive method was applied, the subject *believed* in the method, and expected it to be effective. It was. Thereafter each suggestion worked because the subject *believed* it would and *expected* it to. This explains to a great extent the entire mechanism of suggestibility. *Expectation* generally brings forth its own fulfillment. If the subject is fairly convinced that his arm is becoming paralyzed, it almost certainly will.

Assuming that we have induced such a condition, we observe that the subject's mental faculties become confused and disturbed. We have excited in him the feeling that he can hardly muster enough power to resist any of our suggestions. He has lost interest in the use of his capacity of volition, and he submits willingly to the therapist's suggestions. Each submission strengthens the hypnotic influence. Early suggestions, however, must never seem fantastic to the subject; the effect would destroy his state of expectation. An anaesthetic or hallucinatory suggestion to a subject unconvinced of volitional inability would cause him to rebel and conquer the situation by returning to the waking state.

One point here will precipitate the full magnitude of this device of expectation: *It is harder to start an action than to stop it.* If we tell a wide-awake person to raise his arm, he will resist, for he maintains his power of volition. If he agrees to cooperate experimentally and obliges us by raising his arm at our request, that arm will tire quickly. Now, with the obliging fellow's physiology to assist, we can suggest that his arm is becoming so tired that it is beginning to fall. No sooner have we uttered these words than the arm drops a little, as though some mysterious weight were tugging on the muscle. We have weakened his resistance, proving to him that he cannot rebel against our suggestions. From here on out, his expectation is on our side, and we won it, not by fighting his normal bodily processes, but by working with them.

In a sense, expectation accounts for many of the extraordinary phenomena that hypnosis can cause. If a hallucination is suggested, it is made manifest because of the subject's expectation. Like other hypnotic effects, this can be demonstrated in waking states. Let us tell a friend that a ferocious dog is about to leap upon him; he will jump to protect himself against the attack. In his mind—before he has an opportunity to confirm our statement—he will visualize the physical aspects of the animal as vividly as though it were present. (We can imagine what would happen were our friend blindfolded and unable to check the situation!) A definite fear-emotion mastered him, and his reaction was purely one of expectation.

When we treat of *suggestion,* we shall have occasion to examine the true nature of the procedure by which we make use of expectation in the induction of hypnotic states.

D. IMAGINATION

Among the faculties everyone uses is the ability to alter the scope of things. When a situation becomes difficult, the tendency to juggle environmental factors to conform to personality fancies arises. In some cases, these become defenses against life situations and can only culminate in neurotic patterns. Here, the insurmountable problem is temporarily driven from consciousness, and in its stead arises a mechanism of escape, which enables the victim—for the moment—to withdraw from the painful situation. There is little wonder that Charcot concluded that hypnosis was a hysterical manifestation, for it compared well with hysteria neurosis. The hysteric almost "suggests" physical symptoms to himself, as the hypnotist causes suggestions of a different nature to take effect.

As previously mentioned, psychosomatic medicine has furnished conclusive testimony to the effect that a great number of human ailments are functional rather than organic in origin. The symptoms are valid, but the most exhaustive examinations will yield no organic pathology. There simply is no "physical" cause.

If the emotional conflicts at their roots be dissolved, these symptoms disappear as swiftly and mysteriously as they came. There is no longer doubt that strong emotion, states of mind, and unconscious psychological conflicts can and do cause organic symptoms. Suggestion, implanted strongly enough, has been known to cause glandular changes. Every physician knows of patients who have literally "talked themselves" into malignant diseases.

In a sense, the very nature of ordinary conversation gives us a bit of insight concerning these mentally caused illnesses. The person who is "tired of it all" suffers from chronic fatigue; the woman whose "heart is broken" complains of a cardiac difficulty. The man with "business headaches" feels the same pain that migraine would cause; the wife who cannot "stomach her husband" is unable to digest her food, and the boy who cannot "stand" school loses his equilibrium and is forced to stay at home.

Every organ of the body seems to respond to a certain colloquial language.* Hippocrates, father of medicine, believed that it was more important to know what sort of person had a disease than to know the kind of disease the individual had!

In cases of hysterical paralysis a patient can lose total control of a portion of the body, thus providing a solution to the problem; perhaps, in the case of a woman, to force attention from a neglectful husband. In such an instance she may employ a narcissistic device that served her as a child. Whenever she wanted something, she got it if she cried loudly enough. Her paralysis has become a substitute for the crying, and a potent weapon it is, with which she can enslave her environment. Many blind people have lost their sight because of things they did not wish to "see"; and similarly there are "deaf" people who did not wish to "hear."

The extent of the control that the mind exerts over bodily processes is receiving wider and wider recognition. Everyday experiences furnish us with many indications. For instance, we know that an emotional shock of sufficient intensity can cause a pregnant woman to abort. Fear causes the body to shake, and if such stimulus becomes sufficiently heightened, the blood leaves the brain and the person faints. If a man unaccustomed to such sights witnesses an accident with much blood while on his way to lunch, he loses his appetite because his entire glandular apparatus has been altered by his reac-

* The reader will profit immensely in this connection by making use of two excellent books dealing with this subject: Dunbar, F., *Emotions and Bodily Changes,* Columbia University Press, New York, 1938; and Weiss, E. and English, O. S., *Psychosomatic Medicine,* W. B. Saunders Co., Philadelphia, 1949.

tion to the scene. Every muscle of the body, voluntary or involuntary in its action, can be affected by changes in emotion or by thoughts.

In conditions of psychogenic origin we find hypnotic suggestion working in a negative manner, for just as symptoms can be relieved by suggestion, they can likewise be produced. It is possible to suggest illness to a hypnotized subject. In fact we shall see by the following example that it is possible that people's health can be influenced by suggestion even in the waking state:

A perfectly healthy college student became the victim of a planned conspiracy in her psychology class. She was first approached by a co-ed who asked her how she was feeling since she did not "look too well." Next, a second classmate indicated with a look of concern that she "looked quite ill." Four encounters later, the girl was actually pale and sick, so sick, in fact, that she was bed-ridden for a week! Her friends may have "talked her into it," but the illness itself was perfectly genuine!

We are all susceptible to suggested sensations. You might like to try this little demonstration at the next party you attend. Choose some likely individual from your group and tell him convincingly that within five minutes he will have to scratch his nose, for it will itch annoyingly. Then, ignore him completely and go about your usual conversation. Within the suggested time, your victim will be forced to obey the suggestion you previously instilled in his consciousness, though he may make amusing efforts to resist the compulsive urge.

Boerheave, the physiologist, requested the courts to assign a condemned criminal to him for experimental purposes. In the presence of interested observers, he placed his victim on a stone slab, blindfolded him, and pretended to draw blood from his veins while buckets on each side received drops of water from pipes to stimulate blood pouring from the body. A few minutes later, the blindfold was removed, and when the observers bent over to examine the unusually pale body of the convict, they discovered that he was dead!

In a famous English legal case, a tutor perished in an odd manner. The boys at the school where he taught disliked him intensely and prepared to "rag" him. They erected a makeshift guillotine in the school yard, and when it was completed, they captured the frightened instructor, covered his eyes with a cloth, and told him that soon the blade would release and chop off his head. One boy imitated the sound of a falling knife; another threw a wet rag on the man's neck. He died instantly.

Before modern anaesthesia the famous Italian surgeon, Porta, would become very annoyed with patients who succumbed to shock on the operating table. He would scowl and dash his instruments to the floor, shouting, "Coward! You died of fright!"

Whether we call these manifestations fright, illusion or fantasy, they all fit into the category of *imagination*. All belong to the constructive faculty and hence modify mental images as products of the reproductive imagination.

With hypnosis, we create a modification of a mental image to such an extent that we summon a remembered effect from the subject's memory and reproduce the same emotion that he experienced when the occurrence first took place. Thus, we create an illusion in a subject's mind of events which he has previously experienced, either actually or vicariously. In accordance with this remembrance, the subject relives the recreated experience evoked by the hypnotic stimulus. Therefore, when a physical change results from suggestion, the body reacts as it did when the original experience took place.

It is my theory that a subject will only enact a suggestion which has been enforced by actual previous experience, either in reality, imagination, dream, or fantasy. Events in his life prior to the hypnotic session have conditioned him to react according to a certain pattern.

We can suggest changes in body temperature by telling the subject that he is becoming very warm. He obeys the suggestion because experience has taught him the feeling of being uncomfortably warm, and he reacts as he did when he felt that heat. He perspires, because we are recreating a remembrance of a situation in which he perspired before.

Analysis of a common occurrence will clarify this. When we think of a horrible situation, we shudder, regardless of how long ago, in point of time, it happened. Hypnosis, then, merely recalls the effect of a previously experienced stimulus. That stimulus need not be immediate. If imagined with sufficient intensity, it assumes all the aspects of reality. We have already seen that imagination and reality are closely connected; if one is convinced that what he thinks is there, it may as well be there for all practical purposes. There is no doubt that imagination can magnify the senses out of real proportion. When an object at night is mistaken for something else, fear and all its physical concomitants will grip and hold us until we discover our error.

Sensory changes become effective through imaginative distortion. This type of illusory success can be attained by hypnosis. Burot, an early hypnotist, produced nasal hemorrhages and bloody sweats by suggestion. The Frenchman, Focachon, obtained blisters on a patient's shoulder blades by suggesting to her that the postage stamps he pasted on her back would give off great heat. The burns, though simulated, appeared real and took two weeks to heal!

The Nancy School proved, with these and other demonstrations, that hypnosis directs the subject's *imagination* along a determined channel, thereby exerting control. Probably, however, their most significant discovery was their simplest; namely, that ideas and physical agents are capable of producing the same results.

There was a time when the dangerous practice of blood-letting was a "cure" for all ills. Today such methods are in disrepute, but while they were accepted, they had their many successes. Only a short time ago, turpentine was the panacea universal. It was common practice for doctors to tell their patients, "Quick! take this medicine while it still cures."

Imagination is certainly the greatest therapeutic adjunct at the physician's command. He knows that if the patient's imagination can be captured in the right channel, there is little doubt of recovery. The trained hypnotist has a strong advantage over the physician who lacks such training, in that he is able to exert direct control over the imaginative faculty.

E. THE HYPNOTIC FORMULA

The actual mechanism of hypnosis depends upon a fixed formula; when this formula is carried out meticulously, hypnosis *must* follow. It will be important for the student to consider its factors over and over again with each one of his subjects.

MISDIRECTED ATTENTION+BELIEF+EXPECTATION=THE HYPNOTIC STATE

Let us review briefly how each factor becomes operative in its direction toward our goal:

1. *Misdirected Attention*: It is essential that the subject concentrate his attention upon something irrelevant to the actual hypnosis: his mind, focused on a diverting channel, becomes unable to harbor doubt.

2. *Belief*: The prime requisite of effective hypnosis is the belief of the subject in both the competence and integrity of the hypnotist. He must believe that the therapist can do what he has promised; he must believe in hypnosis as an actual phenomenon; and he must believe in the inevitability of his personal surrender.

3. *Expectation*: With belief as a starting point, the sub·

ject must be conditioned to expectation. One suggestion works; the subject expects the next to take effect. When he expects to go to sleep, he will go to sleep and not before. Any effective technique, then, must include among it activities, pyramiding expectation.

4. *Imagination*: Imagination is the integrating factor which welds belief and expectation into an irresistible force. Fear can be utilized for added stimulus; the subject's wish to depart from "reality" causes him to welcome hypnosis as a desired experience. The subject's entire personality must be aligned with the aid of imagination in a definite course to aid and abet the experienced hypnotist.

REFERENCES

DUNLAP, K., *Habits, Their Making and Unmaking*, Liveright, New York, 1933.

FOREL, A., *Hypnotism and Psychotherapy*, translated by H. W. Armit, Rebman Company, New York, 1907.

GERRISH, F., "The Therapeutic Value of Hypnotic Suggestion," *Journal of Abnormal Psychology*, 4, 99, 1909.

HOLLANDER, B., *Methods and Uses of Hypnosis and Self-Hypnosis*, Allen & Unwin, London, 1935.

HOLLANDER, B., *Hypnotism and Suggestion in Daily Life, Education and Medical Practice*, G. P. Putnam's Sons, New York, 1910.

HULL, C. L., *Hypnosis and Suggestibility*, D. Appleton-Century Co., New York, 1933.

HUNT, J. M., (Ed.), *Personality and the Behavior Disorders*, Ronald Press, New York, 1944.

JANET, P., *The Major Symptoms of Hysteria*, Macmillan Co., New York, 1907.

KENNEDY, F., "The Inter-Relationship of Mind and Body," *Journal of the Mount Sinai Hospital*, IX, 4, 607–616, 1942.

HUNSTERBERG, H., *Psychology and Life*, Houghton Mifflin Company, Boston, 1899.

PRINCE, M., *Clinical and Experimental Studies in Personality*, ed. by A. A. Roback, Sci-Arts, Cambridge, 1939.

SIDIS, B. AND GOODHART, S. P., *Multiple Personality*, D. Appleton & Co., New York, 1905.

WHITE, M. M., "The Physical and Mental Traits of Individuals Susceptible to Hypnosis," *Journal of Abnormal and Social Psychology*, 25, 293–298, 1930.

5

Characteristics of Hypnosis

A. HEIGHTENED SUGGESTIBILITY

We have already indicated that every one maintains some degree of susceptibility to suggestion. A man may be logical, with cold and calculating reason and a file of scholarly indices to help him find a solution to every problem, and yet be consciously taken in by unproven concepts which appeal to his emotional fancies at the time of their expression.

Closer study of the hypnotic method reveals the tremendous import of suggestion as a means of creating the state, perpetuating the condition of control and especially of returning the subject to normal consciousness in which he executes the suggestions administered during trance.

We proceed to hypnotize the subject by first of all suggesting to him that he can be hypnotized. (Belief) Next, we describe to him both the method we shall use and his own probable reaction. (Expectation) When he experiences the effect we have suggested, he responds further because he believes he will and fully expects to. (Belief plus expectation)

The patient's imagination is a potential that can be exploited as an adjunct to belief, for it gives impetus to the patterns of integrated response created by suggestion. Positive reaction to a specific suggestion is always enhanced by the hypnotist's use of the patient's own faculties.

Heightened suggestibility implies the increase of the patient's *own* faculty of suggestibility. It does not indicate a particular endowment granted the therapist. At best he is comparable to a catalytic agent, having the tendency to make a composition change, without himself becoming involved in the process. His actions stimulate an increase in function of a potential which has always been present in the mind of his subject.

B. IMPULSE

The evidence of most observers indicates that hypnosis reaches its height with a subject who is impulsive by nature rather than with the one whose mentality seeks rational explanations of an idea before acceptance. Cannon stated that if he had a choice between two candidates for hypnotic séance: one, a man who, robbed by an armed thief, fights back, and the other, a man similarly situated who waits until he has been robbed before seeking help, he would select the first as the ideal subject without any question.

Hypnosis, then, depends to some degree upon the impulsiveness of the subject submitting to it. The most learned scholar has a degree of thoughtless action when confronted with certain situations. In the development of learning capacities, impulse inevitably precedes rationalization. Hypnosis utilizes the impulsive characteristic dormant in all human beings, for only when the subject's integrated patterns of behavior are temporarily thrown out of commission by situations which he cannot "think through" will he revert to a lower behavior-intelligence level or to an age when he did not have to think for himself. Here, the hypnotist replaces the father or other powerful authority, and every suggestion translates itself into a command which must be obeyed. The subject loses his power of resistance and accepts suggestions blindly, executing them faithfully.

In mob grouping, impulsiveness seems to be spread by contagion. Once, in the South, I saw a mob in action. One lone sheriff stood at the door of the city jail, facing oaths and threats from the milling crowd. The situation looked grim for the Negro inside, who was rumored to have assaulted a female of the town. Some of the most intelligent men and women in the neighborhood were present; yet I asked questions for hours, only to find that no-one had proof of the prisoner's guilt. No evidence, circumstantial or otherwise, was available to uphold the charge. Some insignificant rabble-rouser had "spread the word," and the impulsiveness of humanity did the rest.

Every malicious dictator who ever rose to power did so on the impulsiveness of the "mob." He owed his successes to the efficacy of his influence over the emotions of the people. Dictators know that when hate-emotion is strong enough, reason can never seep through. One Nazi dictum stated, "Whenever there is a conflict between faith and reason, follow faith!"

Behavior and action normally result from sufficient stimuli; indeed the very definition of behavior denotes this. Suggestion, however, brings definite *behavior patterns* into play by assuming the role of an adequate stimulus. Thus, hypnosis provides a reaction control resulting from stimuli which would ordinarily be incapable of producing the given response in the waking state.

We can easily illustrate this; a man in possession of full consciousness sees a vicious dog before him. He cringes with terror and makes every effort to protect himself. His reaction is governed by the sight of the stimulus, in this case, the dog. The stimulus is certainly sufficiently alarming to cause the terror. Hypnosis, on the other hand, can provide a false stimulus, which in the waking state, would not cause the reaction. As previously described, if the hypnotist causes his subject to "see" a vicious dog and further suggests an imminent attack, the subject will behave *as if* he were actually under attack.

C. THE AS IF PRINCIPLE

Why does the subject accept the ideas we plant in his mind? We have so influenced his logical faculty that he now accepts everything we tell him "as if" it were actually true; he reacts to suggestion as a stimulus, even though it may exist on non-logical grounds. When we nullify one sensory-perception or produce another; when we introduce a thought into his mind or condition one already present; when we cause an action or dispel a contemplated one, we are causing an important manifestation in the subject, for he is acting "as if" everything we have told him were true.

The voluntary subject preparing for hypnosis bestows his confidence on the therapist, and he conditions himself to satisfy every command. He shows himself perfectly agreeable to the other's control over his mental apparatus as far as its use and function are concerned. But above everything else he is willing to adopt the "as if" attitude during the entire procedure. Once the state of hypnosis has been attained, the subject will act upon stimuli that have no appreciable value in any other circumstances. By regarding each suggestion "as if" it were feasible and authentic, his behavior changes as it would in the presence of real stimuli.

The subject demonstrates his willingness to assume the role of an actor who must act, emote and feel according to the dictates of a director who calls every move. "This is a chair; this is a table," orders the director, pointing toward an empty alcove on the stage. "Your mother enters. You see her and are overjoyed at the meeting." The actor regards the table and chair as being present, and complies with his director's instructions, acting "as if" his mother were actually entering the room. It is said that a good actor can place himself in any set of circumstances and in every sense live the role of the character he portrays. The creation of reality from sheer imagery is the mark of distinction toward which every thespian strives.

The hypnotic subject and the stage actor have one qualification in common: both must be capable of accepting the falsified impression "as if" it were true.

D. SUGGESTION

1. *Definition*

From a strictly conservative definition, the term "suggestion" as applied to an order given to a subject is a misnomer. The hypnotist does not "suggest"; he "persuades." He does not say: "Don't you think that you would better keep your eyes shut?" Instead, he commands authoritatively, "Now you cannot open your eyes!"

It is certainly not my intention to change a word that fits so satisfactorily into a universal scheme which is standard throughout the world. Instead, before continuing, I shall attempt to fix a definition that is applicable to the sense in which the word is used.

Hypnotic Suggestion is the process of controlled alteration of human actions and reactions through thoughts, objects, or actions.

2. *Nature of Hypnotic Suggestion*

The tardy emergence of hypnotism from the wallows of quackery was caused by erroneous views propounded by early experimenters and adopted intact by later observers. Statements were made rashly on the basis of uncontrolled experiments. Findings were accepted or rejected according to the popularity of their proponents.

Deslon, one of Mesmer's immediate successors, made an evaluation of prime importance in relation to the mystery of the hypnotic process by stating that *imagination alone produced all of the hypnotic effects.* This assumption was much too simple an explanation for acceptance by later observers.

Bernheim was bolder in his experimental analysis than Braid, Charcot and others who denied hypnosis as an extra-physiological condition. His key to the phenomenon was summed up in the statement that "suggestion is everything." He even dared to conclude that "there is no hypnosis; there is nothing but suggestion!" Professor Dubois, who discounted most of the hypnotic theories, reproached Bernheim's scientific conduct:

"The practice of hypnosis has accustomed one to immediate success, to theatrical effects. It leads its patients by the nose, making them believe everything that it wants them to believe; its therapeutic scepticism has no limits; everything is suggestion."

The controversy between the "physical" and "mental" schools has been perpetuated intermittently to this day by arguments resulting in retardation rather than advancement of the science. The adherents of the physical school have repudiated the idea of suggestion as the principal cause of the phenomenon, and still persist in the techniques of blinding lights, mysterious objects and other such elementary agents. The methods of some modern hypnotists appear to be the method of James Braid of a century ago, with slight, pseudo-scientific variations.

One psychotherapeutic fact is certain, and we might base all of our curative ability on this one premise, so aptly phrased by Dubois:

"*The patient with a functional malady will get well when he is convinced that he will be well; he will be cured*

at the exact moment he convinces himself that he is cured!"
Dubois presented this statement with unreserved conviction,
claiming that its accuracy had been authenticated by unlim-
ited clinical experience. If true, it explains the suggestive
quality that the average physician uses instinctively, although
it is—in most cases—unknown to him.

As a result of my own clinical experience with hypnosis
I would agree with Bernheim that suggestion is the governing principle behind all hypnotic manifestations. It begins its
activation long before the subject submits to the therapist's
influence. Hypnosis initiates its primary effect at the time
the subject scantily learns of its existence.

Let us consider a typical patient's first association with
hypnosis. It wears an aura of mystery, which renders him susceptible to his own imagery. Newspaper accounts of fabulous
claims connected with it, coupled with fictional stories of di-
abolical villains who preyed upon defenseless damsels with
their hypnotic power, serve to accentuate the acuity of his
imaginative conception. His feeling is not that of the acade-
mician; it is, instead, one of curiosity mingled with fear. On
the one hand, he would like to experience the sensation; on
the other, his ardor is dimmed by the fear.

The patient becomes afflicted suddenly with a malady
that defies treatment. He journeys from doctor to doctor,
from clinic to clinic, eventually submitting to observation at
Rochester, with no gratification. As he is about to settle down
to a lifetime of semi-invalidism, a neighbor hesitantly tells
him of Doctor Brown and of the wonders he performed with
her. His method is "peculiar," but she is certain he can help.
By now, the patient is clutching at straws with the frantic
grip of a drowning man and is readily convinced.

He appears at Doctor Brown's office a half-hour early.
His fingers fumble nervously through every magazine in the
ante-room. He expects the worst. Two patients sit within
hearing distance, comfortably discussing their troubles and

the miraculous help they have received from the doctor. Heretofore, he had been harboring the doubt that maybe he could not be hypnotized. Now his doubt is shaken, for the doctor is unquestionably successful. How else could he afford this beautiful suite of offices. . . . and if all those others could be hypnotized, why should he be the exception?

The expected moment arrives. He is ushered into a consultation room whose walls are lined with numerous books, another indication of the doctor's learning. The consultation is brief; the hypnotic session ready to begin. The doctor's confident demeanor removes the last trace of the patient's doubt. He is requested to watch a gleaming gold fountain pen while the doctor tells him that he is becoming drowsy. Within a few moments he submits completely to hypnosis.

This brings up a curious question: *what hypnotized the patient?* or rather, *who* hypnotized him? Was it merely the doctor's continuous, monotonous suggestion of drowsiness? or the shining pen held before his eyes?

I am inclined to think that both of these were purely incidental to the main process. First, we know that the patient's initial curiosity had been aroused; this was of extreme value. Secondly, the neighbor acquainted him with the wonders of Doctor Brown, and in so doing, gave him the most important suggestion: she stimulated his *imagination,* provided him with *belief,* and informed him of what he might *expect.* Basically, it was she who hypnotized him, aided by the conversation he overheard in the ante-room, and assisted a bit more by the impressive display of books in the doctor's office. The patient was conditioned for hypnosis before the doctor opened proceedings. Any method used would have accomplished the hypnotic result; in effect, the patient hypnotized himself, aided by the gadgets of the doctor.

Now, we must consider a fundamental axiom: *Suggestion creates the hypnotic phenomena, and in turn, the phenomena create heightened suggestibility.* Analysis of all methods of hypnotic induction will show this to be apparent.

We have already referred to suggestibility as a quality which we all possess in varying degree. No one likes to be called suggestible, because that smacks of mind or character weakness. We much prefer to give our friends the impression that we are the "masters of our fate"; that we—if no one else does—think for ourselves. But while we all enjoy such fantasies, few of us ever outgrow the "follow-the-leader" games we played as youngsters. Our fashions in clothes give us away on that; to be in style, we wear what others wear. A woman changes her hair-do because it is "all the rage" at the moment. And where is the man brave enough to wear a purple suit? It is "not done." Language also expresses suggestibility in the use of slang and colloquialisms.

Tremendous fortunes have been amassed by clever executives whose one impetus has been the burning desire to have what the Joneses have. Politicians juggle their constituents with suggestion; the religious cultist fills his tabernacle with hordes of suggestible people. It is this very suggestibility of the human race that bestows the tremendous benefits available through hypnosis!

When we are convinced of one thing which we would ordinarily disbelieve, it is easier to be convinced of additional facts which in themselves would be incredible. (Remember the White Queen in Lewis Carroll's story who always believed five impossible things before breakfast just to keep in practice?) We have already seen this mechanism in action. Suggestion proves to be the mainspring of the hypnotic machine. Every characteristic of the hypnotic method presents verification of this hypothesis.

In my opinion, those who cling to the physiological explanation for the hypnotic state have been misled by erroneous conclusions drawn from the evidence. From my observation it is not necessary for the therapist to speak in a monotonous voice, to dangle outré objects before one's eyes, or to burn strong incense to win hypnotic response. The subject's normal capacity for suggestibility sets the wheels of the process in motion, and external suggestion merely gives impetus to the human susceptibility to it.

3. *Mechanics of Suggestion*

One fact towers above all others in connection with the hypnotic state: the acceptance, obedience and docility which are found in every hypnotized subject, in accordance with the commands of the hypnotist.

Professor Janet attempted to account for this by postulating a resemblance between conditions of hypnosis and those of hysteria. Both represent a peculiar departure from normal brain activity, arising as special deficiencies of energy. These in turn affected the cerebral hemispheres, thereby causing mental disassociation. According to Janet, only hysterics can be hypnotized because of their dissociation of mental activity.

This stigma, which Janet stamped on hypnotism, has long since been disproven by clinical data; nearly everyone can be influenced by hypnosis, and marked hysterics definitely do not make the best subjects.

The only reasonable inference is that suggestibility springs from that belief which the subject has accepted, although the basic evidence rests upon not always logical grounds. Once the belief is established, the therapist impresses the subject with his helplessness in the face of the hypnotist's prestige. With each acceptance, the subject sinks into deeper stages of hypnosis, the final depth being dependent upon the subject's willingness and ability to comply with suggestions.

Let us consider a typical method of hypnosis. The patient is seated in a comfortable chair and requested to fix his attention upon a bright light overhead. When his eyes begin to water, the hypnotist takes his cue. He accentuates the physical effect by suggesting that the subject's eyes are tiring (of course they are, but the therapist is calling his subject's attention to the fact, increasing the degree of suggestibility!), his eyelids are beginning to flutter (another muscular reaction upon which the therapist capitalizes!), his head is becoming very heavy, and soon he will be asleep.

Each suggestion has had its premise in logic; each suggestion increased the subject's susceptibility to the acceptance of a future suggestion. But one fact becomes apparent; had the subject not *expected* hypnosis, he could have gazed at the light indefinitely without experiencing more than burning eyelids and a fatigued optic muscle. Therefore, it is reasonable to assume that the responsible factor in induction of trance was a combination of the subject's normal aptitude for suggestibility plus skilled exploitation of this aptitude.

The therapist's words must closely follow the subject's actions without his growing aware of it. The interaction of these two factors leads the subject to believe that he is following the operator's suggestions, although the reverse is true.

It is easy to see the value of this innocent artifice. Anyone's eyes will water and become fatigued when stimulated by bright objects of unusual intensity, and this uncomfortable situation is taken advantage of by the therapist in repeatedly focusing the subject's attention upon that discomfort. The latter inevitably accepts the reality of the influence; everything he is told is true. This acceptance lends weight to the therapist's prestige; the subject is increasingly aware of the hypnotist's leadership, and consequently accepts more complex suggestions with decreasing conscious resistance until he becomes entirely submissive.

4. *Suggestion and the Unconscious*

Modern psychology has demonstrated the role of the unconscious in its scope of activity, leaving little doubt that the control of certain physiological functions rests with the unconscious mind, whose spectacular power has been proven again and again by that elaborate research laboratory, hypnosis.

When we visualize a tremendous card-file with millions of neatly assorted fragments of acquired knowledge and a like number of corresponding pictures of people and objects that we have unknowingly committed to our memory, our perception still scarcely does justice to the broad function of this unconscious mechanism.

Once we assume that the unconscious directly or indirectly influences bodily functions, we can reasonably account for the many hypnotic phenomena that have hitherto been inexplicable. That assumption explains the process of induced anaesthesia, hysterical paralysis, or the blanking out of a sensory perception. Hypnosis produces these and many more curious phenomena by establishing greater access to the unconscious. It does not pretend to cause a change in it; it merely inhibits conscious activity, creating a free channel to the mechanism responsible for so much of body control.

The unconscious mind, despite its apparent omnipotence, is a childlike mind—infantile to the degree that it neither concludes nor rationalizes. Such duties are consigned to the conscious faculty. The unconscious merely accepts the result of conscious reasoning, transferring these deliberative consequences into action. It yields with supple indifference to the dictates of the higher conscious influence.

To clarify this process, we might consider an automotive vehicle and its driver. The machine is gifted with definite functions, but none of these are put into operation without the direction of the man at the wheel. He is the motivating factor behind every functional quality of the machine. He turns the key in the ignition, steps on the starter, and by these actions sets a thousand parts of the mechanism automatically into motion. Thereafter, the combustion system will burn the gasoline properly, the oil will provide necessary lubrication, pistons move up and down in proper rhythmic sequence, and sparks will jump across the wires. Every function of the motor has become automatic, but only upon the initial direction of the man in control of the vehicle. Without such direction, the machine is nothing more than a powerful potential; with control, it is a mechanism capable of amazing feats.

At this point, the illustration may be broadened to extend our knowledge of hypnotic phenomena. Now it does not really matter to the automobile who drives it. Anyone with an ignition key and requisite knowledge of the mechanism may sit behind the wheel to direct its activity. Such an operation would be extremely difficult if the original driver stubbornly refused to relinquish his control of the vehicle. His obstinacy might be overcome by a blow in the right spot or a threat, and the aggressive aspirant for the wheel could assume control with no opposition from the vehicle involved.

We may understand the unconscious in just these terms. It is an impersonal contrivance which puts itself beneath the direction of anyone who will command it. It does not have the discriminative faculty to discern by reason who its master should be. It enacts every decree commanded by the conscious mind with utter servility, whether that mind be the one of its original master or of one who interposes.

It seems logical to suppose that if the conscious mind be deposed from its authority, then the unconscious could do little but follow the dictates of another consciousness with compliancy. We have already spoken of the factors requisite for the hypnotist's leadership of the subject's unconscious. The only way such control can be achieved is to cause a break in the conscious-unconscious relationship. This dissociation provides the hypnotic access to the unconscious without interference from the conscious volition of the subject, making the depth of the hypnotic state dependent upon the subject's degree of diminished conscious activity.

When the unconscious partially loses its former motivation, it becomes subject to another force (the hypnotist) and acts in accordance with the dictates of that force. This process may be termed "heightened suggestibility." It is the all-powerful force behind every hypnotic phenomenon; without it there can be no hypnosis.

5.   Can Suggestion Be Dangerous?

While many investigators have discounted the harm which can befall the subject during hypnotic trance and in the post-hypnotic period, I frequently recall the words of Hollander in his excellent book on hypnosis:

> "I cannot understand authorities on hypnotism declaring, on the one hand, what a wonderful power hypnotism is, and on the other hand that hypnotic subjects can protect themselves against deception by a mountebank or a rogue." *

My own inclination is such that I am in absolute accord with Hollander's view. Elsewhere in these pages I have expressed the opinion that with adequate conditioning criminal acts can be facilitated through the use of hypnosis. This is of course hypothetical as I have no specific case in mind; nevertheless, I would not underestimate the potential capacity of a strong suggestion in an adaptable mind.

Björnström cites a widely reported experiment, having its initial appearance in the French journals, which was based upon an idea borrowed from Clareties' novel, *Jean Mornas*. In this instance suggestion succeeds in persuading a girl through hypnosis to steal a bracelet and later accuse a man of having committed the crime. Björnström also reports an experiment by Liégeois in which a girl under hypnosis is made to confess to the hideous murder of her friend before a justice of the peace, though she had been informed of the consequences of her confession.

* Hollander, B., *Methods and Uses of Hypnosis and Self-Hypnosis*, Allen & Unwin, London.

A case in point was called to my attention recently in which a girl at a summer resort asked a psychology student to hypnotize her with the intention of suggesting to her that her fear of water would be overcome, and that she would thereafter be able to swim. The student, throwing caution to the wind and seeing only the immediate popularity to be gained, readily consented to the girl's wishes. Before an audience of assembled guests he succeeded in producing a fairly deep stage, during which he administered the suggestions. In her confident enthusiasm the subject arose the next morning before the other guests and plunged into the lake for a swim. Her bloated body was recovered from the water a few hours later.

The overtaxing of the subject's abilities, especially in the hands of the untrained, constitutes the real danger of hypnosis. This is of utmost importance, and is by far the most logical reason why it must not be used as a toy for the amusement of the novice. The doctor, on the other hand, understanding the physiological capabilities of his patient, will find much in hypnosis as a therapeutic device, knowing too, the dangers which can result from its abuse.

A professor of psychology, whose works have gained much attention, has written up an experiment conducted before college students. The subject, upon being hypnotized, was commanded to clasp his hands as tightly as possible and was told that he would not be able to open them until he was instructed to do so. A burning cigarette was forced between the clasped hands in such manner that he would suffer severe burns if they could not be pulled apart. True to form the subject made several attempts, screaming the while. The odor of burnt flesh was noticeable. Finally after the subject pleaded for release from the suggestion the professor relented.

As the professor did not exercise the precautions of medical training, he was undoubtedly not aware of the infections that can ensue from burns, even in hypnotized subjects. Normal human beings do not become immune to bacteria, nor do they manifest superhuman qualities during hypnosis. An excellent axiom to follow in this regard is that *if a subject's compliance to a suggestion will be injurious to him in the waking state, it will have the same effect upon him during hypnosis.* The excuse, "It was just an experiment," is never justification for injury.

E. COMPARATIVE ANALYSIS OF SLEEP AND HYPNOSIS

Anyone who has had the opportunity to observe a subject under hypnotic control would assert that hypnosis differs in many ways from ordinary sleep. The essential characteristic of difference, immediately evident, is the subject's activity in response to suggestion. Though he manifests the classical signs of the hypnotic state, upon suggestion he is able to speak, laugh, cry, walk around the room, play a musical instrument or perform any action considered normal in a state of wakefulness.

Physiological sleep, on the other hand, is attended by greater or less depression of waking activity. It denotes a period of rest; control of posture and skeletal muscle tonicity, respiratory movements and vascular tone are relaxed; higher nervous activities are depressed.

When the comparative differences of the two states have been examined, one might conclude that they bear slight similarity. Yet closely related factors prevailing in both states lead us to believe that the phenomenon of sleep and that of hypnosis are not entirely antagonistic to each other. Most of us have experienced at some time a sensation of total relaxation while lying in bed in readiness for sleep. In this state we are neither awake nor in slumber, but we are not aroused by the lesser extraneous sensations around us. There is considerable reason to believe that this sensation and hypnosis are one and the same condition.

In an attempt to reach some conclusion on this point, I chose seventeen patients for experiment under suitable conditions of control. None of these subjects had previously submitted to hypnosis, nor were they aware of the fact that I employed such a method of treatment. I proceeded by requesting each subject to lie on a bed situated in a darkened room, most factors of which were conducive to relaxation. He was asked to try to get some rest as his relaxation was necessary for the treatment that was to follow. I impressed him with the idea that if he could take a nap for a little while, the later treatment would have greater effect on him. When the patient had reclined I took a chair several feet from the bed, which afforded me vantage ground for view of the subject. No further suggestions were given for the moment, every effort being made to avoid the suggestions which would normally bring on hypnosis. After periods ranging from eighteen minutes to one hour and forty-two minutes, depending upon the subject, I noticed certain signs which informed me of the fact that the patient was giving way to relaxation: respiration was becoming slower and deeper. This was generally concurrent with predominantly costal breathing and weaker diaphragmatic contractions. Frequently I would notice with these subjects a deep intake of air followed by a sigh. At this time I would approach the bed and issue the suggestion that the patient's arm was rising and he could not stop it from doing so. In several of these experiments this suggestion would at first elicit no response except, perhaps, a deep breath and another sigh. On these occasions I would repeat the suggestion a few times and, eventually, it would be acted upon. In four of the seventeen cases the patients responded by complete waking, though later, upon questioning, three of the recalcitrant subjects attested to the fact that they were in states preparatory to sleep when the intrusion of the suggestion awakened them. One of these patients asserted that she experienced "a weird feeling of fright."

The remaining thirteen patients made satisfactory response to the suggestion and reacted successfully to commands that followed, finally enforcing post-hypnotic suggestions upon being returned to the waking state.

In the cases which showed changes in respiratory movements, it was interesting to note that the costal breathing, which was predominant in the first phase of relaxation, remained costal during the period of suggestibility and was not replaced by the diaphragmatic respiratory movements of waking, until these patients were returned to normal wakefulness. The rate of respiration quickened in every case at the institution of the initial suggestion, but soon leveled itself, probably due the fact that the voice came as a jolt to the patient's tranquillity, as it imposed upon the silence of the room; the later leveling off was very likely due to his adjustment to the intervention of the sound.

In anticipation of arguments concerning the validity of the nature of the experiment, I shall be the first to state that certain weaknesses in it prevent assertion of conclusions. First, the signs which I noted as preliminary to the sleep state are merely personal observations; second, could my cursory suggestions hinting of sleep be comparable to the suggestions which antecede hypnosis, and if this was the case, were my later suggestions given to a hypnotized subject? I shall not attempt to enter into altercation concerning the first point as our present knowledge of sleep can only permit speculation. The second point is in the form of a question, to which I would answer, "Yes."

When sleep is not based on sensations of irresistible fatigue, it is brought on by indirect auto-suggestion. The person, before retiring for the night, indicates to himself or others: "I feel tired, I think I'll turn in," or "It's past my bedtime," which immediately initiates a conditioned response and thus assumes the force of a suggestion to be enacted. In his bedroom he arranges things so that they will be most conducive to his rest. When he has made himself comfortable in his bed, with lights out, he is now mentally and physically prepared for the sleep that will follow. He closes his eyes, sheltering himself from extraneous visual sensations which might distract his attention from the sleep process. One might say that he eventually falls asleep because he wills himself to do so. Would it be very difficult to assume that the methods finally causing him to sleep are so different from the methods that produce hypnosis?

Pavlov's inhibitory theory has it, as one of its contentions, that sleep is caused by the spreading of an inhibitory influence over various parts of the brain; that certain conditioning stimuli cause a rapid and profound inhibition of the cortex. For some period afterwards the inhibition remains and can combine with other inhibitory stimuli, causing a summation of effect. When this occurs, the inhibition grows in intensity and soon involves other areas of the brain. These areas, though not originally affected by the stimulus, now lose their ability to be stimulated due to the spreading of the inhibitory influence. In this interval, the brain is in a state of diminished excitability, no longer being able to exhibit conditioned reflex response to normally appropriate stimuli. The state produced by the spreading inhibitory influence is, according to Pavlov, known to us as sleep. For a more comprehensive description of these concepts the reader is referred to the original treatises.

Pavlov also observes that the person does not make an immediate jump from wakefulness to sleeping, but travels through certain intermediate stages before reaching the sleep state. In this defined period between waking and sleeping exists the state of hypnosis.

Though Hull, on the weight of Bass' experiments, takes

issue with Pavlov's contentions,* my personal observations are in accord with Pavlov's placement of hypnosis. One can reasonably entertain this view in the light of apparent hypnotic phenomena. If, as an example, the subject is placed in a hypnotic state and left alone, i.e., not given suggestions for a period of time and not offered previous suggestion as to specific time for waking, he will react in one of two ways, depending upon his depth of hypnotic response: if the hypnotist has brought him to light stages he will awaken within a short time; if in a relatively deep stage his state will progress to normal sleep, and he will awaken as the result of stimuli which would affect the average sleeper.

This point would express the fact that the hypnotist holds his subject's attention by keeping him in a state of activity by frequent suggestions that the subject has little alternative but to enforce. Therefore, when activity ceases there is little to maintain his attention and he either returns to consciousness or descends the scale to lower levels.

Many investigators have written about the kindred characteristics of sleep-walking and hypnosis. The fact that sleep-walking or somnambulism will arise from a sleep state, under certain conditions, is no longer a matter for dispute. The fact, too, that the somnambulist will act upon suggestion is known to every person who has ever had close association with one. He can walk without stumbling, converse with persons who intercept him, and follow a command to return to bed. After varied experience with patients who were known to exhibit this phenomenon periodically, I would contend that its likeness to hypnosis is unquestionable.

In the course of my work in sanitariums I had the opportunity to observe at close hand several cases of somnambulism. In every instance the patient, during this state, ac-

* The reader interested in an experimental approach to hypnosis will profit from Hull's *Hypnosis and Suggestibility*, D. Appleton-Century Co., New York, 1933.

cepted suggestions without difficulty in the same manner as if he were hypnotized. Each of the subjects was likewise brought to full consciousness by the usual waking suggestions employed in hypnosis. From these and other observations I have concluded that the sleep-walker is aroused from his sleep state by one or several stimuli, which may take the form of a dream, a sudden sound or a light penetrating the window. The latter stimulus might account for the effect of a full moon upon the somnambulist. Such stimuli, not being of sufficient intensity to result in complete waking, nevertheless, are ample to arouse the patient out of normal sleep and convey him to a state between waking and sleeping.

That such a state is an actuality can be demonstrated in everyday life. All of us have experienced the intrusion of a ringing telephone upon a sound sleep. At first it is difficult for us to get our bearings. We might rationalize for the moment that the telephone is not ringing. Finally we give way to its insistence, but only after a tedious struggle to awaken. The stimulus has made entrance upon our slumber. Momentarily we are in condition of torpor—we are sluggish, apathetic and dull. In this brief interlude we are neither awake nor asleep, and probably in a state of suggestibility.

If a subject is later asked to describe the sensations he has experienced while hypnotized, he will usually tell of a feeling of "wavering." For example: "It seemed that I was on a wave going up and down—up and down. Sometimes I felt a tingling, first in my fingers and arms and then in my legs. The tingling continued while you were suggesting, but the wave stopped going up and down. It started again when you stopped speaking."

Another patient reports a similar sensation: "Have you ever been on a boat that was rocking back and forth? That's the feeling I had—as if I was moving back and forth with the boat. When I heard your voice the sensation stopped immediately. It was a nice feeling. I liked it. When your voice came on, the rocking stopped and then I was doing everything you were telling me to do. I was absorbed in what you were saying. I could have refused to do it; still I didn't care one way or the other. When you stopped talking for a few minutes the rocking started all over again."

As similar sensations are reported by many of our patients we might hypothesize that the subject under hypnotic influence, if not offered suggestion for a time will waver between wakefulness and sleep, yielding to either if left in this state. As a moot point it is still open to investigation.

REFERENCES

BERNHEIM, H., *Suggestive Therapeutics,* translated by C. A. Herter, G. P. Putnam's Sons, New York, 1899.

BJÖRNSTÖRM, F., *Hypnotism,* translated by Baron Nils Posse, Humboldt Publishing Co., New York, 1887.

BRAMWELL, J. M., *Hypnotism,* Wm. Rider & Sons, London, 1913.

BRENMAN, M., "Experiments in the Hypnotic Production of Anti-Social and Self-Injurious Behavior," *Psychiatry,* 5, 49–61, 1942.

BRENMAN, M. AND GILL, M. *Hypnotherapy,* International Universities Press, New York, 1947.

CANNON, A., *Science of Hypnotism,* E. P. Dutton Co., New York, 1936.

CUDDON, E., *Hypnosis: Its Meaning and Practice,* Bell, 1938.

DEJERINE, J. AND GAUCKLER, E., *The Psychoneuroses and Their Treatment by Psychotherapy,* translated by S. E. Jelliffe, J. B. Lippincott Co., Philadelphia, 1913.

DUBOIS, P., *Psychoneuroses and Their Psychic Treatment,* Francke, Bern, 1905.

ERICKSON, M. H., "An Experimental Investigation of the Possible Anti-Social Use of Hypnosis," *Psychiatry,* 2, 391–414, 1939.

HULL, C. L., *Hypnosis and Suggestibility,* D. Appleton-Century Co., New York, 1933.

HULL, C. L., Patten, E. F., and Switzer, S. A., "Does Positive Response to Direct Suggestion As Such Evoke a Generalized Hypersuggestibility?" *Journal of General Psychology,* 8, 52–64.

JANET, P., *The Major Symptoms of Hysteria,* Macmillan Co., New York, 1907.

PAVLOV, I. P., "Inhibition, Hypnosis and Sleep," *British Medical Journal,* 256–267, 1923.

PAVLOV, I. P., "The Identity of Inhibition with Sleep and Hypnosis," *Scientific Monthly,* 17, 603–608, 1923.

PAVLOV, I. P., *Lectures on Conditioned Reflexes,* translated by W. H. Gantt, International Publishers, New York, 1928.

WHITE, R. W. AND SHEVACH, B. J., "Hypnosis and the Concept of Dissociation," *Journal of Abnormal Psychology,* July, 1942.

6

Necessary Considerations
in Hypnotic Procedure

The reader who has followed us so far should accept with little difficulty the importance of an adequate technique of hypnosis, and may easily recognize the factors upon which such a
technique must be based. Of course, it would be impossible to
evolve a method that would prove equally efficacious with every patient. The worth of any method depends upon its ap-
plicability to the subject; from my experience no one method
can be universally successful.

The competent therapist is adroit in his choice of a suitable method of induction. He will take various facets of his
subject's personality into consideration before deciding upon
its particular approach. What proves to be inspirational in
one circumstance will be completely worthless in another.

Before proceeding with induction methods, however, we
should analyze those constants which invariably demarcate
success from failure in all hypnotic approach:

A. EDUCATION OF THE SUBJECT

An ordinarily successful technique can resolve into failure when the practitioner has overlooked the possible prejudice of the patient against the process. Even when his tendencies and disposition preclude the possibility of disbelief in the over-all picture, each subject will have a natural, purely individualistic orientation which will lead him to accept one method and reject another. For instance, the spectacular method with occult trappings, which would have gratifying results with a superstitious person, would prove worthless for the sophisticate. By the same token, a college professor will readily respond—and indeed, require—a method which seems scientifically admissible to him, but that same method might fail lamentably with the "man-on-the-street" who lacks the scientific foundation for comprehension.

The value of any method depends purely upon what the subject can be made to believe. You will recall that Father Gassner's experiments relied upon theological authority. He used all sorts of religious effects, including a diamond-studded crucifix, to gain his supremacy, but all of his embellishments would have failed had his subjects been either of another faith or free of superstition. Similarly, the word construction of any spoken suggestion must be in strict conformity with the subject's personal familiarity with the language. In this respect, limited education provides a considerable hazard.

A friend of mine was temporarily frustrated by a case of this calibre. He was employing a practically "fool-proof" method on a difficult subject. He iterated and re-iterated the suggestion that the patient's body was becoming "increasingly lethargic." After an hour or so of futile effort, the subject opened his eyes, and mildly inquired, "What is 'lethargic,' anyway?". . . . Fortunately my friend has enjoyed enough success with hypnosis not to fling his career to the four winds!

He had forgotten the fact that suggestions and techniques must be tailored to the subject! Also a great deal of success or failure in hypnosis necessarily depends upon the previous conditioning of the subject. Some hypnotists rely greatly on fear and superstition. Occasionally their cold, fierce, piercing "hypnotic eyes" will throw a cowering subject into deep somnambulism through fear alone; more often that same diabolic stare sends a sophisticate into gales of hysterical laughter. This, of course, induces a strong hostility between hypnotist and subject; the hypnotist does not like to be found amusing, and the subject resents having his intelligence insulted. In such a case complete failure is inevitable.

Too many hypnotists become impatient with new subjects who fail to respond readily. Some go so far as to reprimand difficult cases for lack of concentration, or to accuse them of spiteful resistance. These, however, can boast only of meager success, and what little ascendancy they gain is over subjects who would succumb even to a weak influence. To bolster their own egos and maintain their self-esteem, they censure their victims, not realizing that they fail largely through faulty technique. These hypnotists do make it difficult for subsequent practitioners to hypnotize the subject with whom they have failed. Some are brazen enough to tell the subject that he is an impossible case. At any rate, they have destroyed what belief or expectation that subject once had!

The conscientious practitioner realizes that failures in hypnosis are rarely caused by the subject's unwillingness to cooperate or his lack of concentration. In most cases where hypnotic procedure has failed, it is because the therapist has lost sight of his subject's total personality in relation to the choice of method or has not succeeded in winning the subject's complete confidence. Recalling the hypnotic formula previously mentioned, the alert reader will readily grasp the need for this consideration. Both belief and expectation are vitally essential for hypnotic induction; both can be attained only by patient handling of the subject. A modicum of belief has already been established through hearsay; authentic accounts in newspapers and magazines of the value of hypnosis in psychotherapy have created interest among the laity. In certain instances tales of fiction have introduced fantasies of varied sorts of hypnotic situations to promote greater appeal. While it is unfortunate that false impressions are promulgated by them, one can do much to offset their effects by adequate re-education of the patient when he seeks this method of treatment. The medical acceptance of therapeutic hypnosis as beneficial in specific ills of mind and body has been successful as a means for counteracting the fictional information that had previously been presented for public consumption. The popular awareness of hypnosis and its manifold therapeutic advantages is becoming increasingly apparent. This has done much to further its prestige.

The experienced hypnotist will select that phase of acceptance which is already present, fortifying this belief to facilitate induction. Whenever I suspect that the patient's belief is inadequate for the purpose, or when he is openly resistant, I attempt to overcome his obstinacy by a trick which would be inconsequential or silly, save for one attribute; it works.

I walk toward him and casually lift his eyelid, impressing him with the fact that I am seeking for some sign in the corneal structure. After a moment, I remark authoritatively that, from all indications, I can see no reason why he should fail to respond to hypnosis. This is generally the turning point and will insure success when a hypnotic method is used. Actually, the condition of his eyes has furnished me with nothing more than increased prestige—but increased prestige is indispensable in the conditioning of a new patient. Incidentally, this preliminary technique is no respecter of education. I have used it with people from all walks of life, and on one occasion it even had its effect upon an oculist, who, because of his training, should have known better.

B. THE SUBJECT'S EXPECTATION

Where belief exists, expectation will probably follow, although many potential subjects are completely unaware of *what* to expect. This situation can be most disheartening to the hypnotist struggling with a difficult case. Some people expect to fall into deep sleep and lose consciousness entirely. They are very much disappointed when this does not happen and steadfastly deny that they have been satisfactorily influenced. The subjects have difficulty in accepting the fact that total unconsciousness would automatically block the channel for any suggestions.

The idea that hypnotism consists of inducing sleep is universal and false. Were this the case, the art would be useless, for the doctor would need only wait to administer his suggestions until his patient went to sleep of his own accord. This would simplify the matter, certainly, but unfortunately it does not work.

Coué wrote of excellent results with a method that proves efficacious with young children. After the child has fallen into natural sleep, the parent stands at the foot of the bed, repeating a positive suggestion. This suggestion will become effective when the child returns to consciousness. This process has been substantiated by clinical data. The Nazis, by an elaborate recording device planted in children's nurseries, disseminated their vicious propaganda with startling results which can be seen at the present time. Despite the efforts of psychologists in war-torn Germany, the harm created by these methods cannot be undone.

It must be realized, however, that while this method is effective with young children, it is worthless applied to sleeping adults. The child's mind is supple and pliant; fears have not had time to become deeply rooted. He trusts his parents implicitly and considers their voices as part of the scheme of things in his little world. He does not waken when he hears them, for he regards them as constant factors of his environment.

The adult mind, on the other hand, is startled by any sudden sound in the night. It has been conditioned to regard any unexpected disturbance of sleep apprehensively. This has become an integral part of the behavior pattern. The slight portion of the conscious mind which remains awake as a precautionary protector of the adult's being—that portion which prevents him from falling out of bed when he reaches the edge—will in turn awaken him to consciousness at the sound of a strange voice.

It is possible to convert natural sleep into hypnotic sleep, but the methods, which appear to be quite simple, do have their complexities. When the subject falls asleep, the hypnotist begins by speaking in a low tone. If the subject does not rouse, the hypnotist, assuming that the subject has become adjusted to his voice, continues: "Your arm is rising. It is rising. Your arm is rising," and so on. He repeats this suggestion until the sleeper's arm does rise. This is the signal; if the subject accepts one suggestion, the chances are that he will obey others, and he continues as if the subject were under hypnosis. However, this method can become embarrassing to the hypnotist. During one of my experiments with this conversion technique, the subject woke in the middle, harshly demanding, "What the h. . . are you doing here?"

Although these conversions are not impossible, they are difficult. Adequate evidence is available to clarify the differences between the normal sleep and hypnotic states. However, it is usually trying to attempt to convince the average subject not to expect sleep. Some do fall into slumber because that is what they expect, but they are practically inaccessible to suggestion. The same difficulty occurs in certain levels of Depth Hypnosis, where the subject has become too listless to respond.

The hysterical panic produced by Mesmer was merely the sequel of imitation. Patients experienced what they expected to experience; rumor had it that first one must become hysterical to the point of mania; then would follow the cure. One did. When Mesmer commenced treating his patients *en masse*, each saw how others reacted, and each adopted the same ritualistic fashion.

Every hypnotist has pondered over the diverse responses he finds to precisely the same methods. Each subject is reacting in the way that he expected. Some snore because they expect to snore; others respond as if they were in the midst of a dream, impervious to the reality about them, because this is what they expected.

Many patients, whose credivity is unquestionable, fail to react merely because they do not know what to expect. Offer them a satisfactory explanation of the hypnotic phenomenon, and they become splendidly adaptable, regardless of previous failures. Most subjects, when properly conditioned, exhibit a favorable predilection toward hypnosis and find it thoroughly enjoyable.

Once a subject has been hypnotized, his future response will be satisfactory. Where the first method required complex manipulation to produce a suitable state, devices may be discarded after primary success. This is natural. The subject has become familiar with the experience; has been convinced of the state as an entity beyond possible denial; he has no doubt as to the authenticity of his own reaction. This strengthens his belief in future sessions, where he will readily accept deeper stages.

Another reason for this change is that the subject is now fully aware of what to expect. His previous conditioning has provided him with a pronounced predisposition to hypnosis, and he knows what is expected of him. He enters into the spirit of the thing, cooperates whole-heartedly, and is inspired to enter the more profound levels.

Once a subject has tasted the serenity of hypnotic relaxation, he no longer requires the original *imagination* that provided the spark from which *belief* and *expectation* flamed. Given one successful session, the subject will look forward to the second with eagerness and zeal. If fear and apprehension were retarding factors earlier, these will have been eliminated through his own pleasant experience.

C. QUALIFICATIONS OF A SUBJECT

It is generally agreed by hypnotists that the majority of people are highly susceptible to hypnotic influence under proper conditions. We have already discussed some of the reasons why hypnosis can result in failure through the negligence or error of the therapist.

In all fairness to the practitioner, it is necessary to consider the various types of subjects who resist despite all precautionary considerations.

We are occasionally confronted with the subject who professes a keen desire to undergo induction, but, because of an unconscious diathesis of which he is unaware, fails in achieving the hypnotic state. Basically, he does not wish to be hypnotized, and this inconsistency will prevent his submission. Consciously he desires hypnosis; unconsciously he rebels. The inner reclacitrant will nullify his outward expression of co-operation.

Although we are apt to deny the fact, the opinions we cherish—and more, the feelings we bring toward situations in life—are conditioned by our past environment, and because of their relegation to unconscious mechanisms, they frequently cause us to act and react without our own awareness.

One patient who responded poorly to the various techniques finally confided that she had every desire to submit to my suggestions, but some "inexplicable feeling" prevented her whole-hearted submission. A few days later she showed me a photograph of a man whose features bore a remarkable resemblance to my own. She had identified me with the man who had "left her at the church." I earnestly assured her that I had no intention of leaving her in trance; she laughed and submitted quickly and easily to a method which had been inadequate earlier.

Our clinical day is frequently upset by the patient who analyzes our every move. He is like an infant, fascinated by the tick of a shiny watch. He has not the slightest desire to rebel; he merely wants to know what is going on. This type of subject is always an upset to a peaceful practice. The hypnotist, beset by such refractory subjects, might well envy the position of the surgeon who saves himself the annoyance of the patient's curiosity by the simple process of placing him under deep anaesthesia! This analytical subject can be satisfactorily handled only by one of the "quick" methods to be discussed later. If the hypnosis depends upon some lengthy technique, this patient will probably "analyze" himself completely out of the condition for which we have been working.

Another subject who may present many difficulties is the one who has been under the care of other therapists and has met with no success. He may be most willing to submit, but his many past failures have so conditioned him that he is virtually resigned to the idea that, for him, hypnosis is unattainable. Occasionally a sensible chat can turn almost inevitable failure into success.

A good subject is not the *rara avis* that some hypnotists claim. A friendly introduction, familiarizing the prospect with what to believe and what to expect, plus correct procedure, will produce wonderful results for the majority of those who need help. Mass hypnosis proffers substantial testimony to the effect that most people can reach a deep state of hypnotic trance.

Most of us are basically similar; our emotional reactions to fundamental stimuli are similar. Otherwise, film writers would face a hopeless task. The scenes pictured on the screen are tailored to produce universal emotions. When a situation is meant to be funny, everyone laughs; when it is sad, we cry or suppress a tear.

While we can list those traits which render some subjects more susceptible than others, no therapist can possibly forecast the degree of susceptibility to be found in a given subject without actual trial. Sometimes we can hazard a guess; that guess may be lucky but that is all. The best subjects as a whole are those who:

1. have been accustomed to taking orders; this category includes the timid office underling, the henpecked husband, the subservient wife, and the professional soldier.
2. are impulsive rather than logical. This person favors impulse to reason when faced by new situations.
3. tend to accept whole theories without adequate proof.
4. have previous favorable experience with hypnosis.
5. whose belief in hypnosis is so strong that it never occurs to them to doubt the efficacy of it.

This list, of course, is not all-inclusive. From it, one might gain the mistaken impression that only weak-kneed, weak-willed, superstitious people are particularly susceptible. That is definitely untrue. In my own practice, I have discovered that intelligence and concentration are indispensable to hypnosis. I have greater success with college professors and other professional men than with subjects without this training. The one trait, *belief* is something all men have in varying degree; intelligence does not diminish its potency. Where *belief* prevails, *expectation* generally follows. With hypnotism we desire to create an automaton, but if the subject were already of such mental calibre, he would lack the necessary concentration. Feeble-minded patients are rarely affected by hypnosis, for they are unable to concentrate sufficiently to grasp the proffered suggestion.

D. CONDITIONING THE NEW SUBJECT

Proper handling of a subject about to undergo induction for the first time is fully as important as the inductive method selected. We have already considered the fears which prevent complete submission; we have composed a formula which must work when correctly applied. Whatever technique is chosen, it must follow careful preconditioning of the patient.

The explanation given the subject must be altered to suit the needs of the individual. If our explanations are too fantastic for the subject's acceptance, he will feel that his intellect has been insulted, and promptly resist our influence. Therefore, it is essential to proceed warily, carefully considering all the qualifications of the subject lest we blunder in the approach. *Belief* is the one important prerequisite to the advent of hypnosis. Repetition of this cardinal point is intended. Any approach which inadvertently destroys this consideration results in ultimate failure. Each word of the therapist must be carefully weighed in relation to its specific purpose.

This does not mean telling the subject the entire story; to do so would eliminate the cooperation of his imagination. We are trying to condition him for a successful hypnotic session, not to teach him the trade! Anatole France was most apt in his expression when he mused: "To know is nothing at all; to imagine, everything." Therefore, we try to provide the new subject with just enough knowledge to start speculation, permitting his imagination enough leeway to do the rest.

Voice intonations must be soothing and sympathetic, reflecting an attitude of confidence. The patient is hypersensitive to his surroundings; a facial expression which seems harmless to the therapist can evoke fear and distrust in the sensitive subject. The mingled austerity and spiritual aloofness of the mysterious yogi belongs in the realm of the "occult," not in the doctor's office. Usually, a few words of logic establish a confident placidity, where preposterous gibberish would destroy what serenity the patient brings.

A basic preamble which, modified to fit each individual, pretty much covers the territory is the following:

"Hypnotism is a new experience to you, and it is only natural for you to be a bit uneasy. That is to be expected. You will find, however, that it is one of the most enjoyable states you have ever experienced. You will become supremely relaxed; supremely serene. I assure you, you won't want to wait for "next time." I can't describe it for you; you will have to feel it for yourself.

"First of all, please understand that hypnosis is not sleep. When you are asleep you are unconscious, and hypnosis is anything but a state of unconsciousness. Most people waken, forgetting everything that has happened, but they have not been "out." You will remain partly conscious the whole time; you do not abandon your judgment at all. Momentarily, you do surrender your consciousness to my will, of course, but you do it entirely of your own accord.

"When you submit to the scalpel of a capable surgeon, you know his only purpose is to help you. The active thoughts which I place in your mind to help you are what we call 'suggestions.' They are for your own welfare. You must have the utmost confidence in me or hypnosis cannot possibly succeed. In effect, you hypnotize yourself. I merely help it along a bit.

"They say that only weak-willed, moronic people can be hypnotized. That is false. Your job is concentration, and concentration requires both intelligence and will. You have both.

"The only drawback to intelligence is that a tendency to analyze what is going on may arise. Don't give in to it; it will destroy your concentration. Hypnotism *is* fascinating, and after our session I shall be glad to answer all your questions, but first, let me have your concentration and cooperation. When you begin to feel drowsy—relax. Don't try to analyze what is happening in your mind; don't try to force yourself into deeper stages. What will happen will happen, and no mental bearing down on your part will help it.

"Instead, try to be completely indifferent, for indifference opens your mind to suggestion. When you have reached a deep enough stage of hypnosis, I will implant certain suggestions in your unconscious mind. These suggestions will be of tremendous benefit to you. When they have been absorbed, your mind will follow through by enforcing them.

"Hypnosis will help you, not because of any "dominating power" of mine, but because my suggestions will integrate your own forces, enlisting them in your behalf for your welfare. In other words, I will help you to do what you would very much like to do but have not been able to accomplish alone.

"This is what to expect as you sink into hypnosis. (After all, hypnosis is merely the state which separates your waking from sleeping, and you know how you feel when you first 'drop off.') You will be drowsy; your eyes feel tired, fatigue creeps on you and you experience a delightful feeling of relaxation. This happens naturally for a brief second when you go to sleep at night, and again just as you are about to waken in the morning. Hypnosis is simply a means of inducing this state artificially, and of prolonging it to your own advantage.

"Now, will you please. . . ." and the technique may begin.

This is only a suggestive outline, of course, but it contains all the points necessary for successful conditioning. It must be modified to suit the understanding of each subject;

116

simplification of language is particularly essential in the case of children and those adults who are unfamiliar with the English language. This approach does include the requisite factors for conditioning, and it requires a minimum of time.

Some hypnotists insist upon several consultations with a subject before proceeding with hypnosis. I would most fervently question the wisdom of a method which provokes an anticipatory mood, only to dismiss the subject at the very height of his zeal with a curt request to return next Tuesday! The let-down involved might destroy all the conditioning for which the hypnotist has labored.

For greatest success, conditioning must be rapid. The hypnotist is, in a sense, a salesman selling his product. The good sale is the quick one; too many factors intervene when the customer "goes home to think it over." Conditioning the subject is a matter for good salesmanship. It means presenting your wares in such an enticing fashion that the subject cannot resist them!

E.   QUALIFICATIONS OF THE HYPNOTIST

Hypnotism was slow in emerging from the realm of superstition largely because of its practitioners, who steadfastly opposed any scientific methods. Their motives were two-fold. By encouraging the popular opinion that the ability to hypnotize was "divinely endowed," they enhanced their prestige by being set apart from the common herd, and they discouraged competition. Even today, some hypnotists continue to promulgate the "we-alone-have-been-chosen" *motif*. Any intelligent investigator quickly discounts this idea.

The ability to hypnotize and to be hypnotized is latent in everyone. Those who have mastered hypnotic techniques have done so by constant study and practice. Ability stems from proper training. Proficiency in hypnosis requires basic knowledge of the *modus operandi* of the process plus a deep understanding of human reactions.

Hypnosis is not merely a technique; it is an art. Anyone can learn to play the violin by mastering the finger manipulations and learning the fundamentals of music. But a Kreisler or a Menuhin is an artist, not a technician. Just so, the outstanding hypnotist must be an artist. Technique is not enough. He must evolve an individual method of handling every patient, of analyzing that patient's needs, and selecting the pertinent approach to conform to those needs.

Recognizing that *imagination* and *belief* are basic in any technique, the hypnotist must utilize these factors to the utmost. Usually this requires a masterful showmanship that demands "flair" plus interminable practice. Again we note the parallel to salesmanship. All the advantages of the item are useless unless the salesman has a flair for presentation. The timid soul is hopeless; the over-eager lad talks himself out of more sales than he makes. The clever salesman presents the salient features of his product, but allows the customer's own awakened enthusiasm and desire to close the sale.

Confidence in himself, his integrity and his technique then becomes the first aim of the novice. If his movements are halting or uncertain, the patient will sense his hesitancy and fail to respond. The hypnotist must convey a sense of authority.

Patients resent being treated as guinea-pigs. Therefore, if the hypnotist stammers through an explanation or suggestion, if he shows any hesitancy at any point, the subject's fears will outweigh his confidence and the session will end in hopeless failure.

In view of these facts, the beginner must unalterably follow specific rules:

1. He must give the impression of authority; he must be matter-of-fact.

2. He must enlist the confidence of the subject, though he be forced to assume it himself. We might mention here that people who know us too well make bad subjects, for they remember when we were without this knowledge.

3. He must prepare, word for word and action for action, everything he is going to say or do in order to avoid hesitancy in presentation. To the patient, diffidence spells lack of ability.

4. He must develop the proper use of his voice that it may be at once comforting and dynamic. This combination is rarely found in nature. It requires vocal training under proper guidance, but it can and must be acquired for consistent success. The smoothness of the therapist quite frequently draws the line of demarcation between success and failure.

5. The surroundings must tend to conduce a suitable *rapport* between patient and therapist. The stage must be set with the care and precision of a theatrical technician. Everything must be designed to enhance the subject's confidence in the procedure, to crescendo his *belief* and *expectation*.

a. *Cleanliness*: If the office be unclean, unconscious repugnance may constitute a block.

b. *Noise*: Traffic noises are repetitious and do not present much drawback. Sudden noises, however, such as horns, unexpected shouts, banging doors, are definite hazards to adequate response. It is wise to guard against these by selecting a quiet spot and installing soundproofing if necessary. Another very definite noise hazard is a ringing telephone. This is easily overcome either by leaving the receiver off the hook for the duration or by disconnecting the bell, permitting the telephone to ring in another room. These simple precautions save the practitioner a great deal of aggravation in the early stages of induction.

c. *Temperature*: Heat, cold, drafts, electric fans, and so on are disturbing features to any sensitive subject. The room must be well-ventilated and the temperature comfortable.

d. *Odors*: Stagnant odors of cigarette and cigar smoke clinging to the drapery are frequently responsible for failures.

6. The therapist's person must carry prestige.

    a. *Cleanliness*: is again the first consideration. Disagreeable odors emanating from the fingers of the operator are fatal. Nails, clothes, shoes must all be immaculate. The wise therapist goes out of his way to conform to the idiosyncrasies of the most fastidious.

    b. *Time*: the practice of hypnosis must allow ample time for each patient, particularly the newer ones. The therapist ensures his own failure by attempting to "rush through" a session because of another appointment. The patient must be allowed enough time to orient himself to his surroundings and to accept this new state. If the practitioner is anxious to complete the session, the subject senses that anxiety and may misinterpret it as apprehension. Either way, he resists. At the same time, if the subject fears he will not "wake up" in time to keep an appointment of his own, that fear will block the proper reaction. When this is the case, the appointment should be shifted to another time.

7. *Audience*: Occasionally, the patient will invite a curious friend to accompany him. This can cause serious snags. Sometimes in the middle of the session the bystander bursts into laughter or unsuccessfully attempts to stifle a giggle. Any interference with the subject's concentration must be eliminated. If the guest is a mere curiosity seeker, let him wait in the ante-room until the subject has achieved a state which cannot be disrupted by outside influences.

It is frequently wise, however, to have a third person present throughout the entire session for one's own protection, particularly during the treatment of minors. This precaution can save a good deal of involvement, legal and otherwise, by precluding preposterous claims of any kind.

It is always unwise for a practitioner to deviate too far from the established rules of caution. The majority of patients seeking his aid are neurotic; some possibly psychotic, and he must always be on the lookout for the unexpected.

When an audience *is* deemed advisable, it is a simple matter to include the witness in the conditioning of the patient, taking a few minutes to win his cooperation before embarking upon induction.

F. SUMMARY

The various considerations outlined in this chapter are the sum total of long experience in the field. By considering hypnosis as an exact science and working accordingly, the novice will be enabled to succeed where many practitioners have failed because of lack of consideration of one or more of these very points.

One final point contains in itself the epitome of all others: the person who learns to place himself in the position of the patient, who learns to "look at things" through that patient's eyes, limiting his vision with the prejudices and pre-formed emotional reactions of the subject under consideration, will develop an awareness, a sixth sense of technique that ultimately will preclude any possibility of failure.

REFERENCES

COUÉ, E., *How to Practice Suggestion and Autosuggestion,* American Library Service, 1923.

HEYER, G., *Hypnosis and Hypnotherapy,* C. W. Daniel Company, London, 1931.

KRAFFT-EBING, R., *An Experimental Study in the Domain of Hypnosis,* G. P. Putnam's Sons, New York, 1889.

KUBIE, L. S. AND MARGOLIN, S., *A Physiological Method for the Inductions of Partial Sleep, Etc.,* Transactions of the American Neurological Association, 1942.

LEVBARG, J. J., "Hypnosis—A Potent Therapy in Medicine," *New York Physician,* 14, 18, 1940.

LLOYD, B. L., *Hypnotism in the Treatment of Disease,* Bale & Danielsson, London, 1934.

WILLIAMS, G. W., "Suggestibility in the Normal and Hypnotic States," *Archives of Psychology,* 19, 122, 1930.

7

Objective Methods of
Hypnotic Induction

Hypnosis, as a scientific procedure, had its early beginnings in a labyrinth of wild and idle speculation. In the middle part of the nineteenth century there evolved so many diverse opinions of the nature of the phenomenon that an impasse threatened its advancement. As sparing knowledge of the mind was available to him, the investigator of that day sought explanations for hypnosis which might seem fantastic in the light of modern reasoning. In pursuing his laudable purpose of producing hypnosis in the most expeditious manner he reserved little time for assessing the methods of contemporary hypnotists of other schools.

Fundamentally there were two schools of thought about hypnosis. One arbitrarily relegated all phenomena to the realm of matter, claiming that hypnosis is a condition of the nervous system resulting from sensory fatigue or induced nervous reactions (through stroking, passes, pressure, etc.) which affect a portion of the brain; the other placed all manifestations in the realm of the psyche, considering suggestion the causative factor, and deeming physical adjuncts mere window-dressing, useful as tools to assist in misdirecting attention or implementing or dramatizing suggestion, but unimportant in themselves.

Leaving the merits of each theory for later evaluation, in this chapter we shall present those methods in general use by the proponents of the physical or objective (as opposed to the suggestive subjective) premise. To avoid confusion, it is well to keep this basic formula in mind throughout the analysis of each technique.

A. MESMER'S METHOD

The method from which all others have been derived was that of the father of "mesmerism," Anton Mesmer himself. He would sit facing the candidate for mesmerization. He would take the person's hands in his own, staring deeply into his eyes. Within a quarter of an hour, he would release his grasp and begin to make stroking passes over the patient's body, keeping his fingers a few inches above the body. The pass started from the top of the head, extending slowly downward, stopping at the eyes where momentary pressure was exerted, down to the chest where the fingers rested again, and then at the pit of the stomach, finally ending at the knees. This gentle pass was repeated about fifteen times. If a desirable effect was evidenced, Mesmer would continue with the séance; if not, the patient was requested to return for another sitting. When his practice grew to impossible proportions, Mesmer evolved the theory that his magnetic fluid could be stored away in certain objects, which would then emanate therapeutic vibrations. By resorting to this indirect method, he was able to dispense with the personal touch. But his success was equally outstanding with the aid of his magnetized *baquets,* flowers and trees. Mesmer also contended that his followers could discern the difference between unaltered and magnetized water.

The student will readily ascertain from the above description the degree to which a subject's response was conditioned by his belief, expectation and imagination. *Belief* was firmly implanted by Mesmer's popularity; *expectation* grew from constant repetition of miraculous successes, while *imagination* began the process of inducing the desired response, long before the time of submission.

B. ESDAILE'S METHOD

Doctor Esdaile, whose work in Calcutta (1840–1850) commanded contemporary attention, used the following procedure:

The subject, partly undressed, was ushered into a dark hall and made to lie on his back in bed. Esdaile stood at the head of the bed, leaning directly over the subject so that their heads were almost in contact and their eyes meeting in a steady stare. With one hand the magnetizer brought pressure to bear on the subject's stomach; with the other, he affected rhythmic strokings over the eyes. Frequently, he blew gently in the subject's nose, on the eye-balls and between the lips. Esdaile insisted upon utmost quiet throughout the entire séance.

Although Esdaile's technique theoretically depended upon several very involved principles, the hypnotists Cullére, Teste and others have succeeded in producing the same effect by merely fixing their vision in a fierce stare upon the subject, eliminating Esdaile's other manipulations.

C. BRAID'S METHOD

James Braid devised a bright object, centered a few inches above the subject's nose, at which the subject stared, a method still used in one form or another by hypnotists of our own time. Focusing his vision upon the object causes the patient's eyes to converge, bringing about a twitching from over-irritation of the nerves and muscles. Braid further demanded that his subject concentrate upon the advent of sleep. This abnormal tension frequently brought headaches, tears and other discomforts in its wake.

Later, Braid forsook the idea that straining to a point of convergence was a formal necessity before induction, but he still insisted that straining of the eyes, despite its painful effects, rendered the subject more responsive to the hypnotic influence. He discovered that similar results could be obtained if the subject's eyes were centered upon an object far above the root of the nose, so that strain of the optic muscles would result from centralization of vision upon the object.

This method is still perpetuated by most modern practitioners with a few minor variations. Some have abandoned the use of objects of bright intensity, replacing them with curios or even their own outstretched fingers, upon which they command their subject's attention, while others have adopted the use of blinding lights.

The value of this abnormal tiring of the senses is questionable, considering that identical results can be achieved without sensory manipulation. Fixed attention can serve a few very useful purposes, although to qualify it as an essential ingredient merely adds to hypnotism's already well-steeped confusion.

What is there about Braid's technique—or any other dependent upon sensory fatigue—that can motivate a subject to assume the hypnotic state? With our present knowledge, we may venture a substantial explanation.

First, the object projected before the subject's vision provides a means of *misdirected attention,* as described in Chapter IV. By fixing his gaze on the object, the subject's mind is concentrated upon something which eliminates all thought of possible failure. Similarly, he is made to concentrate upon "sleep."

Secondly, as his eyes tire, the idea of sleep is impressed upon the patient's mind, as fatigue seems to be a natural preliminary requisite to sleep. The more fatigued his eyes become, the more effective will be the suggestion that he cannot keep awake any longer. Thus, the subject, believing that hypnosis will ultimately result because his eyelids feel heavy, fortifies the sleep suggestion through his own thought process, and drowsiness ensues. Sensory stimulation for the purpose of fatigue alone will not produce hypnosis unless the subject *is aware* that hypnosis is being induced; unless he maintains *belief* in the phenomenon, and unless he *expects* that hypnosis will result.

If you will experiment by fixing your attention for some time upon an object suspended above your head so that you must strain your eyes to bring the object into your visual field, you will soon be convinced that nerve muscle fatigue cannot in itself produce hypnosis.

Thirdly, the resulting sensory stimulation serves to justify the phenomenon of hypnosis to the subject, for he would prefer to respond to an external motivation which acts upon him physically than to one that relies solely upon his own imagination.

Doctor Braid himself did not overlook the power of the subject's own intellectual ability in the matter of response. He always brought the patient's thoughts to the expectation of sleep. In his considerations of hypnotism as a therapy, he proved himself in accord with the view that *imagination* accounted for a good deal of his success. In his book, *Neurypnology,* published in 1883, he stated:

"Many skeptics have endeavored to throw discredit on the importance of hypnotic processes as a means of cure by attributing the whole results to the power of *imagination.*

They are willing to admit that certain effects are produced and are content if they can only damage the importance of the facts by associating them with what *they* consider *a bad name*. Their admission of the *facts*, however, is something, and we shall now devote a few minutes to the consideration of the power of imagination over the physical organism of man. Those who suppose that the power of imagination is merely a mental emotion, which may vary to any extent without corresponding changes in the physical functions, labour under a mighty mistake. It is notorious to those who have carefully studied this curious subject, that imagination can either kill or cure; that many tricks have been played upon healthy persons, by several friends conspiring, in succession to express themselves as surprised, or sorry or shocked to see them looking so ill; and that very soon a visible change has come over the patients, and they have actually gone home and been confined there for days from bodily illness thus induced. Not only so, but there are even cases recorded in which we have the best authority for the fact, where patients who were previously in perfect health, have actually died from the power of imagination, excited entirely through the suggestions of others. Nor are the suggestions by others of the ideas of health, vigour, hope and improved looks less influential with many people for restoring health and energy both of mind and body. Having such a mighty power to work with, then, the great consideratum has been to devise the best means for regulating and controlling it, so as to render it subservient to our will for relieving and curing diseases. The modes devised, both by mesmerists and hypnotists, for these ends, I consider to be a real, solid and important addition to practical therapeutics; and not the less curious and important that it is done simply through appeals to the *immortal soul*, to assert and demonstrate its superiority and control over the *mortal body*."

D. CHARCOT'S METHOD

While the Salpêtrière experimented with many modes of operation, stimulation of the various senses seemed to be the basis of their procedures. The Charcot School appealed to hearing, touch, and smell, in addition to concentration upon the visual sense. Charcot's method presented a lengthy modification of the technique to which Braid attributed his success. To promote tiring convergence of the eyes for the purpose of facilitating the advent of sleep, Charcot placed pieces of glass close to the bridge of the patient's nose. Later he discarded this method in favor of one that did not depend upon forceful strain on the optic nerves with its resultant painful squinting. On the contrary, he sought to prove that the same effect could be obtained by fixing the subject's eyes upon an object centered in his habitual field of vision. This device relieved pain and discomfort, and brought forth identical symptoms within the same span of time required by the earlier methods.

At times he would appeal to a technique based upon monotonous stimulation of the auditory sense with the purpose of arousing the subject's drowsiness. In other instances, he would place a motor close to his subject's ear, relying on the supposition that its constant, tiring hum would produce the same effect. Sometimes he used the rhythmic beating upon a hollow-sounding bell, or resort to the sudden clanging of an ancient Chinese gong.

It must be remembered that Charcot was first and foremost a neurologist, and it is not surprising that he clung fanatically to the physical theory of hypnosis, disdaining any idea which would relegate its effects to the category of suggestion. With this in mind—as if to discount the possibility of such accusations—he and his disciples avoided entering into lengthy conversation with their patients, frequently dispensing entirely with speech. They omitted anything that would smack of *suggestion*. (Despite all precautions, however, they did find it necessary to announce their purpose to the patient and to tell him what to expect!)

Charcot, too, entered into experimentation with the sense of touch for the purpose of obtaining more effectual hypnosis. He contended that pressure on certain zones of the body helped to induce the condition; that these *hypnogenic zones,* properly stimulated, brought about sleep. He listed several spots on the body as the most susceptible, namely, the root of the nose, the crown of the head, the elbow, and the thumb. According to him, a gentle scratching of the neck could likewise produce hypnosis, as also a like stimulation of the head and the soles of the feet. He later affirmed that light pressure in the region of the cervical vertebrae was an excellent preface to induction.

However, with all his reliance upon physical stimuli, it must be remembered that Charcot's hospital contained over four thousand patients. His experiments were famous with scientists and lay people alike in every portion of the civilized world. It was only natural for his authority and reputation to create *belief, expectation* and *imagination* in the minds of prospective patients long before they arrived at this hospital. His magnificent professional acclaim rendered suggestible all of the patients who sought his help. Thus well conditioned, is it strange that subjects reacted properly regardless of the inductive methods attempted?

Through this perplexing maze of methods, each endeavoring to supersede something of the past which had brought temporary fame to its user, one principle, almost an axiom, seemed always to be outstanding: *tire the senses and hypnotic sleep will follow.* From a confusing network of inconsistencies, the hypnotist still produced the soporific result. Even the scholarly Charcot, though he claimed that sleep would follow a mere touch on the forehead in susceptible subjects, could never become convinced of the validity of suggestion as an operation of induction. If he ever faced the problem of why some people are easily susceptible while others are not, his answers to that question have remained obscure.

E. MOUTIN'S METHOD

Louis Moutin, a French demonstrator who became world-famous, used a means of induction which was presumably physical in its aspects, but which did not rely upon the usual sense-stimulations. He describes it in this manner:

"To discover whether the subject under examination is apt to receive the hypnotic influence, I apply one of my hands with a notable amount of pressure, between his shoulder-blades, at the base of the neck, and I ask him to tell me his sensations as they occur. If, after three or four minutes, he tells me that he notices a certain heat at the spot my hand is pressing, I transfer the pressure to both shoulder blades, allowing my fingers to quiver slightly. In all hypnotizable subjects, this method rapidly brings about an almost unbearable heat. The subjects who feel but a slight degree of warmth would need more time, and probably several sittings, before reaching the hypnotic state. I have noticed sensations of intense cold to be developed in place of heat, also electric discharges, slight cramps in the muscles of the shoulder-blades and neck, or even in the arms and lower limbs. These are positive symptoms of a natural disposition to hypnosis; therefore, this preliminary experiment allows me to eliminate all the individuals in whom hypnotic tendencies are either absent or too weak to be worth developing. I also decline to proceed further with anyone who has proved, in his first attempt, to be subject to fits or hysterics, or shows a disposition to over-excitement detrimental to mind and body.

"When I have decided to proceed with my experiment, and after the sensation of heat or of extreme cold, etc., over the region I have touched has become very marked, I gradually withdraw my hands, without saying a word, and the subject follows me, walking backwards; should he not do so the first time, I resume my hand application on the shoulder-blades until the complete effect has been produced, and then the subject gives up the struggle—sometimes with amusing contortions—and follows me backwards. I act here as a magnet and he as the attracted metal. I have no trouble in producing the reverse effect and compelling the subject to walk away from me." *

The reader will notice that words have been uttered during the technique; conversations have taken place between operator and subject. One might, therefore, be very likely to conclude that the idea of suggestion can be entertained as a factor of this method. Yet this curious physiologic anomaly remains true; different subjects have assumed different physical symptoms in the presence of like stimuli. In the preliminary operation for the purpose of detecting suitable subjects, Moutin exerted considerable pressure between the shoulder-blades. It is rather perplexing that his manipulation should bring unbearable heat to some, produce intense cold in others, and have no noticeable effect at all upon subjects who did not have hypnotic tendencies.

Moutin did not define this tendency to hypnosis, nor did he hazard an explanation of the qualities which make one person susceptible to hypnotic influence while another remains unresponsive.

We have already seen in our analysis of other methods the subtle way in which effective suggestion can be administered. Like Charcot, Moutin's reputation was assured. His public experiments were greeted with amazement by thousands of people. When a subject volunteered for hypnosis, it would be reasonable to suppose that he had witnessed or

* Moutin, L., *La Nouvelle Hypnotisme* (translated by C. Fowler from original treatise), Perrin et Cie., Paris, 1887.

had heard of the responses of previous subjects. By this introduction to Moutin's work, again, *belief* was established, *expectation* existed resulting from imitation, while natural curiosity contributed *imagination*. Once more, we find the three bases.

Pressure upon the shoulder-blades had a double effect: first, it served as an excellent object toward which to *misdirect* the subject's attention; second, it enabled Moutin to distinguish the suggestive transitions produced by the subject's own *imagination,* making him aware of how well the suggestions were taking hold.

The latter part of Moutin's demonstration is not explained away as easily. I have engaged in countless experiments to determine whether a hypnotized subject will follow a force emanating from the operator to the extent that he will move in the direction of the hypnotist's hands. To my astonishment, I have discovered that this act, while scientifically inexplicable, can be carried out. The practical proof lies before us, but the scientific explanation for this hypnotic phenomenon still waits for its discoverer.

This is one of many hypnotic manifestations which have never been explained. The field is wide open for future scientific explorers who will correlate the known principles of chemistry and physics and apply them to the phenomena of hypnosis. Until then, all one can do is to record those methods which appear to reproduce such demonstrations without benefit of explanation.

If the hypnotist's fingers are held above the subject's hand in such a manner that they quiver slightly, the subject, with eyes closed, deprived of natural means of sensing the position of the operator's fingers, lifts his hand toward the hand of the therapist. This has been the result in every case with which I have experimented, but it is to be regarded purely as experimental data.

How this is accomplished I have at present no means of

explanation. However, the experiment has been successfully duplicated many times under the most rigidly controlled conditions. Only the ancients ventured an interpretation in the light of "mysterious fluids" and "magnetic forces." Their views have been dismissed as superstitions by modern experimenters. What I shall present herewith is conflicting, confusing—and yet, to disregard it for want of original explanation would stunt the progress of modern scientific hypnosis, which must necessarily proceed on the basis of earlier findings. The presentation of the following theory is meant only to provide an empirical basis for further investigation; it by no means constitutes my own opinion.

F. MAGNETISM

A book on hypnosis could not fail to include an account of magnetism. Little exploration which could be called scientific has been made of the phenomena offered as evidence by the proponents of the magnetic theory. However, the material is presented here without bias, as a matter of interest, and judgment as to its validity will have to await the results of research.

The theory that unseen "fluids" exist which can penetrate material bodies has flourished throughout all recorded history. The seventeenth century magnetizers were certainly not the first to claim that a force emanating from one body can influence the body of another. It is comparable to the bond of affection or sympathy, which finds interplay between two persons, only to change to antipathy and abhorrence given certain stimuli. Thus, the direction of a definite force transforms itself from convergence to divergence.

The magnetizers further bulwarked their attraction-repulsion theory by comparing it analogously to the attraction of the north and south poles of a magnet with the consequent repulsion of two north poles. Therefore, they maintained that, as in the physical sciences, "like attracts unlike; like repels like."

Now if emotions of various intensity emanate from the same force, the individual empowered with magnetic control could change the emotional curve completely or alter its dimensions. The basic contention of the early magnetizers, then, was that all forms of magnetism and electricity are but manifestations of this subtle, all pervasive fluid. Human beings are apparently known to emit electrical currents without conscious effort. Certain cases of the period seemed to offer adequate substantiation of this. Doctor de Farémont's patient, Angélique (1846), a robust girl of thirteen, presented an interesting example. People experienced slight electric shocks upon touching her body; objects strewn about the floor would move as though physically shoved when she entered a room.

In a somewhat similar case, described by Doctor Féré in 1884, crackling sparks were emitted when his patient's body came in contact with her clothing. Sometimes her dress would cling so closely to her skin that she could move only with difficulty. Under emotional stress, these effects became intensified to a noticeable degree.*

Doctor Binet and Doctor Féré, while investigating certain phenomena of attraction, described a state in which the awareness and sensibility of the subject were affected only by a particular hypnotist, and which were highly developed, particularly during the somnambulistic state of hypnosis. They termed this phenomenon *"elective sensibility."* They found that in this state, the subject frequently develops a definite attraction for the hypnotist who has induced sleep through

---

* This might easily be explained away by the phenomenon of electrical conductivity of the atmosphere or of static electricity. Whether there exists a greater interplay between positive and negative ions as a result of emotional tension is an interesting problem for investigation.

pressure upon the crown of the head. If the pressure was secured by any other object than the actual hand, a state of *indifferent somnambulism* resulted, in which any person apart from the hypnotist could manifest control over the subject and impart suggestions. The influence was no longer individual and might be assumed by any person present.

The state of elective sensibility presented a totally different picture. When the hypnotist—according to Binet and Féré—pressed upon the top of the subject's head with his hand, the subject felt a strong attraction for the hypnotist. If the latter left the room, the subject indicated restlessness and unease until his return. While the hypnotist's touch was pleasing, a foreign touch was immediately discerned, bringing with it intense pain.

According to these observers, the state of *indifferent somnambulism* can be easily converted into the *elective state* by placing the hand upon the subject under control. If the subject be touched by two hypnotists, each will command the sympathy of that half of the body corresponding to the hand that touches him. The subject becomes aware only of the hypnotist who has placed him in the elective state; all of that person's suggestions will be obeyed, while those offered by the subsidiary individual will be ignored. This degree of personal influence manifested by the hypnotist over his subject can be classified as the old *"en rapport"* condition, or, to use the modern term, *"transference."*

A specific example may help to clarify the picture. Doctor L. tells his subject: "You cannot lift your arm." Subject S. hears the command and demonstrates to her own satisfaction that she cannot lift her arm. If Doctor L. makes so-called "passes" of a mesmeric nature up and down S's arm, insensibility of the limb follows. This may also be attributed to suggestion, for the subject is fully aware of what the hypnotist is attempting. Thus, this suggestion is carried out by enlisting the subject's imagination. Now, let Doctor X. enter the picture, making mesmeric passes, and the response will be entirely negative! Again, *suggestion* offers an explanation, for the subject believes that only his original hypnotist is capable of producing the effect. Therefore, we may say that the results of the experiment depend upon the belief of the subject.

However, suggestion as an explanation is not entirely adequate, since the subject, unaware of *who* is making the passes, will still react only to those of the *original hypnotist*. To paraphrase Gertrude Stein, it may be to the rest of the world that "a pass is a pass"—but not to the hypnotized subject. He, oblivious to any but his temporary master, responds only to that master.

Mesmerists believe, then, that the original hypnotist has some specific influence which suggestion leaves unexplained. They believe that such a power is inherent in the hypnotist, existing in some but not in others; that a man possessing this influence, can cause cessation of pain, contractions of muscles, and even cure habits and diseases. They stipulate that it is possible to exert a magnetic influence over children less than a year old, producing all sorts of curative manifestations. Infants do not normally respond to suggestion, because of undeveloped mental faculties; a child under one has no grasp of language. Therefore, they believe that if a child can be successfully subjected to magnetic influence, a fluid interplay between child and hypnotist affords the only possible explanation.

Duprel, one of the closest adherents of the magnetic theory, has made some rather startling statements. He contended that animals can be magnetized—which would eliminate any idea of suggestion as an operative factor. For example, if an animal has been held in such a way that he could not move of his own volition, we might conclude that he is unable to move after release, but we cannot prove it. Many widely experienced practitioners of hypnosis hold this view.

Secondly, Duprel contended that he could exert a magnetic influence over sleeping persons—those who are unaware of being magnetized. The opponents of this school have an answer to this; they affirm that the sleep state is not necessarily a state of absolute unconsciousness; suggestions could be obeyed even by a sleeper.

In Duprel's third argument, he tells us that each subject reacts differently, thus placing suggestion out of the question. It is simple to dispute this contention on the basis of the fact that the subject's reaction is governed by his expectation of effects. As these expectations differ between subjects, reactions are likely to vary.

Fourth (and quite unanswerably, this time, except that he did not prove it), he mentions certain plants undergoing magnetization for the purpose of stimulating growth.

Fifth, the inference that magnetism can be conveyed to inanimate objects would indicate that those objects were permeated with the same magnetic "fluid" present in the hypnotist.

Sixth, he claims that the processes of telepathy furnish final proof of magnetism and the powers of the "subtle fluid."

It is difficult to judge the value of Duprel's statements. The mechanism of magnetic influence is generally encompassed either by "mesmeric passes" or by the fixed gaze of the hypnotist into the eyes of his subject, by touch, or by pressure upon the eyes and temples of the subject. While many observers contend that the will and concentration of the mesmeric operator originate the magnetic "flow," certainly the magnetic "passes" are most universally utilized.

Much is left unexplained, of course, but to assume that magnetism is sheer myth would be unscientific. However, we cannot, as yet, classify the magnetic theory as an authentic, scientific fact.

G. MESMERIC PASSES

Of all the methods in general practice, mesmeric passes have been most widely used. Much data has been correlated with regard to the effects of various passes. Some believe that the direction of the pass—upward or downward causes considerable difference in its effect upon the patient; others state that the outward portion of the hand manifests a different effect from that of the palm. Still others feel that those who have been mesmerized on the right side will react differently from those who are mesmerized on the left.

Among the many theories about magnetism, its methods and precepts, let us return to the fountainhead of them all. Mesmer's ideas may be summarized as follows:

He propounded that the entire universe is filled with a fluid less perceptible than such gases as ether; that this fluid carries vibrations in its substance, even as air, water, ether. Mesmer opined that light-ether was the cause of light, air-ether, the cause of sound, and that consequently the vibrations of this fluid, permeating all the universe, cause all mesmeric phenomena. Like the astrologers of his day, he believed that the universal body exercised a peculiar influence over all other bodies; that the actual earth and all other planets were the direct cause of the vibrations conducted through this fluid. He also believed that each animal body causes a direct influence upon other animal bodies, resulting in vibrations of the fluid. To this theory, Mesmer gave the name "Animal Magnetism."

Mesmer's concepts are frequently confused with other fluid theories, however. He had in mind a fluid which extends throughout everything, which fills all space between all substances, organic and inorganic.

Conversely, a theory was presented that presumed a fluid emanating only from the nerves of living creatures to cause response in other living creatures. Alexander von Humboldt and the German physician, Johann Reill, supposed that a specific force was manufactured in the nervous system which could produce physical effects even at a distance.

Although Mesmerism is out of scientific fashion today, his theories were accepted by some of the greatest minds of his and later days. Mesmerism claims that sleep is not a necessary factor to magnetic influence. We are well aware of the fact that hypnosis in itself does not cause sleep (although the sleep state may be induced through suggestion); hence, Doctor Braid's differentiation between hypnosis and magnetism, namely, that magnetism ignores sleep as a factor of influence, no longer applies. The present theory is that those states assumed by the mesmerizer to be magnetic are merely minor manifestations of hypnosis which fall naturally within the category of hypnotic stages.

However, after all scientific explanations are produced, after we exhaust the possibilities of suggestion as an explanatory factor, we still find the fact that it is possible to record the magnetic influence which one animal body can exert over another where there is no direct contact between the animals themselves. It may be scientifically embarrassing, but there it is.

A magnetometer, evolved by the French Abbé Fortune of Chalet, provides a part of this record, the original instrument being in the Academy of Sciences. It was used for many other purposes than a mere denotation of magnetic waves and influences. The needle, which was magnetized, could determine variations in weather and warn of an approaching storm. Like the ammeter, the needle moved back and forth when a hand approached it. If the hand was clenched in a position over the instrument for approximately five minutes, the effect seemed to disappear completely, and the needle returned to its normal position. The magnetic needle recorded a different degree of movement with each operator. Can these movements be entirely attributed to variations in the degree of electricity emanating from various bodies of individuals? Again we find an unexplored field for experimentation.

The most commonly used magnetic technique shows a close similarity to the so-called hypnotic method. The subject is seated comfortably in a chair or reclines upon a professional couch. The magnetizer stands before him, raises his hands and moves them in a continuous slope downward, the palms of his hand toward the subject. This pass proceeds from the top of the head to the pit of the stomach, with the hand held at a distance of from one to three inches from the subject's body, in such a way that there is absolutely no physical contact. When the hands reach the stomach, they are brought forward in a wide sweep upward until they regain their original position above the subject's head. The same movement is repeated many times in the same direction. Only rarely is it used from the pit of the stomach to the head. This procedure continues for approximately ten minutes, after which the subject breathes deeply and restfully, his eyes having closed at some point during the process. If he has not reacted satisfactorily, the passes are continued for as long as an hour or an hour and a half if necessary to achieve the desired effect, no further step being taken until this is accomplished.

As soon as the subject is obviously affected, he is requested to raise his arm, only to find that his arms lie so heavily by his side that a barely perceptible motion is the most he can accomplish. Immediately, he is asked how he feels—which is "tired." Next, he is forbidden to open his eyes, and he cannot. The operator raises the subject's left arm; it remains in the air in a cataleptic state until released. By now, everything is proceeding according to schedule. As other more complex suggestions are given, the subject becomes more and more confused; he discovers himself unable to disobey any command given him by the operator. His face assumes a strange expression; the features evidence a peculiar waxen expression, the stare is wide, eyes focused directly ahead, all of which spell a trance state to the casual observer.

Those who are familiar with the scientific explanation of hypnotism are reluctant to accept the arguments for the magnetic theory or to agree with its practitioners' line of demarcation between hypnosis and magnetism. It is clear that a hypnotic state has been induced in the subject. If we analyze the hypnotic technique previously presented, we quickly spot the similarity between the magnetic and hypnotic methods; it is simple to recognize our old friends, the three bases.

Although apparently no adequate suggestion was given, the subject, of course, realizes what is *expected* of him; he has sufficient *imagination* to bring about the effect; he originally *believed* in the magnetizer's ability before submitting himself to his methods, in addition to which the current of air induced by the operator's continuous motion intensified the original belief. The entire hypnotic formula has been followed quite adequately, and the subject is in the desired state. What difference can we find between it and the state attained with any other hypnotic methods?

The possibility of a scientific basis for the "magnetic fluid" theory is sheer conjecture at the present time. Those arguments which certainly appear valid in the light of early experiments are largely discounted by present-day investigators because of their easy explanation by the theory and practice of hypnotism. We have undoubtedly reaped the benefits of the work of the early magnetizers, and due credit should be given them; they provided the foundation for our scientific hypnotism, but, again, there is little residue from their work which cannot be classified within the limits of that very scientific hypnotism.

At the same time, we must not arbitrarily dismiss all the ideas which have been presented under the name of magnetism. Experimentation in physics makes us aware of the reality of some governing factor in the body, perhaps electricity, perhaps some other force, which serves as an active principle in life processes. The physiological system or the process of an impulse travelling along the nerve path leads us to believe that there is an electrical manifestation which creates the harmonious inter-relationship between the nerves, glands, bloodstream and the cells of the body. We can conscientiously subscribe to the existence of this force, although it has never been adequately defined, and its phenomena have never been satisfactorily proven. Those who are interested in further study on this phase are referred to the older textbooks on magnetism.

H. LUYS' METHOD

Doctor Luys, of the Charité hospital school, seeking for a method which would hypnotize a group of persons, devised a variation of the lark's mirror, an instrument for hunters. This apparatus consisted of a rotary mirror, a multitude of tiny specks of glass glued into a wooden object. The surfaces of these glass specks were finely polished to produce a dazzling effect as the facets of the mirror revolved. The instrument, supported on a pivot, was turned rapidly by hand, and as the hypnotic subject gazed at it, he developed a very strong feeling of optic fatigue, which, if continued from three to ten minutes, produced a deep state of hypnosis in susceptible individuals. Later experimenters have evolved a machine similar to Doctor Luys' revolving mirror which works on a similar principle. A mirror is fastened to a revolving phonograph turn-table. One side of the mirror is painted black; the other side is very highly polished. A light is placed directly behind the mirror, and as the turn-table revolves, the mirror reflects the light from a bulb directly back of the turn-table. This creates a fatiguing effect, and may be used in the induction of hypnosis. It must be remembered, however, that while this is a contrivance for producing quick hypnosis through fatigue of the optic nerve, other methods are equally effective, and weariness is of value only in its implementation of the subject's own imagination. The procedure has unpleasant by-products, for it causes a fatigue which the subject retains upon awakening, and consequently should be used only as a last resort.

In fact, because Doctor Luys' method or any modification of it tends to produce undue fatigue, its use tends to increase the difficulty of future hypnotic sessions. A patient only seeks hypnotism as a relief from some unpleasant condition, and if the method causes concomitant unpleasantness, then that very method will destroy the *rapport* which is so important for the ready acceptance of suggestion by the subject.

I. THE FASCINATION METHOD

All fascination methods proceed from a single process; that of having the subject stare intently at an object in such a way that intense ocular fatigue is created. Some hypnotists use their own eye as the object of fixation; others use the brilliant surface of a pocket watch, a small shining flashlight, or even a spot upon the wall. The object is usually held directly above the subject's normal range of vision, so that the subject must strain his eyes slightly to bring it into focus. The ocular fatigue forces him to close his eyes, which, although not in itself an indication of sleep (for one may be thoroughly fatigued and still remain awake) provides the hypnotist with a springboard for sleep suggestion.

The technique of fascination is probably the most widely used method of hypnosis. Briefly, it consists of this:

The subject concentrates his attention upon an object overhead (or before him) so held that he must strain his eyes slightly. When the eyelids are sufficiently fatigued, suggestions of sleep are instituted. The subject is told that he is becoming more and more drowsy, his eyelids are becoming heavier and heavier, his entire body will soon feel a tingling sensation, and his arms and legs are becoming numb. When the subject presents the appearance of fatigue, drowsiness and mental clouding, sleep is suddenly commanded, at which time the patient's eyes close tightly. Following suggestions are obeyed, and with each command the subject falls into deeper stages of hypnotic trance. There are many variations of this technique, but all of them work on the basis of the same principle not, in my opinion, on the principle of sensory fatigue (as the objectivists claim) but merely on that of misdirected attention. In other words, the hypnotist causes the subject to direct his attention upon the object solely to keep him too occupied either to analyze the hypnotic technique or to speculate as to its result.

It is important to use the proper wording and to be extremely careful in your presentation to the subject. There is a certain patter that the student might well memorize. We shall present it, in conjunction with another method which operates along the line of fascination:

A round black circle is attached overhead in such a way that the patient, provided he strains to focus his eyes, has the circle in the scope of his vision. With this method the subject may be either seated or reclining, but the black circle must be so placed as to cause very slight fatigue. The hypnotist uses the following words or some variation of them:

"Breathe very deeply, relax as much as you possibly can. Relax as much as you possibly can. Above, you will notice a circle. Watch that circle, watch it very carefully. Concentrate all your attention upon that circle. Watch it very carefully, do not take your eyes from it for even a moment. Breathe very deeply. Now think only of sleep. Think only that you are going into a deep, sound, heavy, restful sleep. Breathe very deeply. Soon your eyes will become so very tired, your eyelids will become so very heavy, you will hardly be able to keep them open. You will have to shut your eyes. When you shut them, you will be in a deep, sound sleep. Deep, sound, heavy, restful sleep. Now breathe very deeply. Do not take your eyes from the circle for even a moment. Watch it very carefully. Strain your eyes just a little to see the circle. Soon your eyes will become so very tired. Now they're beginning to water, they're beginning to water, now they're becoming very red. Your eyelids are becoming so heavy. Keep watching the circle. Watch it; watch it. Now the eyelids are becoming so very heavy. Your arms and legs feel very numb; you are so tired now, you want to go to sleep. Do not resist going to sleep. Do not resist it. Try your best to go to sleep. Think only of sleep, think only that you are going into a deep, sound, calm sleep. A very relaxing, peaceful sleep. Breathe very deeply. Now your eyes are becoming so very tired, so very tired and so very heavy. You cannot keep them open. You cannot keep them open. They're beginning to close, you're trying your best not to blink your eyes, you're trying your best but you cannot keep them open. You must shut your eyes. Do not resist going to sleep, do not resist it. You have to shut your eyes. You have to shut them. Shut your eyes! Shut them!!! Shut them, shut them right now. Shut your eyes!!! Keep them tightly shut. Keep them tightly shut. Breathe very deeply. Breathe very deeply. With each breath you take, you are falling deeper and deeper into sleep. Breathe very deeply. With each breath you take, you are falling deeper and deeper into sleep. Breathe very deeply. You will fall into a deep, sound, heavy, restful sleep. Breathe very deeply. Now you will follow every suggestion I give you. These suggestions are given you for your own good, and your own welfare. You will follow every suggestion I give you."

REFERENCES

ARTHUR, R., "A Commentary on the Methods of Esdaile," *India Medical Gazette*, Calcutta, xxvii, 40, 68, 1892.

AZAM, F., *Hypnotisme et double conscience, et alterations de la personnalité*, Préface par J. M. Charcot, J. B. Baillierres et Fils, Paris, 1877.

BEARD, G. M., "Trance and Trancoidal States in the Lower Animals," *J. Com. Med. and Sur.*, Apr., 1881.

BELFIORE, G., *L'ipnotismo e gli state affini Prefozioni del Prof. Cesare Lombroso*, L. Pietro, Naples, 1887.

BINET, A. AND FÉRÉ, C., *Animal Magnetism*, D. Appleton & Co., New York, 1888.

BRAID, J., *Neurypnology*, George Redway, London, 1899.

CHARCOT, J. M., "Hypnotism and Magnetism," *Forum*, vol. viii, p. 566.

CHARCOT, J. M., *Comptes rendus de l'Academie des sciences, 1881*, Progrés medical, 1878, 1881 et 1882.

ESDAILE, J., *Natural and Mesmeric Clairvoyance*, Hippolyte Baillière, London, 1852.

LUYS, L., *Leçons cliniques sur les principaux phénomènes de l'hypnotisme dans leurs rapports avec la pathologie mentale*, G. Carré, Paris, 1890.

LUYS, L., *Hypnotisme experimentale. Les émotions dans l'état d'hypnotisme et l'action à distance des substances médicomenteuses ou toxiques*, J. B. Baillierres et Fils, Paris, 1890.

MESMER, A., *System der Wechselwirkungen Theorie und Anwendung des thierischen Magnetismus als die allgemeine Heilkunde zur Erhaltung des Menschen*, herausgegeben von Wolfart, Berlin, 1814.

MESMER, A., *Mémoire sur la découverte du Magnétisme animal*, Genéve, 1779.

MOUTIN, L., *La Nouvelle Hypnotisme*, Perrin et Cie., Paris, 1887.

TESTE, A., *A Practical Manual of Animal Magnetism*, translated by D. Spillan, Hippolyte Baillière, London, 1843.

8

Subjective Methods of
Hypnotic Induction

So far we have paid most attention to those objective methods which depend solely upon sensory fatigue for the production of hypnosis. Earlier we mentioned the methods by which hypnosis can be attained without benefit of physical methods. The success of the methods thus far presented seems to be based upon the tiring of the senses; however, no such physiological response is essential, for equal success can be attained by the use of subjective methods; i.e., those which rely entirely on suggestion for both their causation and results.

Although methods of induction as devised by various experimenters seem at first glance to differ, that difference is only apparent on the surface. Disregarding their few inconsequential deviations, the observing student will notice a startling basic similarity. The formula which we have already presented appears to account for the efficacy of all techniques, while the physical attitudes of the operator or the object upon which the patient concentrates are of no real importance. Any statement pronounced by the operator or any action which he institutes will have the desired effect if the subject *believes* that it will; if he *expects* it to; and if he mingles his belief and expectation with sufficient *imagination* for it to come about.

A popular psychological experiment, originally employed by Coué to demonstrate auto-suggestion, will prove the validity of this principle. The stage hypnotist frequently uses this device, with slight revisions, to enable him to select suitable subjects for his demonstration. He asks members of the audience to clasp their hands together as tightly as possible. Then he suggests that their grasp is becoming tighter and tighter. After allowing ample time for them to exert this pressure, he commands, very firmly: "When you try to separate your hands, you will find that you cannot. The harder you try, the tighter your hands will stick together."

The ratio of the audience who find themselves unable to oppose his suggestions contains the necessary subjects. And that ratio is in the majority! The hypnotist can immediately release them from the suggestion by dramatically snapping his fingers, simultaneously shouting: "Free! You're free! Now —loosen your hands!"

He commands no unnatural influence. Instead, he depends upon forces which are naturally inherent in everyone— *belief, expectation* and *imagination*. With little effort he could cause his susceptible majority to act upon other suggestions, once the original submission was obtained. We shall find that every technique, simple or complex as it may appear, rests firmly upon the same device. The hypnotist must capture *belief, expectation* and *imagination*.

We may expect those of you who as youngsters, amused yourselves by "hypnotizing" dogs, cats, crawfish or roosters to rebel at this statement. These animals certainly have no capacity for any of the three attributes!

The crawfish may be caused to assume a motionless position, almost cataleptic, by holding his head and claws and gently stroking his bent tail. Adherents of the objective (physical) theory point with unreserved pride to the experiments of Father Kirchner (1646) and his "sleeping hen." The fowl's head was pressed against the ground and a line drawn so that it extended forward from the beak. After the hen remained in this position for a short while, its wiggling ceased and it lay apparently paralyzed for some time before recovering its normal movement. In this same category we may place the phenomenon of the snake fascinating the frog. The celebrated nineteenth century horse-trainer, Rarey, was supposed to use methods of eye-fascination to accomplish his amazing control over horses.

Observation of these phenomena caused the objectivists to propound that hypnosis is principally a condition of the nervous system produced by manipulation of the sensory nerves which affect a portion of the brain. While that explanation seems feasible, closer investigation bares its obvious fallacies. We have been furnished insufficient proof to warrant the assumption that animals, when stimulated, fall into a state of true hypnosis. The apparent paralysis and inertia do not indicate that they are necessarily hypnotized, for psychological experimentation provides us with adequate evidence that fear can produce identical symptoms without sensory stimulation. While these states undoubtedly demonstrate physiological similarity, the primary requisite of hypnosis is suggestibility. The rabbit appears to enter the same condition as a mechanism of defense. When he is frightened by strange sounds or sights, he immediately immobilizes himself for his own protection. He appears as part of the bush, and thus assures his safety. Nature has not adjusted him to the changing times, for on the highway he uses that same faculty for defense against an onrushing vehicle and perishes as a result of his own defense. To propound that nature has taught him self-hypnosis would verge on the ridiculous. Insects also are attracted to light, and when in the presence of this stimulus they react as if fascinated; by some physiological compulsion, they swarm around its glowing surface. Human beings are known to react in like manner when unconsciously their eyes become fixed upon a light globe; sometimes it is only with effort that they are able to remove their attention from this object.

All this, however interesting, is not hypnosis. Hypnotism implies acceptance and enactment of suggestions, a feat only possible with beings of higher intelligence. Other conditions resembling hypnotic states do not produce response to suggestion and therefore cannot be classified under the title of hypnotism. It is my contention that if the "physical" were entirely stripped from the various methods which supposedly rely upon physical devices, the methods would succeed equally well. Hypnosis will occur independently of physical means if the basic factors prevail at the time of pre-induction.

It is customary for thinking individuals to seek material explanations whenever possible for phenomena which are inexplicable. Their very zeal defeats their purpose. One frequently hears a pseudo-realist dismiss hypnotism with, "There is not much to it; it is only imagination." With this statement he ignores the manifold advantages which accrue from that very despised "imagination," and discards the most potent of man's resources. "Reality is the only truth," and yet when man charges a fable with sufficient intensity of imagination, that fable becomes a reality to him. *Suggestion,* created verbally or by other means, signifies an idea which has been translated into involuntary action through the collaboration of imagination and reality. It thus becomes control of the individual by an externally caused idea.

Although the objectivists are reluctant to admit that suggestion and suggestion alone is the ultimate cause of hypnotic induction, that, nevertheless, remains the exact definition of the process. Methods given hitherto have apparently relied upon physical implements for induction. This appearance is illusory. There are methods beyond the process of fascination, which create a sufficiently deep state to enable the subject to obey any given suggestions, although the state depends upon a method purely mental in scope.

It is not necessary for the individual to gaze intently at some dazzling object, or even to be subjected to passes of the hypnotist. We shall find that a mere suggestion issued from the therapist's lips will not only produce the desired state, but produce it more effectively, more predictably and with more practical results. In the furious disagreement between the adherents of the objective and subjective schools of thought, it is obvious that those professing the use of physical methods completely ignore any implication of suggestion as a modality for the production of hypnosis—and one cannot prove a point by ignoring a basic component. In extreme opposition to hypnotic induction through physical techniques, I shall present here several methods with which any stage of hypnosis can be induced without the use of physical "props" or passes.

One of the most successful of the "mental school" of thought was Doctor Bernheim, who describes his procedure as follows:

"I proceed to hypnotize in the following manner: I begin by saying to the patient that I believe benefit is to be derived from the use of suggestive therapeutics, that it is possible to cure or to relieve him by hypnotism; that there is nothing either hurtful or strange about it; that it is an *ordinary sleep* or torpor which can be induced in everyone, and that this quiet, beneficial condition restores the equilibrium of the nervous system, etc. If necessary, I hypnotize one or two subjects in his presence in order to show him that there is nothing painful in this condition and that it is not accompanied with any unusual sensation. When I have thus banished from his mind the idea of magnetism and the somewhat mysterious fear that attaches to that unknown condition, above all, when he has seen patients cured or benefited by the means in question, he is no longer suspicious, but gives himself up, then I say:

" 'Look at me and think of nothing but sleep. Your eyelids begin to feel heavy, your eyes, tired. They begin to wink, they are getting moist, you cannot see distinctly. They are closed.' Some patients close their eyes and are asleep immediately. With others, I have to repeat, lay more stress on what I say, and even make gestures. It makes little difference what sort of gesture is made. I hold two fingers of my right hand before the patient's eyes, or persuade him to fix his eyes upon mine, endeavoring at the same time to concentrate his attention upon the idea of sleep. I say, 'Your lids are closing, you cannot open them again. Your arms feel heavy, so do your legs. You cannot feel anything. Your hands are motionless. You see nothing, you are going to sleep.' And I add in a commanding tone, 'Sleep.' This word often turns the balance. The eyes close and the patient sleeps or is at least influenced." *

We notice that Bernheim's method calls for little physical display of any sort; it seeks to establish the state entirely by suggestion. A patient's entire body is made to react to the implanted idea. In his method Bernheim calls upon the patient's own natural imaginative resources to compel him to obey the suggestions which are offered. The length of time required for the patient's concentration upon an object is admittedly shorter than would be adequate for production of sensory fatigue. The patient is induced to sleep merely on the basis of suggestion. The suggestions issued by Bernheim are accepted by the patient's imagination and obeyed.

Bernheim's method produced phenomenal responses without excessive consummation of time. Time is frequently an essential factor in hypnotization. When the procedure depends upon suggestion alone, the process should be short

* Bernheim, H., *Suggestive Therapeutics,* translated by C. A. Herter, G. P. Putnam's Sons, New York, 1899, p. 1.

enough to preclude any possibility of the patient's "talking himself out of it." Bernheim provided his patient with a serviceable explanation, thereby replacing suspicion with credence. Confidence is a vitally important element in hypnosis, for it exaggerates the feeling of the subject and enlists his own imagination to heighten the response. When long-drawn-out procedures are used, the subject has time to analyze his feelings and is likely to retain acute awareness with eventual loss of *confidence*. The attack must be rapid to be *effective*.

The stage hypnotist, hampered by the time limit on his act, has been forced to recognize this sooner than the doctor in private therapeutic practice. He creates such expectation and such belief that the subject, unable to analyze the situation, is quickly netted into deeper and deeper states by his own stimulated imagination. The physician, on the other hand, must necessarily limit his techniques within ethical borders.

One of the shorter methods uses a physical stimulus but relies mainly upon suggestion for its effectiveness:

I place thumb and forefinger of my left hand upon the bridge of the subject's nose, pressing firmly but gently. The fingers of the other hand press against the inferior portion of the occipital bone, that is, directly where the back of the neck joins the protruding bone. The fingers are pressed against these bones. Both hands are exerting their pressure, which means that the fingers of the left hand are pressing the head back, while the fingers of the right hand are pressing forward. Both hands exert an equal amount of pressure. I suggest at the beginning of this procedure that I am pressing upon certain nerves which will cause the patient to fall into deep hypnotic sleep. The suggestion is this:

"I am now pressing on certain nerves; when I release my fingers, you will fall back and be in a deep, sound sleep. Do not be afraid of falling; my arm is directly behind you and I will catch you. Now breathe very deeply; think only of sleep, think of nothing else, but concentrate all your attention on sleep."

Now when the therapist releases his hands, he releases his *right* hand first in such a way that, although the patient does not notice, the right hand is removed from the back of the subject's neck, and the fingers of the left hand are applying the same pressure on the front portion of the patient's head. As a result, when the right hand is released, the left is *pushing* the patient back to conform with the suggestion. It is advisable to assure the patient that he *will* be caught when he falls back, and the therapist must not only take this into consideration verbally, but also have a chair close-by where the patient may rest during the hypnotic state.

Let us analyze this method for a moment. First, the patient is told by the therapist that there are certain nerves in a portion of the head which, when pressed, will induce sleep. He is also advised of the fact that when the fingers of the operator's hands are released, he will fall backwards.

The subject is given these two suggestions at practically the same time. The hypnotist facilitates the suggestion by releasing the fingers of the right hand a fraction of a second more quickly than he removes the fingers of the left hand from the bridge of the patient's nose, and, as a result, he is pushing the subject back with a slight, unnoticeable pressure. When the subject falls back, he is immediately convinced of the fact that the suggestion has been obeyed; he was told he would fall and he did fall. He was told that he would be caught, and he was caught. Each further suggestion gains power from the one preceding it, until the patient is guided into the hypnotic state—because he is convinced that the nerve pressure is able to produce that state. Each further suggestion increases the pressure of that belief.

At the point of the fall, the therapist must immediately seize his advantage; he instantly directs the subject to keep his eyes tightly shut; then he announces that the subject can-not open his eyes—and, lo, he cannot. As soon as the patient relaxes and accepts the fact that he is obeying the therapist's suggestions, the hypnotist places the subject's arm outward, suggesting that the arm is becoming extremely rigid and cannot be lowered. This follows. In other words, each sugges-tion creates a still firmer stronghold on the subject; each leads him to firmer conviction that he is in the state where every order must be obeyed.

When the therapist observes that each suggestion is be-ing accepted, he may continue with other suggestions im-portant to the subject's welfare. He can suggest the abolition of pain; he may regress the subject year by year with the pur-pose of bringing to the surface certain experiences which might remedy the patient's condition, or he may create illu-sion for therapeutic purposes, or induce anaesthesia for the relief of pain. These suggestions are actually obeyed because the stock suggestions have been carried out. It is therefore ap-parent that the subject's normal compliant response to sugges-tion is the foundation upon which heightened suggestibility can be developed—the suggestions functioning as the build-ing blocks for its construction. Thus upon the acceptance of the uncomplicated primary suggestions (i.e., those which seem reasonable for acceptance by the subject), and later the increasingly more complex ones that follow, he gradually be-comes more susceptible to intricate suggestions which, in ordinary waking states, would elicit poor response. This process of conditioning is achieved by the full and complete recognition by the subject of the fact that he is hypnotized and that he must obey every order of the therapist.

Analysis of this method might lead one to suspect that it is based upon some physical factor exerted on the nerves. That is not so—there are no nerves in that portion of the hu-man anatomy known to be capable of inducing a hypnotic state; we have merely flourished a suggestion that sounds reasonable. The subject unfamiliar with the nerves of the body can easily be *misdirected* into *belief* that such pressure causes sleep. When he falls back, it is not because of a physiological device but rather of suggestion (aided by a slight push). The nature of the specific auxiliary technique is not important; nor are these the decisive factors: the nerves need not be mentioned. The therapist can, instead, suggest that when he presses on the subject's forehead he will feel extremely weary, fatigued and sleepy—the subject will still react. Any modification of this technique can be used, provided a certain element of showmanship is added to the suggestion in order to capture the subject's *imagination*. The single criterion of success with any mental method is the patient's reception. Therefore, it is important that the *expectation* of the patient be considered in the choice of the device to be used. The consistently successful practitioner takes time to learn the patient's own ideas on hypnosis. If the subject has read a bit and *believes* that the "only way" is through a wild glare from the doctor's eyes, by all means let the doctor glare wildly. By so doing, he inflames the subject's imagination through catering to his expectation. Other subjects believe that they must take a potent pill they have heard about. A vitamin or sugar-and-water concoction will do the trick nicely, especially if accompanied by intricate instructions as to the method of swallowing water.

For the new patient, it is wise to fortify his degree of expectation and increase his imaginative capacities. Give him a pill to take or a glass of colored water to drink while he is waiting for his appointment. Ten or fifteen minutes later, ask him what effect the pill has had. Usually he will answer that he is just a bit drowsy. This, of course, is due to the suggestion implanted with the pill. Now the therapist can begin with a great deal of certainty, for the patient is conditioned to respond to any further method; also he feels that the substance offered him has already removed a certain amount of his capacity for control.

Should the subject express doubt, or should the therapist suspect doubt, may I refer you to the stratagem, mentioned earlier, of walking over to the subject, lifting the lid of one eye and staring intently into its structure, walking away casually, stating firmly, "There is absolutely no doubt that you can be hypnotized!" This serves as an extraordinarily powerful suggestion, to which almost any patient will respond.

It is important to repeat, however, that the method must be cut to fit the patient's measure. It would be foolish to attempt a method implying mysticism for induction in a subject without such inclination; again, it would be useless to attempt technical language to a person with no technical vocabulary. Appropriate methods can be devised to conform with each patient's ability to understand.

The fact is, any method may be used satisfactorily if adapted to the patient's knowledge, education and cultural background. In most cases of failure, the therapist has attempted to adjust the patient to the method, rather than adjusting the method to the patient.

Sometimes unconsciously negative suggestions have crept in to trip the therapist. A friend of mine, in practice for thirty years, could still count only one successful induction out of every twenty subjects. Together, we checked his methods thoroughly. I was baffled; the formula was exact; every specification met, every possible contingency was apparently provided for.

Finally, in desperation, I accompanied him to the office and witnessed an entire day's work. To each patient, at some stage of the patter, he was repeating: "You will fall into a *dead* sleep from which only I can awaken you."

The *"dead"* was the trouble, of course. Nineteen out of twenty people will unconsciously repudiate the word. Other pitfalls we discovered were these: "You will *succumb* to hypnosis." "You will be absolutely *paralyzed* and not able to move."

The inquiring student can easily discover other "word-traps." It is a good idea to list them, and devise one's own "patter" completely free of implied or uttered negativity or threat.

Another method that works with refractory patients and, incidentally, has remarkable effect on children is this one:

Two lines of identical size are drawn in such a way that they cross each other. An object is tied with a string to the patient's fore-finger, and his elbow is placed upon a table in such a way that he must hold the object on the string directly above the place where the lines cross, at the same time directing his vision toward it. While he is staring at this crossing point, the therapist suggests that his arm is becoming very tired, and that the object is becoming very heavy. As the subject's arm begins to quiver, the suggestions of weariness are repeated with increasing monotony. It is also suggested that the subject's eyes are becoming heavy and that the diagram before him is changing and assuming many different forms. It is further suggested that his eyes are becoming so heavy that they cannot stay open any longer; that his arm is dropping; that the object he holds is becoming too heavy to hold. When the effects are evident to the therapist, he fortifies his suggestions by telling the subject that he is falling into a deep sleep; he can no longer remain awake. By now the subject realizes that his arm *is* tired (the position is awkward!); that the diagram *is* distorted (a device of optical illusion!); consequently, he convinces himself that he is responding. When the sleep suggestion comes, then, his arm begins to fall down, he feels the heaviness, realizes that sleep is overpowering him. His eyes close, and generally his head falls forward on his forearm which, by this time, rests on the table. The usual suggestions follow, to convince him that he cannot disobey, and very shortly he is deeply asleep.

This technique is particularly adapted to children, especially if mystical drawings or ancient Chinese symbols be employed as a focal point for the eyes.

Another effective method, which dispenses with sensory fatigue, is to have the subject stand erect. The therapist stands behind him, and causes a rather strong pressure upon his back, carrying his hand in a swift pass from the nape of the subject's neck to the small of his back, pushing him slightly forward with each pass. The subject, to protect himself from falling forward, swings back to the normal position and slightly beyond. This method is highly effective, for before the patient fully regains his balance he is given another stroke forward. This is repeated until the therapist suggests that the subject can no longer keep his balance, at which point the subject falls back completely into the arms of the therapist. Now the usual suggestions are brought into play; eyelids becoming tighter and tighter, the eyes will not open, et cetera.

This works entirely upon the patient's suggestive capacity, assisted by the normal fear of falling forward. The patient feels that he is falling forward too far, and, upon suggestion, lets go completely, falling backward into the arms of the therapist. Here we appeal to the subject's own normal method of protection, utilizing his own resistance to gain our end.

When the basic principles of hypnosis are thoroughly understood, many methods may be devised to suit particular needs. The method must be personally constructed with an eye to the talents or limitations of the therapist, on the one hand, and the background of the patient, on the other. The skilled therapist makes it a point never to adopt one method for habitual use; his methods vary according to the circumstances with which he is confronted. If a patient be accustomed to one method, he is careful not to make a change.

Most important is the receptivity of the patient. The method must conform to his limitations, background and prejudices, for it is his imagination which must be captured.

Using the hypnotic formula, a method may be tailored to any subject almost instantaneously. First, a point of fixation for the purpose of *misdirected attention* must be provided. This may be done with either an actual object or an idea. If the subject is concentrating on the idea—let us say—of sleep, his attention cannot wander to speculation about this new experience he is undergoing. Next, an appeal must be made to the subject's *imagination,* and for that appeal to be effective it is absolutely essential to have a thorough knowledge of the components of that imagination. What has the subject heard about hypnosis; what is his emotional reaction to the idea; what are his fears concerning it, and so on? This knowledge enables the practitioner to select a method which will fit his subject's orientation and easily capture that all-important *imagination.*

He must also know what the subject expects, and he absolutely must live up to that *expectation* in every way possible. The subject's *belief* must be conditioned to add its weight to the prospective technique.

To increase one's skill and confidence, it may be a good idea to perform the various experiments I have cited throughout the book. They do prove beyond doubt the tremendous value and assistance rendered by the patient's own powers. In the final analysis, all suggestion is auto-suggestion; all hypnosis, auto-hypnosis. The therapist merely serves as the presenter of tools and instruction, and his success or failure depends entirely upon the wise selection of those tools. All that is really necessary in hypnosis is to provide the patient with some attractive idea which will fire his imagination to such a degree that a physiological change takes place within his own body. THIS PHYSIOLOGICAL CHANGE—*caused by himself*—IS THE ACTUAL HYPNOSIS.

One experiment which gives a vivid picture of the hypnotic situation is this:

A group of subjects—two, three or four—sit beside each

other upon chairs. I have them raise their arms in the air, stretching straight ahead of them, clasping their hands. I tell them to concentrate on sleep; that soon their arms will become very tired, and although their hands will remain clasped, they will fall into their laps. At this point, I institute another suggestion; namely, that I will remove my presence from the room, and although I shall be in another part of the house with the door locked, I shall be able to exert my influence upon them by remote control. I then walk out of the door, read a book in another room, exerting no mental influence whatsoever; I forget all about them for five or ten minutes. Upon my return, I discover that the majority of those chosen for the experiment are hypnotically influenced. There has been no mental pressure from me; but the subjects respond, just the same.

They are responding because I have given them a thought upon which their own mental faculties worked. Also, I added the suggestion that soon their hands would become so heavy they would drop, they would have to drop. Hence, as soon as the strained position of the arms made them uncomfortable, the subjects were made to realize that my "influence" was still there, was still being exerted. Again, we find the basic principle: if one suggestion is followed, the next will be obeyed; each suggestion carries with it the increasing pressure of preceding successful suggestions.

A fifth method which contrives hypnosis without concentration upon any physical object operates in the following way:

Several subjects are placed facing the wall. They are requested to put both arms forward in such a position that the palms of their hands press against the surface of the wall as hard as they possibly can. After a moment or so, the hypnotist requests them to press even harder. After another moment has elapsed, he dares them to withdraw their hands from the wall. They try with all their strength to pull those hands from the wall, but they cannot.

Here again we see a definite mental control which has been manifested over the subject without resorting to sensory fatigue. There is no doubt that all of these methods have to do only with imaginative processes on the part of the subject.

We return to the stage hypnotist, only because it adds to our knowledge of the mechanisms involved in induction. Here he chooses a technique that always assures success. He calls several people from the audience to hypnotize each other. A row of chairs is prepared in such a way that one person is seated between two others facing in the opposite direction. The five or six subjects first agree to follow the operator's instructions. Then the hypnotist begins:

"I am going to count slowly; when I say, 'one,' you are to turn your head and look straight into the eyes of the person on your right. At 'two,' swing your head quickly to the left, gazing into the eyes of that person. At 'three,' shift to the right; at 'four,' to the left, and so on. I shall continue counting, and soon you will find that you are being influenced— not by my power—but by the power I have extended to you and your neighbors."

The hypnotist proceeds, and his result depends largely upon the percentage of extremely susceptible individuals in his group. Of five or six, it is probable that two will manifest the required susceptibility, but the wary hypnotist will carefully "plant" two previously conditioned subjects, for this reason:

Perhaps the normally resistant person looks to his right and finds his neighbor noticeably affected; on the left, the person may or may not be reacting. But if one person on either side shows signs of being influenced, the one in the middle will eventually imitate that influence. He says to himself, "I wonder if I look like that?" and his physical expressions will change imitatively. This method relies entirely upon the phenomenon of imitation, and of imitation by suggestion. The suggestibility of the subject becomes altered, and he must follow the effect of those who have already been influenced. He might even say to himself: "Jones on my right is going under; Mac on my left is responding; how do I know that I'm not reacting too?". . . . and this very train of thought will eventually overcome him.

If we recall, this is merely a modification of Mesmer's original process; one person touched a magnetized tree and promptly became hysterical. The next, having observed the first, produced the exact symptom through imitation alone.

A slightly different approach, relying on suggestion alone, is this one: The subject is seated in a chair and requested to close his eyes. The therapist opens: "I want you to imagine a star. The star is suspended far, far in the distance. I want you to imagine that star. I want you to concentrate all your attention on that star. Now the star is moving forward, moving forward, closer and closer, becoming larger and larger in your radius of vision. Soon the star will be almost upon you. Now in your own imagination you can visualize that star; it is almost upon you. And now, it is going farther and farther away. It is retracing its path, going farther and farther away into the atmosphere. Soon it will be barely perceptible to you; soon it will be entirely out of your range of vision. When you can no longer see that star, you will be in a deep, sound sleep; you are falling deeper and deeper into sleep now. The star is moving farther and farther away. Now you can hardly see it; now you cannot see the star at all. It has escaped completely. It is not within your vision any longer. You cannot see the star; it has escaped your vision completely. Breathe very deeply. With each breath you take you will fall deeper and deeper into sleep."

We shall find that the subject has succumbed to a satisfactory state of hypnosis entirely through his own imagination, facilitated by our suggestions. The experienced therapist with an ingenious turn of mind can devise all sorts of methods which will fall within the schematic pattern of his subject's mind.

At times a method which appears entirely inconsequential and rather impossible will be capable of causing deeper stages than one which seems more practical to the therapist. We must always keep in mind the fact that *minds are different*: emotional qualifications are different. The approach, the pre-conditioning of one person, is always completely different from the attitudes, ideas and approach of another. The responsibility of selection rests entirely upon the therapist. If he fails, he has failed to conform his method to his subject's bias.

Any method which insures the thorough application of every portion of the hypnotic formula is definitely sure to produce the hypnotic effect, regardless of the subject who confronts us, and regardless of the number of failures he has experienced at the hands of other therapists—providing we are able to *inflame his imagination brilliantly enough to counteract the memory of those failures.*

A word of caution may be inserted at this point. Many of the illustrations I have used required a flamboyancy of technique because of their inherent nature and problems. For general practice and for the majority of patients, a firm, quiet, professional manner is the best approach. Once again, the attitude, "patter" and technique of the practitioner must be adapted to each individual case. Flamboyancy may be essential for Mr. Jones and fatal to the confidence of Professor B.

In any case, respect for the patient is a *sine qua non*. Respect, in this sense, goes beyond any mere formality of a professional manner and includes the recognition of the patient as a person in his own right. It is important to establish in him a feeling of his own dignity. This can never be brought about by making a spectacle of him and aggravating his feeling of helplessness, nor by encouraging an attitude of dependence on the manipulations of the therapist. Although in certain circumstances the effects of hypnotherapy seem to be the result of trickery, it must constantly be kept in mind that it is the patient's own activity and response to suggestion that bring them about. Further, when a feeling of awareness and understanding is encouraged in the patient, not on the level of manipulation or trickery but on examination and revaluation, the therapy is more effective and extends itself dynamically.

A. INCREASING THE DEPTH OF HYPNOSIS

Contrary to those observers who contrive to assign stages of differentiation in the hypnotic process, I have observed that the various "stages" are merely the result of the therapist's suggestion. If complete catalepsy of one portion of the body is suggested, with appropriate response by the subject, it need not mean that the subject has reached a "cataleptic state"; the state is one from which many phenomena, including somnambulism, catalepsy or even extreme lethargy, can develop, depending entirely upon the suggestions of the therapist. A deep hypnosis is not necessary to put the subject into so-called "cataleptic trance." The fact is that if the subject obeys the preliminary suggestions, he will progressively follow really difficult suggestions presented to him during this phase. For instance, in the "somnambulistic state" it would not be necessary to increase hypnosis to a deeper degree to secure cataleptic reactions. If he be informed that a certain part of his body will become rigid, and if the suggestion is enhanced by stroking or passes, that part will become rigid, not because hypnosis has been deepened but because the suggestion has been implemented. This can be done at any stage, for once a person is convinced that he cannot lift his arm against orders, he will not be able to do so. It stands to reason that if he be receptive to these suggestions, he will respond to other suggestions as well.

The very pyramiding of suggestions serves to increase the depth of hypnosis, for as each suggestion is obeyed, the subject inevitably falls deeper into the state. One method which I devised, and of which I can find no previously written record, is that of waiting for a few minutes after hypnotizing the subject, to repeat the entire process from the beginning, despite the fact that he seems already to be in the desired state. In other words, I pile Pelion on *Ossa*; after hypnosis, re-hypnosis. This causes the subject to enter a very deep state, similar to that deep lethargic state of which early observers have written. I find this method most satisfactory, although it may be unnecessary. If a subject will obey simple suggestions, he will obey difficult ones; once difficult ones are accepted, there is no resistance to therapeutic suggestions, which are intrinsically as simple for the subject to accept as are suggestions of catalepsy or of partial or total amnesia.

B. STATES OF HYPNOSIS

For the sake of clarity and simplification, we may enumerate three general stages of hypnosis, which, although they overlap, are useful for the sake of interpretation.

1. Light Hypnosis

The subject is extremely drowsy, although he may not feel as though he were affected. He is fully aware of everything going on about him; will obey simple suggestions, but will not react favorably to those of a complicated nature. He droops his head, breathes heavily, and finds distracting influences disturbing.

2. Medium Sleep

To all intents and purposes, the medium sleep suffices for almost any purpose which is pursued during hypnosis. It is occasioned by marked obedience. The subject makes no effort to resist; he accepts all suggestions readily. All of his senses are made available for utilization by the theraptist; he can feel or re-live any suggested event. This is the stage where regression for analytical purposes is most facile. A sensory suggestion may be either given or removed. From every standpoint this is the most desirable state, particularly for inducing post-hypnotic amnesia. Catalepsy, light anaesthesia for the relief of pain or for minor surgery, is also most satisfactorily induced during the Medium Sleep.

3. *Depth Hypnosis*

This stage, as its name implies, is the most complete state. The respiration and heart action of the subject are markedly lower; he presents the familiar signs of sleep, although he will halfheartedly listen to suggestions offered to him. While this Deep Sleep is not dangerous, it can bring with it many disagreeable experiences. The subject takes a complete "don't give a d. . . . ." attitude toward suggestion; he feels so good that his only desire is to be left strictly alone. When an order is suggested to him, he ignores it at first and only obeys reluctantly upon iterated commands.

The chief value of the Depth Stage is for major surgery. Painless amputation is possible. My method of achieving depth is to hypnotize the patient repeatedly without allowing him to waken in the interim. By hypnotizing him over the hypnosis already present, he will be caused, sooner or later, to arrive at the Depth Stage. Generally it requires from twenty minutes to an hour to accomplish. However, it is not a good thing for the novice to experiment with; he will find that his end can be served in Medium Hypnosis, and it is wiser not to resort to Depth Hypnosis until one has a healthy background of experience and feels equipped to attempt pioneer work in the field.

The inexperienced practitioner, whose knowledge of hypnosis is derived from books and lectures, would do well to leave this stage alone in his trial and error experiments. Authors generally do not write of the unforeseen occurrences that can beset a subject who has been guided to this stage. As a result he is at a loss when faced with the unusual; his bewilderment being reflected in his behavior. The consequences are usually panic for the patient and despair for the practitioner.

I shall relate a disagreeable incident which occurred several years ago, which will help to clarify this point. It concerned a rather mettlesome physician who had read a number of books on the subject and had attended a few of my lectures. The demonstration that I had given on this particular night impressed him with its simplicity. Upon arriving home he spoke enthusiastically with his wife of the facility with which my subject responded. His wife's interest in the procedure was the signal of a long awaited opportunity, and he made the best of it. With surprising ease the woman made immediate response to his suggestions, but soon began to display signs of uneasiness—shifting nervously in her chair, wrinkling her brow from time to time, her head pivoting from side to side. While such expressions would instantly provoke certain observations on the part of the trained therapist, they merely led the doctor to believe that his wife had not responded to sufficient depth. By further manipulation he succeeded in bringing her to deeper levels and finally he could achieve no further response. She showed little if any activity. Her rate of respiration was shockingly low; her pulse was hardly perceptible. The doctor, not having formal training in hypnosis, was stricken by panic. He shook his wife fiercely, but she remained unresponsive. He thought of several remedies for her condition, even an intracardiac injection of adrenaline, but fortunately he went to the telephone instead. A short time after being summoned I was at the physician's house. Surprisingly she made immediate response to my suggestions and within a few minutes she was returned to her normal state of consciousness.

Upon my request she visited my office the next day. As her husband had informed me of her discomfort during hypnosis I was interested in her mental impressions throughout the experience. The reasons for her reaction became increasingly apparent as she related an incident that had occurred soon after marriage. Her husband would take every opportunity to question her about her premarital experiences and she had been reluctant to tell of them. Because of his insistence in the matter she had been forced to maintain a "tight lip" whenever conversations of this sort transpired between them. Only after reaching the first stages of hypnosis did it occur to her, and rather suddenly at that, that in this state she could be made to answer her husband's questions. This accounted for her nervousness, for she felt "trapped." While she perused one of her husband's books on hypnosis she had read that a subject forsakes his capacity for resistance to the suggestions of the hypnotist. This led her to conclude that if he had queried her in this state she would have no alternative but to give him the right answers. Finally as a method of defense she assumed a state wherein she could no longer perceive the sensation of her husband's voice. Yet, paradoxical as it may seem, my voice was perfectly audible to her, and in her words, "It came on as a relief." The suggestions which I had administered were acceptable to her and therefore she responded eagerly to them, for she knew that I had no desire to question her about her past. There is no doubt that this stage would have progressed to normal sleep and eventual waking if my suggestions had not intercepted the state.

Lately I have experimented with a particular phenomenon in this state, which, early findings indicate, produces gratifying benefits to the subjects. I have placed patients in Depth Hypnosis for a period of seventy-two hours, affording them complete repose of mind and body, to discover entire relief in cases where rest was indicated.

I have also used the method upon psychotic patients in sanitariums, where I discovered that placement here for two or three days has enabled them to become calm and infinitely more receptive to psychoanalytical therapy. The rest has put them into a condition they were totally unable to reach through other means.

Hypnosis of the psychotic is generally very difficult, for that type of patient lacks the necessary concentration, but once accomplished, I have been enabled to win the patient's complete confidence, *rara avis* indeed, which contributed to a more peaceful attitude between analytical sessions. Of course, much investigation, much experimentation and exhaustive tabulation of findings will be required before hypnosis can be used extensively in this capacity; however, again we find in hypnosis that fertile field for the explorer of scientific horizons.

C.   HYPNOSIS BY POST-HYPNOTIC SUGGESTION

Once the subject has responded to hypnosis, we may eliminate the usual methods of induction for later sessions. During the first hypnosis, before the subject is awakened, he can be told that every time the therapist claps his hands three times, he will fall into the same deep sleep that he is presently experiencing (i.e., first hypnosis). Whether or not this is recalled upon awakening, the next time the therapist claps his hands three times (or drops a book, or touches him on the forehead—the signal itself is unimportant) the subject will automatically lapse into his original hypnotic state. This little device saves wear and tear on both subject and therapist. It is particularly useful to a doctor faced with administering a painful treatment to a slightly hysterical patient or to a child, and its possibilities in dentistry are endless.

Particular precautions are necessary in connection with this method for the protection of the patient in his daily life. An idea must likewise be implanted, together with the basic suggestion, that the suggested phenomenon can occur only in the presence of the doctor, i.e., that the "signal" will have no effect on him when it is offered by someone other than the hypnotist.

It is prudent, also, to establish different signals for different patients. Some time ago the door separating my office from the reception room flew open without my knowledge. I clapped my hands three times for the patient in my office, only to discover, to my abashed amusement, that I had inadvertently hypnotized the patient in the waiting room at the same time. That was her signal, too!

The suggestions for future hypnosis work precisely as adequately as do other post-hypnotic suggestions. If we tell a subject that a week from today he will experience an annoying itch on his nose, the chances are that he will carry this through if the suggestion was administered during the first hypnotic session. If he will react to this, there is no reason to doubt the efficacy of a similar post-hypnotic suggestion anent further hypnosis.

Some therapists with a flair for the unusual have discovered that through this method it is possible to hypnotize subjects by telephone, telegraph, or even by letter. While this demonstration is more spectacular than useful, it is based upon precisely the same device of post-hypnotic suggestion.

It works this way: while a subject is under influence, he is told that when he is called by the therapist to the telephone, he will immediately fall into deep sleep at the first tone of the therapist's voice. A similar suggestion, of course, may be given, using a telegram or a letter in the therapist's handwriting as the cue.

These results seem amazing; however, they are readily understood in the light of what we know about the possibilities of post-hypnotic suggestion. In therapeutical work, the principle is most helpful. For an insomniac, it can be suggested that the minute he goes to bed and his head touches the pillow he will fall into a state of hypnosis which will translate itself into natural sleep, from which he will rouse completely refreshed at his usual rising time. The principle is always the same, and its value is limited only by the originality or purpose of the therapist.

D. WAKING THE SUBJECT

Much of the fear propaganda promulgated around hypnosis has been built about the "dangers" of being unable to waken the subject. This is sheer nonsense, ignored by anyone with the slightest knowledge or experience of the science. If the subject is not awakened by the therapist, his state will automatically convert itself into natural sleep, from which he will waken naturally within an hour or so. The only exception I have ever known was that of the Depth Stage, in which the sleep lasted up to seventy-two hours because I so ordered it. There has never been a case in all the annals of psychological history where a subject failed to return to a normal condition, despite the elaborate fancies of professional fictioneers.

It is, of course, advisable to exercise reasonable care in awakening a subject to avoid frightening him. At that sensitive time, he could well be startled into hysteria, it is true. He will waken instantly if told very gruffly, "Wake up; you're all right now," and while this is a method generally employed, I am definitely not in favor of it. It requires a little time to put the subject into the hypnotic state, for he has to be carried over from absolute consciousness to hypnosis; it is advisable to use a similar amount of time in returning him to full consciousness. If the subject wakens startled, it takes time for him to regain his equilibrium, nullifies the good work accomplished during hypnosis, and, most important of all, the trauma has conditioned him poorly for later sessions.

A method of wakening I have found most satisfactory, which avoids this pitfall as well as other unpleasant aftermaths, is that of suggestion: "I shall now count from one to ten; when I reach seven you will be wide awake; you will feel a warm glow of health and well-being; you will be free of all pain, of all discomfort; you will feel relaxed and peaceful." This suggestion I make several times before I start counting.

The value of counting to ten is clear; it gives the patient sufficient time to bring himself out of the state which we have induced. One might, of course, stop counting at seven; the patient will be awake, but he would immediately wonder *what* had brought him back to consciousness, and a slight psychological unease might result. The continued counting answers that question before he thinks of it, which is always useful procedure. When he wakens peacefully, he will welcome rather than resist future sessions.

Likewise, treat his ego with dignity and respect. The subject must never be ridiculed during a state of hypnosis. Silly pranks for purposes of entertainment have been known to throw a subject into a hysterical condition from which rousing is difficult. This point cannot be over-emphasized!

When a subject submits completely to the dictates of the therapist, he does so with confidence and trust. These qualities must never be violated, even in jest. When he is awakened, it must be with thoroughness, kindliness and consideration, else he might emerge from hypnosis with a headache, dizziness, or other distressing symptoms. Whether the hypnosis was induced for therapy or for experimentation is immaterial; the subject must always be left with a restful, happy attitude, completely free of symptoms which can arise from the hypnotic state if not guarded against. This can be accomplished, as I said before, with suggestions to that effect.

At no time is it necessary to use any other means than mental suggestion. Some hypnotists believe that wakening is more thorough if the patient is furiously fanned, hissed at, or shouted at loudly. Nothing in the hypnotic process justifies any of these techniques. The one predictable result would be shock for the patient, leaving him with deleterious effects as by-products.

At the risk of seeming repetitious, once more, I want to underline, emphasize and stress the fact that the desired sequel to every hypnotic treatment is complete and thorough restfulness. *Conditioning the patient favorably for future sessions* is an indispensable factor in hypnotic procedure. It requires a bit of time and trouble, certainly, but the rewards are more than compensatory in every possible way, and hypnosis will always terminate naturally and harmoniously when that principle is habitually followed.

REFERENCES

BAUDOUIN, C., *Suggestion and Autosuggestion,* Dodd, Mead & Co., New York, 1922.

BECK, L. F., "Relationships Between Waking Suggestibility and Hypnotic Susceptibility," *Psychological Bulletin,* 33, 746, 1936.

BERNHEIM, H., *Suggestive Therapeutics,* translated by C. A. Herter, G. P. Putnam's Sons, New York, 1899.

BROOKS, C. H., *The Practice of Autosuggestion by the Method of Emile Coué,* Dodd, Mead & Co., New York, 1922.

COUÉ, E., *How to Practice Suggestion and Autosuggestion,* American Library Service, New York, 1923.

DREUGER, R. G., "The Influence of Repetition and Disuse Upon Rate of Hypnotization," *Journal of Experimental Psychology,* 14, 260–269, 1931.

ERICKSON, M. H., "Concerning the Nature and Character of Post-Hypnotic Behavior," *Journal of General Psychology,* 24, 95–133, 1941.

JONES, E., "The Nature of Autosuggestion," *British Journal of Medical Psychology,* 3, 206–212, 1923.

KELLOG, E. R., "Duration of the Effects of Post-Hypnotic Suggestion," *Journal of Experimental Psychology,* 12, 502–514, 1929.

MORGAN, J. J. B., "The Nature of Suggestibility," *Psychological Review,* 31, 6, 1924.

PRINCE, M., *The Unconscious,* Macmillan Co., New York, 1929.

9

Suggestive Therapy

When all available data on scientific hypnotism have been examined, one fact looms large, inescapable and inevitable: viz., *suggestion* causes the hypnotic state; *suggestion* is the vehicle upon which all hypnotic control travels, and *suggestion* is the most effective means of rousing the subject. In other words, the entire procedure of hypnosis, from induction to awakening, is founded upon *suggestion*.

The word "suggestion," used in hypnotic context, has become a technical term divorced from its meaning in general usage. To reiterate, it signifies the process of controlled alteration of man's actions and re-actions through thoughts or objects. We have already considered the effect of "thought," and are well aware of the fact that the spoken word can alter mental or emotional response.

Speech is probably the most direct route to the brain, and therefore the most direct approach to the acceptance of an idea by an individual. If we wish to institute an idea or initiate an action on the part of another, the simplest way is to tell him so. We are all regulated by words; our very thoughts must be expressed in words. We attempt to formulate every conceivable impression in the language that we speak. We need neither observe nor experience hypnosis to recognize the power of words.

The verbal suggestion, then, is the direct route for conveyance of an idea. However, the situational suggestion utilizing an object or setting for the stimulus, indirect route though it may be, is an equally, if not more potent means of transmission. Whether the suggestion be implanted directly or indirectly, it is undoubtedly absorbed by the recipient.

It is well known that objects or settings may change an entire emotional response. At a funeral one feels sad; at a party, happy. This is an example of indirect suggestion. If a student yawns in class, the contagion spreads until the entire class is agape, and many are the unprepared who have avoided recitation by invoking this mild epidemic!

If I smile at you, while speaking, you smile back. If at a party I "sit down at the piano" and play, I am soon the center of a group.

These examples are self-evident, and they are all stimulated by indirect suggestions. Yet in many ways they carry more weight than would direct suggestions. I can tell you to dance, and you promptly resist; you don't like to be ordered about. But if I use the indirect method, such as playing a lively tune, your whole body responds to the rhythm, and before you know it, you are dancing.

It is my contention that every properly instituted suggestion works on the basis of association. The unconscious recollection of an association pattern already crystallized in memory implements the suggestion to a forceful degree. Each idea suggested by speech or object becomes classified with a series already present in consciousness, and becomes charged with the emotional coloring attendant upon that series. Suggestion can only be visualized upon a basis of experience of some sort, either actual or imaginative. The subject requested to visualize a star will picture the star of his own experience: the Hottentot, one of the stars of the night sky; the American, a five-pointed star, and a Rabbi, the Star of David. Similarly, any suggestion will instantly link itself to a chain of recollection peculiar to the subject; it will be enforced because, in one way or another, it was previously enforced.

Indirect suggestion, then, consists of suggestion offered in subtle forms. Any physician practices it constantly whether or not he is aware of the fact. His very attitude and bearing may unconsciously suggest either: "Of course you're going to be all right. The treatment is a little painful, of course, but with your constitution. . . . ." or else, "Dear me, dear me, this is too bad. I don't quite see how we are going to pull you through. . . ." and the patient responds more readily to these implied suggestions than to all the pills or elixir he may prescribe. Fortunately, the patient rarely develops adequate transference to the doctor whose prognosis is gloomy, and little lasting damage is done.

The effect of indirect suggestion frequently leads to amusing incidents. Sir Humphry Davy, discoverer of nitrous oxide gas, was requested by a colleague to administer the anaesthetic gas to a patient suffering from functional paralysis. (It was to be the first time such an experiment was attempted.) Delighted, Davy readily agreed to the test, offering to serve as anaesthetist. First, as is the custom, he placed an ordinary thermometer beneath the patient's tongue. Suddenly, the paralytic began to quiver. Half-frightened, half-jubilant, he claimed that a strange current was running through his body; already he felt himself deriving immense benefit from the "treatment." Poor Sir Humphry never did have the opportunity to test his gas on the patient. Chuckling inwardly at the medical inconsistency, he effected a truly miraculous "cure" on the paralytic by the simple process of

tucking the thermometer under his tongue, at discreetly
spaced intervals!

A British medical journal reports the case of a severe de-
pressive who committed suicide by swallowing a mild alcoholic mouth-wash, which she mistook for carbolic acid. She
died—although the coroner's report disclosed absolutely no
evidence of physical damage.

A man whom his physician suspected of suicidal intent
begged for "sleeping tablets" to relieve his insomnia. Wishing
to protect him from himself, the doctor substituted Vitamin
C for the phenobarbitol that he requested, cautioning him
not to take more than one at a time of the twelve tablets he
was given.

The next morning, his wife called, panic-stricken. She
could not rouse her husband, and she reported that he had
swallowed all twelve tablets of the "drug." Several hours of
oxygen inhalation proved necessary for his revival, while his
respiration and heart action had dropped dangerously low,
and his abnormal pallor led the doctor to fear for a time that
the case might terminate fatally.

Another patient, who developed violent sneezing spasms
at the bare mention of dandelions, let alone their physical
presence, was brought complete relief by a "drug" consisting
of "imported South American herbs," which were concocted
of bits of pumpernickel rolled into impressive pills.

A woman of thirty-six who had suffered from insomnia
since childhood came to me. It took two to four hours for her
to go to sleep, and this, caused by extreme exhaustion, left
her unrested. Upon analysis of her childhood, one fact was
salient: as a child she had always knelt by her bed to recite
that old prayer of childhood:

> "Now I lay me down to sleep,
> I pray the Lord my soul to keep,
> If I should die before I wake,
> I pray the Lord my soul to take."

The last two lines seemed indicative to me, because she was continually giving herself the suggestion that she might "die before" she awakened. This thought was first amplified in her consciousness, then repressed into the unconscious. It was clear that her trouble had its roots in this experience, and the situation resolved itself almost immediately into complete cure upon her conscious acceptance of it!

There is no doubt that a person may be affected by factors of which he is totally unaware. Many things serve as indirect suggestions which are obeyed by the mind as exactly as though directions had been received in the hypnotic state. Parents tend to give their children one destructive suggestion after another, causing untold damage to the child's psyche, although the suggestions have been devoured by the unconscious through an indirect route.

In this chapter we are less concerned with indirect suggestion than with those direct suggestions, administered purposely during hypnosis, which work their way to the unconscious. However, the value of the indirect suggestion in assisting us to formulate our therapeutic approach to mental and physical disorders must not be overlooked.

We have already discussed the fact that everyone is suggestible to some degree. In a conscious state, this degree varies according to our moods, desires, and the situation confronting us at the time we absorb the proffered suggestion. With hypnosis, we have found an artificial method which greatly increases the individual's capacity for suggestibility. When a new idea is placed in a person's mind, it can only gain a foothold by dispossessing an opposing idea which is already present. In the conscious state, this process causes much resistance and argument; the mind tends to reject or suppress any new idea attempting to invade it. No matter how practical, valuable, or realistic the new idea we wish to institute may be, in the conscious state we face the patient's intellectual biases and emotional prejudices of long standing. With hypnosis, we are able to create a direct pathway to his mind along which the new idea may travel, dissolving the barriers along its way. We can accomplish this with the most stubborn of minds, for once the idea that we institute has become acceptable to the subject, his mental and physical faculties all cooperate to carry out the new idea.

This psychological principle of hypnosis must be recognized and accepted by every student. Humanity as a whole inclines to disregard any new idea in favor of one that is familiar. Two conflicting ideas cannot be harbored at the same time; one must prevail. It is impossible to experience thoughts of love and hate simultaneously without internal conflict; to keep the eyes open and closed at precisely the same instant; or to entertain a precept which seems both right and wrong to us at the same split second. One half of the second it may seem right; the other half, wrong; but confusion and teetering is unsettling to the strongest psyche. Wherefore, any concept presented to the mind exists only by itself; it is unable to co-exist in the same sphere with an opposite without neurotic stress. One must be eliminated, once and for all.

Hypnosis simplifies this process, because the mind is placed in such a position that it cannot resist the new idea. There are many ways to do this. During consciousness there are strategic periods; a person under emotional strain or greatly fatigued is highly suggestible, for he is too tired to resist. (Commercial radio confirms this; the inordinate popularity of evening hours with sponsors has become a by-word in the industry!) It would be impracticable to wait for either condition to appear in a patient; in hypnosis, his censor is removed (i.e., that portion of the consciousness which springs to the defense of earlier concepts).

When we deal with therapeutic suggestions, we must take this fact into consideration. A sick person is "low" in every way; his thinking is negative, his perceptions blurred, and his recovery is hampered thereby. Man differs from jungle

animals in that he emotionalizes his conditions; he suffers more pain than an animal because his imagination exaggerates and over-emphasizes the importance of his symptoms.
The time-span of recovery is conditioned largely by the patient's mental attitude; he himself can speed or retard its
rate. The alteration of that attitude from destructive to constructive is one of the many inestimable services hypnosis can
render.

Suggestion replacement is invaluable in the treatment of
any ailment, but it is vital that the patient's background and
"mental set" be thoroughly understood before any suggestion
is planted in his mind through any technique whatsoever.
The therapist must, of course, know the nature of the illness
requiring treatment; he must learn which type of suggestion
is likely to prove most efficacious; he must analyze the patient
closely for possible hysterical manifestations, and, above all,
he must check thoroughly to be sure that hypnotic therapy is
the one indicated.

One example of the dangers of incomplete background
study was recently brought to my attention. A hypnotist of
my acquaintance encountered great difficulty when attempting to cure migraine headaches in a patient under his care.
Finally the suggestion took effect after an unusual number of
treatments, and the symptoms vanished. Some time later, the
patient developed other symptoms. The diagnostician to
whom he went reported the presence of a neoplastic growth
which should have been removed a long time earlier. It is
vitally important that no hypnotist remove "symptoms" until
the cause of those symptoms has been tracked down. Pain is
nature's way of telling us something is wrong. Even where no
physical cause exists, it is wise to determine whether the
symptoms are the result of a severe neurosis, for in such a case
the symptoms might be eliminated while the patient still retained the neurotic problem which, in the course of time,
might totally incapacitate him. In any event, it cannot be too

strongly stated that the medical picture must be completely understood before hypnosis is initiated.

To recapitulate, four steps are essential before undertaking hypnotic therapy:

First, complete diagnosis. The therapist must know the nature of the complaint, whether its cause is physical or functional, plus full details of any other type of treatment the patient is undergoing at the time.

Secondly, he must analyze his patient's emotional, mental and cultural background thoroughly, and select the type of suggestion to use for best results.

Thirdly, he must check the possibility of hysteria and its attendant complications.

Fourthly, he must determine whether hypnotic therapy is the best treatment for the case. In many neuroses, complete psychoanalysis may be preferable.

It is undoubtedly true that without these precautions the hypnotist can still appear as a miracle man to his patient, but the mere possibility of such a phenomenon leads the ethical practitioner to assure himself that hypnosis is unquestionably the best possible of treatments before going ahead.

We must regard hypnosis as a mere palliative method which *does* remove symptoms that are distressing the patient. Occasionally the removal of these symptoms enables an individual to make a better adjustment to the situations which confront him. There is no doubt that in the final, over-all picture, psychoanalysis provides a more effective and longer-lasting method of treatment, but in certain conditions a time element is involved; during the lengthy analysis, the patient may develop further symptoms and lose what little contact he still retains with the reality about him.

One example of this possibility is in alcoholism. Psychoanalysis can accomplish wonderful cures, but thus far the methods in general use require one to three years to establish its cause and to dig down into its depths to uproot it. During this time the patient retains his urge to drink, and is only too likely to stop off at a bar, completely forgetting about his appointment with the analyst. Such "binges" are especially common when a traumatic idea is brought to consciousness during therapy. The patient will return to his usual means for coping with problems—alcohol. This causes complications both in the prognosis of the analysis and in the patient's home life. Analysis cannot deprive the patient of his habit until its conclusion, and the interim suffering is great both for the patient and his family.

In such a case, hypnosis serves a very wonderful purpose, for it is able to stop the alcoholic's desire for drink, and to stop it permanently. The course of the analysis is expedited, his adjustment to his environment both at work and at home is facilitated, and the entire background becomes infinitely more satisfactory. Consequently, it is always advantageous to employ the hypnotic procedure in conjunction with any other methods used in treatment of the alcoholic.

The same thing may be said for physically caused ailments. Once the cause is identified and under treatment, the use of hypnosis to relieve symptomatic pain becomes perfectly legitimate. In fact, hypnosis is always justifiable if used as an adjunct to other modes of treatment. Its use becomes questionable only when it is handled as an end in itself with no regard for other possible factors. The physician who launches into hypnosis without considering these factors is doing his patient a grave disservice.

A. FEARS

The various fears evidenced by humanity are based on past experiences. The original stimulus was met with an inordinate degree of fear-emotion reaction (logical or illogical) and whenever that stimulus is either repeated or recalled, the sufferer reacts as hysterically as at first.

In other cases, the fear evolves as a cover-up for something the individual wishes—consciously or unconsciously—to hide. For instance, a patient of mine showed a fear and anxiety reaction every time he saw a man with a beard. By regression through hypnosis, we took him back to the age of nine, at which time a man with a beard told him he could summon the devil to punish naughty little boys. The patient was panicked at the time; he was a "naughty little boy" because he "had wicked thoughts"; consequently, he did everything in his power to convince himself that the man with the beard was lying. The conflict became so great that he withdrew from the experience entirely, repressing the whole thing. The surface symptom was all that remained; he retained this phobia of men with beards, a fear that was completely inexplicable to himself. The repression was effective in that he was not haunted by the devil, but the phobia was present. As he grew older, a certain amount of rationalization entered the picture; he conditioned himself logically and religiously to accept the fact that the devil was a myth, and were he not, bearded gentlemen still would be unable to invoke him. Yet the fear reaction within his unconscious remained constant, transferring itself from fear of the devil to fear of gentlemen with beards. This is a substitution device frequently met; the original fear is over, but a consequential result tied in memory to the original fear causes the same illogical panic roused by the basic stimulus.

With other fears, we generally find exactly the same thing happening. We can so condition ourselves as to admit consciously that the fears and phobias are groundless and inconsistent with logical knowledge, yet in time of stress, we react precisely as emotionally as ever. Another experience faces us unexpectedly and the entire fear pattern set by the first experience is thrown into action.

For example, let us suppose a little boy is playing with a mouse. The mouse does not bother him; in fact, he is having a grand time catching the mouse as it attempts to run away. Suddenly his mother enters the room, shrieks wildly and shoos the mouse away. Then, fear in every inflection, she explains that mice are horrible animals; they breed infection; when a mouse bites you, you have to die, and so on.

The boy's first attitude about mice was that they were fun to play with; conflicting with this comes mother's warning, "Mice are very dangerous and can cause all sorts of harm to little boys." This conflict is spot-lighted by the emotional coloring of mother's hysteria.

As he grows older, he will be taught about mice, perhaps dissecting or using them as experimental animals. His knowledge and experience indicate that mice are harmless furry animals, very useful to science. Yet let that same chap be confronted unexpectedly by a mouse, perhaps while disposing of garbarge, and he will drop the can, run away, and react as though panic-stricken. He may stop and say to himself, "Nonsense, I am not afraid of mice"; he may laugh at himself. But the mouse presented itself so suddenly that both knowledge and experience were ignored, and he reacted with the same emotion his mother had conditioned in him as a boy.

Therefore, even though logically we can dispel a phobia, we are only able to dispel that phobia by conscious direction and discipline; the basic attitude still persists, and if the stimulus be unexpected enough, the reaction will manifest itself precisely as in the original experience. At times it becomes necessary to go back to the original attitude of the patient, dissolving the phobia entirely by bringing to his conscious mind the traumatic experience which occasioned it, a matter for thorough psychoanalysis.

If this is not advisable because of the time and money involved, hypnosis offers a possible short cut. We are aware that a phobia is in itself a suggestion, initiated early in the patient's life by either a thought or a painful experience, later repressed into the unconscious, leaving an illogical fear as the top of an iceberg which emerges in consciousness without let or hindrance. Hypnosis is able to dispel the phobia by neutralizing the original suggestion as it exists in the unconscious of the patient. This may be easily accomplished through dramatization.

Hallucination is simple to create in a state of medium hypnosis. With our mouse-phobia lad, all that is necessary is to tell him that when his eyes are open he will see a mouse before him. He will notice that the mouse does not cause either anxiety or fear-reaction, because the mouse is small, furry, and friendly. He will be able to play with the mouse, tame it, and make a pet of it.

By this suggestion, we are actually dramatizing the suggestion so vividly that we make him face the thing that he fears. Afterwards, we tell him that he did face it; that he played with the mouse and it did not hurt him; hence, he will no longer have qualms of any kind about mice.

Another possible technique would be to present an imaginary mouse to him in a state of medium hypnosis, and ask the patient to engage in free association about the mouse. That is, the patient is to say anything that the sight of the mouse brings into his mind. Sooner or later he will arrive at the experience which prompted the original phobia, which, once related, is stripped of its emotional content.

Free association is a device—and a valuable one—of psychoanalysis. In full consciousness it requires months or even years to track down the traumatic experience, but hypnosis offers the orthodox analyst a tool which is as labor-saving as a housewife's kitchen gadgets. Frequently these illogical fears are of such a nature that they interfere with a patient's method of coping with existent problems. If, during psychoanalysis, we use suggestion to nullify the fears, the analysis is facilitated and the patient spared months of unnecessary anxiety.

B. IMPROVING VISION

Some of the newer therapeutic methods which are gradually gaining scientific as well as popular approval have been the eye-exercises, best known of which is the Bates System. This technique seeks to improve the vision of the patient by causing a great amount of optic muscle relaxation. Hypnosis assists this type of treatment by providing an abnormal degree of relaxation, which will quickly afford the patient improved quality of vision. This method shortens the entire exercise process and creates almost instantly an effect which Bates and other investigators in the ocular field have only been able to achieve with their patients after lengthy and tedious exercises. The method is as follows:

The patient is placed in a state of Medium Sleep. Then he is given a suggestion to this effect:

"I shall now count from one to twenty-five. The higher I count, the more you will feel a very definite vibratory sensation in your eyes. They will feel as if they are becoming stronger and stronger. When I reach the count of twenty-five, you will open your eyes quickly, relaxing them as much as you possibly can, and you will be able to see much better than you did before."

The therapist continuously intersperses the counting with suggestions for complete relaxation of the eye muscles and for improved vision, implementing them with vibratory passes and touchings of the eyelids of the patient. When he reaches twenty-five, he immediately hands the patient a book, requesting him to read. This procedure is repeated a number of times during each treatment, and each time it is carefully mentioned that the ocular apparatus of the patient is unaffected and that his condition is purely functional. If his imperfect vision is due to the fact that he cannot relax these muscles as much as he should, each treatment will improve his vision and sooner or later he will be able to discard his glasses entirely.

During the last war, I used this method on men rejected for Air Corps service because of ocular difficulties. After approximately one or two weeks of treatment—seeing each patient three times a week—most of them were enabled to pass the very rigorous eye examinations which they had previously failed. Of those cases upon which I have been able to make follow-up investigations, relapses have not been observed.

Of course, if there are any ocular involvements, the treatment is useless, but it is certainly worth a trial because functional disorders are bound to be accompanied by a physical condition, and some improvement will be noted.

The same technique is useful in cases of functional blindness. Once the patient manages to see fairly well under hypnosis, the chances are that his improvement will carry over to remain with him in the conscious state.

The student will, of course, recognize that during this treatment we are continually dramatizing and demonstrating to the patient that he *can* be better and better, and as his unconscious accepts this, his entire physiology falls into accord with his belief and expectation, resulting in immediate improvement and ultimate cure. This does not imply that physical defects of the eye can be eliminated by hypnosis, but their concomitant emotionalization and self-pity is negated. Even with physical treatment, the patient's symptoms remain for a while, retarding its effectiveness, and hypnotic suggestion, once again, may act as a valuable adjunct to other requisite therapy.

C. OBESITY

It would seem axiomatic that correction of overweight may be assisted by suggestion, which can be utilized to accomplish two effects. First, it increases the metabolism of the body, speeding up its digestive processes and removing waste products as quickly as possible before they can accumulate in the system, and second, it curbs the appetite of the patient, even going so far as to make fattening foods repulsive to him.

The body reacts to external situations, increasing anabolism and catabolism accordingly. The entire metabolic process could be controlled by certain situations as they confront the patient. For instance, extreme anxiety about a problem or situation can cause a swift loss of weight, unless the victim be temperamentally one who resorts to sweet-eating as a relief, in which case the same anxiety might be responsible for just as swift an increase. Undoubtedly, emotions control the digestive and metabolic structure of the body; hence, those functions prove amenable to suggestion.

A possible suggestion might be as follows:

"You will be able to digest your food more rapidly and you will temper and curb your eating habits in every way possible. Breads, pastries and candy will produce a nauseating effect. Your elimination will be normal each day; following the suggestions I am giving you at this time, you may expect to lose approximately a pound every other day. When you will have lost ten pounds, your body will normalize its functions, and you will neither gain nor lose additional weight."

Suggestion may also bring about the complete discharge of waste products. In fact, we can suggest to the patient that within fifteen minutes he will have a complete elimination, and in most cases this suggestion will be carried out. It can even be suggested to him that five minutes after he wakens each morning he will have a complete evacuation.

In this way, we can institute a habit of elimination which can be helpful to the patient suffering from constipation. Suggestions for frequent evacuation may be given with no danger to the patient, provided we keep in mind the fact that extremes and abnormalities in any department have serious results. The loss of weight should be kept down to from one to three pounds a week.

By and large, the use of suggestion in control of obesity has proven gratifying to every practitioner who has attempted it.

D. MENSTRUAL CONDITIONS

The medical profession has long known that emotional states cause irregularity and pain in menstruation. As shock, worry or anxiety can cause premature or delayed periods, just so may suggestion be used to restore regularity. In cases of amenorrhea, if a patient is suffering from delay, it is simple to suggest to her that, within a given time after the suggestion, her function will be renewed normally and painlessly. Before such institution, however, she should submit to a thorough physical examination to assure the practitioner that his suggestions do not interfere with possible pregnancy.

If the flow be too heavy or weakening, suggestion may be used to eliminate the period completely for a long enough time to give her forces a chance to recuperate, or to slow the flow to normality. Again, this type of suggestion must not be used unless physical therapy is being administered to correct the cause of the abnormality.

The one time that medical reference may be dispensed with is when functional pain is involved. This condition, as well as its accompanying nervous irritability, can be permanently alleviated by suggestion—not just for the immediate period, but for many months to come.

Some sexually adjusted women who are free of inner fears and complexes concerning the state find that the menstrual period brings them increased mental power and sensitivity. They so arrange their lives as to ease down on physical activities at that time, using the stimulated mind for reading, writing, letters, or study. I have one patient, a motion picture actress, who reserves this period for memorization of scripts in their entirety instead of the customary piece-meal preparations throughout the month for "morning scenes." When instituting suggestions, this possibility should be kept in mind, that the patient, instead of being negatively free of pain, can learn to use and enjoy all the days of each month.

E. INSOMNIA

The condition of insomnia is perhaps one of the most disagreeable of all symptoms. Six hours of sleep are likely to leave the person who needs eight hours irritable and cross; imagine the state of the victim who lies awake endlessly, night after night!

Generally, a person sleeps because he expects to go to sleep, and, conversely, stays awake because he does not expect to go to sleep. Treatment consists of altering that expectation. The best way is dramatization; that is, proving to the patient that he could go to sleep were it not for certain thoughts which keep him awake. Also, despite all complaints that they "did not sleep a wink," the most consistent insomniacs have dozed off for at least a few hours each night. Men cannot live without *any* sleep.

Another factor for consideration is that only about two and one-half hours of sleep out of twenty-four are absolutely necessary to maintain life and a certain amount of well-being. The insomniac emotionalizes his condition, insisting that he must "die" or "go mad" unless he gets more sleep. He is worrying himself needlessly. The body will get its minimum of rest, although it may not be enough to provide health and energy in addition.

Youth requires more sleep than age; at one time eight to ten hours of sleep are necessary for health, but, as the years pass, many people find five to seven hours adequate. Each person's needs are dependent upon his personal rest habits and over-all conditioning. In this section, however, we are dealing with a certain type of insomnia, the corrective suggestion for which is as follows:

"Listen to these suggestions that I am giving you now. You will follow each suggestion implicitly in the order I am now giving them to you. Each night, as you retire, you will relax every portion of your body, and make your mind ready for sleep. This will be done without the slightest effort. You must not try to force yourself to go to sleep, for conscious trying creates a tenseness in your body that defeats its own purpose. Therefore, you will relax unconsciously as you prepare for bed. Exactly five minutes after your head touches the pillow, you will, with the greatest ease, fall into a deep slumber which will remain unbroken until morning. When you awaken, you will feel refreshed, relaxed and have the utmost degree of rest as a result of your sleep. You will be able to carry on the duties of the next day with perfect relaxation and perfect calmness. You will harbor no negative thoughts about these suggestions, remembering that even a small negative thought is much more powerful than a positive thought. The negative thought would keep you awake, but the positive one, which I am planting at this time, will be powerful enough to dissolve the negative one completely. You will go to sleep, because you will expect to go to sleep, and when you do go to sleep, you will sleep soundly without interruption. You will be perfectly relaxed and refreshed upon awakening. You will awaken in the morning at your usual rising time, awake, alive, calm, rested and happy. Throughout your sleep you will feel calm, contented and ever so relaxed, and you will carry this calm, content and relaxation over to your waking state."

The student will notice that we have not yet dramatized the suggestion we have given the patient. The full import dramatizes itself, when the patient, on the night after he receives the suggestion, lies down on the bed, and exactly five minutes later, falls into a deep sleep. This is sufficient dramatization, post-hypnotic in nature, which will cause the suggestion to be obeyed, night after night, until the patient forms a habit of it.

Once the suggestion is placed in the mind, it amplifies itself with each demonstration. In this case, the patient is actually continuously demonstrating to himself each night that he is sleeping; each night's sleep enforces the strength of the dramatized suggestion of the original suggestion keeping it in action until the "insomnia" is completely edged out by the new habit.

F. NERVOUSNESS

The following suggestive routine may be used by itself, but in special conditions—such as insomnia or asthma—in which nervousness is a by-product rather than a prime cause, it is well to combine the procedure for the treatment of nervousness with other therapeutic suggestions. The idea is to clear up as many conditions as possible in one session. Parts of this may be adapted for use with other suggestions when advisable, but, when used alone, the "patter" is this:

First, place the patient in Medium Hypnosis. Then, when he has passed the tests, say:

"Listen to these suggestions very carefully. Relax every portion of your body. You must accept every suggestion that I give you. Breathe very deeply; relax as much as you possibly can. Soon you will find that every portion of your body relaxes. Your nervous tension will disappear completely; it is disappearing now. Every portion of your body is relaxing; you feel exceptionally free and at ease. From this moment forth, you will be able to release the tension created by stored-up nervous energy harbored in your nervous system. This energy has not been used in its proper channel and has hitherto accomplished no constructive purpose for you. This energy will now be released and flow freely through you for your use as you require it. Problems which have previously bothered you will be solved by you with the least amount of effort. It is only the conflicts and your own dissatisfaction with the way you have handled those conflicts which have created tension in your body. You will be able to release that tension by thinking thoughts of a constructive nature, and above all, you will feel content with, and within, yourself. The thoughts that have disturbed you in the past will cease to disturb you. You will meet each problem that confronts you in your life with a great deal of confidence. You will learn to accept yourself as you are. Your nervousness will be gone; you will be able to relax. You will have peace of mind at all times by accepting yourself, your personality and the many things in you which, thus far, you have not been completely content with. Do not criticize yourself with destructive thoughts, for by doing so, you make yourself your own worst enemy. Do your very best each day, and each day be satisfied with what you have done."

This suggestion is repeated over and over again, as are all other suggestions which are given to the subject. The repetition of a suggestion enforces it in a much more potent way and lends itself to a fuller and more complete acceptance by the patient. After a certain number of treatments, the suggestion will reach the patient's mind from within himself, and as soon as it wells upward from within, the nervousness will disappear in its entirety.

G. FAULTY CONCENTRATION

The suggestions for faulty concentration are self-evident, but we present them here for the sake of showing the student how we evolve and prepare various suggestions for acceptance by the subject.

The standard routine for faulty concentration would be this:

"Listen to these suggestions; you will accept each thought which I place in your mind. You will be able to concentrate better than ever before. You will be able to free your mind of extraneous thoughts and you will be able to concentrate fully on anything you may wish to think or do. In the presence of a task which confronts you, your mind will not wander to thoughts which will distract you. Your mind will free itself of all thoughts which do not belong to the fulfillment of the task you have set out to accomplish. Your mental faculties will respond in their entirety when you need them, and thoughts which do not relate to the idea occupying your conscious field will be quickly dispelled."

It will be noticed that the last three suggestions have not been dramatized in the sense of our dramatization of the mouse, because such dramatization or belittling of the patient's condition or problem would encounter unconscious resistance. In nervousness, insomnia, or any case involving deeply rooted self-pity, the patient is unconsciously convinced that no one has ever suffered as much as he. To suggest the contrary would be to give strength to that feeling; hence, we administer positive suggestions repeatedly, allowing them to root by themselves. Repetition of suggestion lends potency, and accomplishes a much more complete acceptance by the patient.

H. MEMORY TRAINING

Groups of suggestions for memory training are very similar to those for faulty concentration. They proceed in this way:

"You will accept every thought I place in your mind. Your memory capacity will grow day by day. You will be able to remember everything you learn without any difficulty. You will be able to remember everything that you have learned without any difficulty." (It is sometimes wise to repeat the same suggestion several times within each session.)

"Your mental faculties will be able to retain all the knowledge you have acquired in the past. Everything that you have learned in the past will come back to you. You will be able to remember what you wish to commit to your memory. Each day your memory retention will improve. It will be better and you will be able to concentrate on all the things which you wish to commit to memory. Your memory will improve day by day. Your concentration will center around that which you intend learning and once you have placed this knowledge in your mind, you will not forget it. You will be able to recall it whenever it becomes necessary for you to do so."

Once again dramatization may accomplish a more intense effect for it serves to fortify the structure of the suggestion. It is logical to suppose that if we are able to prove to the patient, beyond a doubt, that the suggestions have taken hold, their effectiveness increases. Before waking the patient he is requested to open his eyes. A rather lengthy passage of a book or parts of a poem are given him to read. After he has had the opportunity to read the passage a number of times he is asked to repeat the contents without consulting the printed matter. In most cases he will be able to do so without hesitation, often using exact wordage from the text. If the patient seems mentally sluggish during this interval, the physician may read the passages to him, repeating the words as often as is deemed necessary. Before returning him to normal consciousness the hypnotist must impress a suggestion upon his subject's mind that the passage will be remembered after awakening. Such action serves as a double demonstration of the validity and force of the idea which has been implanted.

I. HYPNOSIS AND OBSTETRICS

Hypnosis is invaluable as a therapeutic and anaesthetic method in childbirth. Its need cannot be over-emphasized. Most of the various drugs which have been tried for anaesthesia in obstetrics are either useless from one standpoint or another or are dangerous to both the sensitive mother and her highly sensitive child. Obstetrics has been in dire need of a safe anaesthetic which would at the same time ease the mother's pain and leave her in condition to give full cooperation to the obstetrician.

Scientific hypnosis is equal to fulfilling this need, but its capacities have hardly been applied on a serious level. De Lee and Greenhill state:

> "Hypnosis has been used in obstetrics for a long time and should be employed more often than it is at present. Even if complete hypnosis is not desired, physicians should remember that repeated suggestion, with or without the aid of medication, can accomplish a great deal in labor, particularly for the relief of fear as well as the pains of labor." *

Read, in his excellent book relative to the subject, clarifies the position of fear as the chief pain-producing agent in normal delivery. He points to the fact that when fear is eliminated in physiological labor the distress of pain is also banished.

De Lee and Greenhill, in their summary of anaesthetic agents used in obstetrics, point to the disadvantages of the various drugs. Chloroform, while it might have the advantage of affording complete relaxation to the mother, causes decrease of uterine contractions, kidney and liver damage, irritation of the lung and sluggish response of the baby. Ethyl ether produces uterine inertia, irritation of the lung, narcotization of the baby and is contraindicated in several conditions. Divinyl oxide can produce hepatic damage and moderate irritation of the lung. Ethyl chloride can cause damage to the liver, the heart, the kidney and the lung. Nitrous oxide produces poor muscular relaxation except in the presence of

* De Lee, J. B., and Greenhill, J. P., *Principles and Practice of Obstetrics*, W. B. Saunders Co., Philadelphia, 1949, p. 266.

anoxia. Cyclopropane causes heart symptoms at times and cannot be used when cardiac irregularities are diagnosed. Gas ether, normally incapable of causing specific visceral damage, causes the baby to respond sluggishly to the extent that it may need resuscitation; and it will increase nausea in the mother. Tribromethanol (avertin) can damage the liver and kidney, produce sluggish response in the child and decrease contractions of the uterus; contraindicated in a number of conditions.

Hypnosis could well be the anaesthetic of choice in every possible way. The mother feels the contractions, but as they are not painful, she is fully capable of bearing down to the fullest extent. She maintains a perfectly calm, peaceful attitude during delivery, suffers no pain whatsoever, and risks no danger either for herself or her baby. What hypnosis does is to remove a portion of the mother's sensory perception, all of her fears and anxieties, and the embarrassment felt by a sensitive woman in the presence of strangers at that time. When a mother is free of exaggerated emotionalism and fear, she may rise from her bed within twenty-four hours after giving birth with no undesirable consequences. It is also possible, at that time, to give her suggestions producing relaxation, removing fatigue, and permitting her to go about her work more efficiently. Looming large above all considerations is the fact that there is no effect upon the baby.

The practitioner need not be present with the mother at delivery; the purpose is served through post-hypnotic suggestions. Post-hypnotic anaesthesia is a simple thing to accomplish, once the patient has been placed in an adequate state of Medium Hypnosis.

Wherever possible, we start hypnotizing the patient as soon as she is aware of her pregnancy. Thus, we can negate all symptoms of fear, anxiety, irritability, physical discomfort and morning sickness as soon as they arise, giving her a pleasurable pregnancy and delivery. We can also control her diet and weight, by suggestively creating in her a desire for the foods proper to her condition and a repugnance to those which would be harmful, and we can entirely avoid constipation with its consequent hemorrhoid irritation. Every conceivable unpleasantness can be alleviated during the pre-natal period, with delivery suggestions first instigated about a month before the baby is due. This may be embodied with any others deemed useful, and should be repeated a number of times for several sessions:

"You will experience no discomfort in regard to childbirth; there will be no pain attending your condition at any time. The first moment of uterine contraction, you will be completely freed of any attendant pain. You will experience no discomfort whatever, and immediately upon the first contraction, you will fall into a state of hypnosis during which you will feel the contractions, but at no time will they be associated with pain. You will maintain a cheerful attitude through labor, during, and after delivery. You will feel absolutely wonderful during this process; you will have no discomfort, no fatigue, no distress, no embarrassment. You will feel extremely peaceful, extremely wonderful, throughout the entire process. All of the fears and anxieties which you may have felt about the delivery of your baby will be completely gone. They have already disappeared; they will not return. I shall repeat this suggestion that I have already given you; at the very moment of the first contraction, you will immediately fall into a state of hypnosis, during which you will help the doctor by bearing down with each contraction, but you will experience not the slightest bit of pain. The hypnosis will continue until the delivery is completely over and your baby is here. You will find then that you feel very refreshed, extremely strong and you will not need to stay in bed for any particular period to recuperate. You will need no recuperation from pain because you will have had no pain; you will need no recuperation from strain, because you will have had no strain. You will feel absolutely strong, your body will normalize itself very quickly, and you will be able to go about your normal duties without any discomfort whatsoever. This suggestion is a post-hypnotic suggestion which will immediately take effect upon the first contraction of your uterus. You will find that giving birth to a baby is an extremely pleasurable experience, one that need not be associated with any pain at all. Generally it is the mental attitude of the prospective mother which causes a great many of the discomforts normally attendant upon the woman who is giving birth. There will be no need for you to suffer through any of these experiences, for you will feel exceptionally good, exceptionally wonderful, before, during and after the birth of your baby."

The doctor should see his patient at least a dozen times before the actual delivery, and repeat these suggestions each time she comes to the office. If during that period she does develop any symptoms which seem disagreeable to her, nullification of those specific symptoms should be incorporated with the other suggestions.

While sometimes the hypnotist's presence in the delivery room will give the mother more confidence and act as a powerful suggestion in itself, it is not necessary. This again is a question for the doctor and the individual patient to decide. In any event, she will obey the post-hypnotic suggestion given her in regard to the discomfort of birth.

Nearly every hypnotist has had occasion to use these methods from time to time, and they have nearly always worked successfully. The student's technique becomes a decisive one toward his success; his wisdom in winning the confidence of the prospective mother and selecting the suggestions for presentation to her carry the day for them both.

In obstetrics as in any hypnotic procedure, we must "temper the wind to the shorn lamb." Study the prospective mother closely and devise a form of suggestion applicable to her, using language entirely within the scope of her comprehension.

J. TREATMENT OF ALCOHOLISM

A number of times throughout the text I have called attention to the gratifying results to be achieved through hypnotic therapy in alcoholism. Since the adoption of this method of treatment, two hundred and seventeen alcoholics have been under my attention. Their ages have been within the range of puberty and old age. Of these cases, at least of the patients I have been able to check periodically, few have had further recourse to alcohol, though several years have intervened since initial therapy. While it must be admitted that in none of the instances cited was the exact root of behavior disturbance uncovered, the effects were, nevertheless, removed, affording these patients the opportunity to regain normal lives. The fact that the patient can once more return to his job, his family and his society and make a fair adjustment to them justifies hypnosis as the therapy of choice for the alcoholic.

In no instance is the dramatization of suggestion more efficacious and, likewise, more spectacular than it is in the treatment of alcoholism. The patient is placed in Medium Sleep. After he has satisfied the therapist as to his susceptibility to ordinary and hallucinatory suggestions, he is told to open his eyes, at which time a bottle of his favorite brand of alcohol is brought before his vision and opened in front of him so that he can see the mark and be convinced that this is a "fresh" bottle. Such action confirms his belief that the contents have not been tampered with, and as a result he is not being fooled. Next, the patient is offered a drink, but requested to take a short sip and keep it in his mouth for a moment before swallowing. This produces a slight burning sensation, which will greatly facilitate the effects of our subsequent suggestions. If the patient refuses the drink, the therapist must be insistent, explaining that it is necessary for the treatment. Once the patient has swallowed the alcohol he is asked if he enjoyed its flavor. The answer is usually, "Yes." Now the suggestion is offered. The therapist calmly informs his patient that he has been the victim of a trick—that it was really not "Old Granddad" that he drank, but actually a concoction of most obnoxious substances (this is, of course, left to the ingenuity of the therapist). If the response is not immediate, the physician should continue with the suggestion, coloring it by whatever means possible to intensify the horrible qualities of the drink so that it stimulates a maximum sensation of revulsion. Careful inflections of the voice aid in heightening the response. In most cases the effect is rapid. The patient's face and behavior will indicate his response. In a large number of alcoholic cases nausea or retching followed by vomiting will be the normal course. If an effect of this nature is not forthcoming, it is wise to insist upon the patient taking another drink. Now he shows immediate signs of being affected.

Before awakening the subject it is important that he be given a habit in exchange for the one of which he has been deprived. I recommend that such a technique be routinely employed for very logical reasons. Primarily, since the cause for the patient's periodic inhibition has not been alleviated, he is most likely to resort to another method of defense or escape which might well be more anti-social than the one that had been removed. Likewise, if the patient returns to the original pattern it is usually because he has not been offered a substitutive device in its stead. This "substitutive therapy" should be used wherever it can be made applicable in suggestive therapy. Thus it is embodied in the pre-waking suggestion:

"Soon you will awaken from hypnosis. You will be very relaxed, and feel very good. Upon waking all that has transpired during this state will be forgotten. You will have no further recollection in consciousness of my suggestions during this state. Instead you will have the feeling that you have been deeply asleep. Alcohol will be extremely repulsive to you. If you take a drink of any substance that contains alcohol, it will be so obnoxious to you that you will be forced to throw it up. Furthermore, you will have no further desire for alcohol in any form. Its taste will be quite upsetting to you. If at any time you are nervous, upset or generally beset with tension, you may eliminate these feelings completely by counting to yourself from one to ten. At ten all of your tensions will have disappeared. In this way you will have no further need for alcohol, etc."

The suggestion is repeated several times, after which the patient is awakened by the usual method. When he has been allowed ample time to regain his composure, he is queried about his recollections of the hypnotic state. Memory retention of the incident does not markedly alter the patient's response to the therapy, but it does allow us to proceed more assuredly, knowing that his susceptibility to our suggestions has been demonstrably accentuated.

Our next move is intended to add substance to the suggestions. This is done by further dramatization, but this time in the waking state. It is assumed that the patient has forgotten the drink administered to him while in trance. Now he is offered still another drink. He will most likely refuse it. Once again the therapist is insistent. Frequently, the patient will bring the glass to his lips repeatedly, each time withdrawing it after some hesitation. Finally, with all of the courage at his disposal, he partakes. The effect is dramatic. His response is usually of the type previously manifested, but now it is even greater. The patient has been so conditioned by hypnosis that even the *thought* of alcohol will repel him!

The effect is lasting, to the extent that if he wanted to defy the suggestion at some future date his attempt would only serve to supplement the therapy, further dramatizing, as it would, the suggestion which had been originally implanted.

It is advisable to institute further treatment, designed for supportive therapy. For later sessions it will no longer be necessary to utilize the dramatization effect; usual suggestions of a simple nature sufficing to add weight to the ones already given. It is important to remember that the method offered here is an uncompromising one and offers little advantage to the patient who intends taking an occasional "social drink."

The doctor must exercise utmost care in his choice of suitable patients. A problem frequently met with in the course of psychotherapeutic practice is the patient who has agreed to treatment, but only after many family scenes and a "final threat." Such patients are openly agreeable "to anything," but only outwardly so. If we succeed, and usually after much effort, in bringing about a hypnotic state, the patient either simulates the effect, or else responds poorly to the suggestions. In one case, where persistent effort eventually met with success, the patient returned to his home, and with bottle and glass ventured to overcome the suggestion. Twelve hours later he gave up in despair.

Large amounts of alcohol, when imbibed immediately antecedent to hypnotic therapy, cause the patient to respond in an unsatisfactory manner. While the preponderance of medical opinion holds that alcohol is a depressant and not a stimulant, its pharmacological action on the central nervous system is particularly noteworthy in this regard. The person who has taken excessive quantities of alcohol loses his shyness, becomes talkative and courageous. This can be explained, not on the basis of cerebral stimulation, but as a disappearance of the inhibitory control normally exercised by the higher nervous centers, thus allowing the person the opportunity to forsake his accustomed modesty and self-criticism. In this way, alcohol, after it has been absorbed, also removes the feelings of worry and fatigue. Although the alcoholic during a "binge" may be ready for sleep, he is certainly not in the best state for hypnosis. As adequate concentration is a requisite for the state, the patient deprived of sobriety is also deprived of the qualities which make for successful hypnosis. As he is not interested in the impression he is causing, and not particularly concerned with his future, a satisfactory response cannot be anticipated.

The wary practitioner will seize the moment for initiation of therapy when the patient has overcome his intoxication, and is in a state of "regret." Being sober and self-critical he will offer utmost cooperation to the physician and thus demonstrate greater accessibility to suggestion.

K.   RE-EDUCATION DURING HYPNOSIS

Considering the increased suggestibility of every subject under hypnosis, it is clear that the patient will accept a therapeutic lecture without too much resistance.

Whenever it is necessary to re-educate the patient pertaining to habits, routines or reaction patterns, the patient should first be placed in such state that his faculties are more susceptible to the words of the physician. In such conditions as inferiority complex, habitual quarreling, or inability to come to terms with a particular problem which is causing worry and anxiety, we can, during hypnosis, effect a complete acceptance of our words. It is wise first to consider carefully the question of whether our ideas are the best for the patient, although he will accept them without question. The re-education technique is sometimes an excellent idea, but it does have its disadvantages. Consequently, it should be resorted to only after due consideration and when all other possibilities have been explored.

I have used it with excellent results in the case of both

alcoholics and drug addicts, but because the forcefulness of the dramatized suggestion is lacking, we cannot depend too much upon the response.

In all cases of reconditioning or re-educating the unconscious, we must replace one habit pattern with another more constructive pattern. That new pattern must be potent enough to destroy the earlier pattern in the mind of the patient. If mere lecturing will do it, then re-education is the proper method. If dramatization is necessary to accumulate the essential force, then dramatization is the method to select. Under certain circumstances it might be advisable not only to prove to the patient that he can do something, but also to give him a lecture about it that he may have logical reasons to obey. In analytical therapy, for instance, when we have brought to the subject's attention some particularly painful trauma which has existed for some time as a repressed cause of neurotic behavior, a suitable lecture will enable him to accept the painful situation and thus obviate any violent abreaction. Therefore, the lecture can suit many clinical purposes, and it is frequently useful.

In conclusion, it might be mentioned that there are four methods by which a suggestion is given to a patient under hypnosis: the first is the indirect one; the second, a direct method of suggestion employing a complete dramatization; the third, the mere suggestion without benefit of dramatization, this requiring many repetitions for its acceptance by the patient; and the fourth is the re-education method.

Practice will show that the proper method of suggestion to any patient is a blend of all four of these methods, continually adjusted to the patient's characteristics and his mental and emotional background. In a way, they go hand in glove, and their selection depends entirely upon the insight and proficiency of the operator and the qualifications of the subject.

REFERENCES

DAVY, J., *Memoirs of Sir Humphrey Davy,* English Press, London, 1831.

DE LEE, J. B. AND GREENHILL, J. P., *Principles and Practice of Obstetrics,* W. B. Saunders Co., Philadelphia, 1949.

READ, G. D., *Childbirth Without Fear,* Harper & Brothers, New York, 1944.

READ, G. D., "Correlation of Physiological and Emotional Phenomena of Labour," *Journal of Obstetrics and Gynaecology, British Empire,* 53, 55, February, 1946.

TOMBLESON, J. B., "An Account of 20 Cases Treated by Hypnotic Suggestion," *Journal of Royal Army Medical Corps,* London, 340–346, 1917.

10

Hypno-Analysis and Hypno-Synthesis

It is not the intention here to present an exhaustive survey of the theory and practice of psychoanalysis. The reader is referred to the extensive literature in the field. I shall confine myself to a brief summation of the more important concepts of psychoanalysis, particularly those which have led to the later developments of hypno-analysis and hypno-synthesis.

The principles of psychoanalysis were formulated by two physicians, Sigmund Freud and Josef Breuer, in Vienna during the latter part of the nineteenth century. Upon graduation from the University of Vienna, Freud became vitally interested in the subject of neurology, and devoted his time to research in conditions of nervous origin, particularly those of diplegia and aphasia in children. Freud's interest in neurological disease led him to investigate the phenomenon of hysteria, and it was during this investigation that he became influenced by Breuer, with whom he later became associated.

Breuer was conducting hypnotic experimentation in hysteria, and Freud shared this interest. Desiring to explore further along these lines, in 1885 he left for Paris to work with

Charcot at the Salpêtrière. Charcot's observations on hysteria were recognized in the field of neurology as being well ahead of those of his contemporaries. Freud was fascinated by his demonstrations proving that ideas could produce actual bodily changes; for instance, paralysis of the arm was both produced and eliminated in a hysterical patient during hypnotic trance.

Freud altered his theories to conform to those of the Salpêtrière, namely, that the condition of hysteria was the result of a mental dissociation. Continuing with his studies in this field, he went to the Nancy Clinic, of which Bernheim was the director. At this time he became absorbed in the phenomena of post-hypnotic reactions, feeling that they were the result of hidden, unrecognizable motives. For example, when a patient who had just carried out a post-hypnotic suggestion was questioned about motive, he would come up with one that was pure fantasy, not referring to the fact that it had been received hypnotically. This indicated to Freud that the subject was entirely unaware of the suggestion that had been given him under hypnosis, which, in turn, predicated that a portion of his mind was divorced from consciousness. He also discovered that when a patient was returned to consciousness, he had complete amnesia about suggestions given him in hypnosis, inventing elaborate explanations for his obedience to them until challenged, at which time, strangely enough, he could instantly recall having received them during the hypnotic state.

Before leaving for Paris to continue his studies, an interesting conversation had transpired between Freud and Breuer. It concerned a case of hysteria which Breuer had brought to a successful conclusion. The patient, Anna O., had been under his care for one and a half years. Breuer related how he had employed hypnosis to relieve the girl's condition, during which the patient talked about the onset of her symptoms, going into exact details as to their development. What appeared remarkable to Breuer was the fact that when her experiences were aired in their entirety and the feelings she had in connection with them were expressed, the symptoms disappeared.

While working in the hospitals of Paris, Freud had frequent occasion to recall Breuer's case, and whenever possible he would interrogate his hysteria patients in order to elicit some clue concerning the advent of their symptoms, searching for traumatic experiences. Such elicitations would, at times, reward him with pertinent information as to the origin of certain psychic manifestations. As a result of the experiences gleaned from clinical and later private practice, Freud was convinced that Breur's method of therapy held magnificent hope for the hysterical patient. Together they published their first paper, which told of their joint discoveries. These findings were presented more extensively in a book that made its appearance a few years later, entitled *Studies in Hysteria*. Breuer's cathartic method was the starting point for Freud's later investigations.

Their combined observations in this work embraced their theories of the origin of hysterical symptoms. Resolution of the illness, according to Freud and Breuer, was brought about by the psychic and emotional "purging" achieved by the patient during treatment. They expounded that hysteria was an affective result of the patient's past. Freud later referred to the symptom as a monument of some disagreeable and forgotten act of the patient's life. Brill adds explanatory comment to this observation: "The patient did not, however, recognize the significance of this monument any more than the average foreigner would understand the meaning of the Bunker Hill monument."*

This theory led to the later development of Freud's evaluation of the unconscious, but more, it laid emphasis upon

* Brill, A. A., *Freud's Contribution to Psychiatry*, W. W. Norton Co., New York, 1944, p. 61.

the importance of the emotional factors as a basis of the neurotic condition. In their presentation of the affective dynamisms that are responsible for the syndrome of hysteria, the symptom, according to Freud and Breuer, originated as a consequence of an imprisoned or a strangulated affect. The patient, by certain mental mechanisms, was restrained from giving vent to his emotions, and as such, the idea with its attendant emotions was driven from consciousness or *repressed*. As the repressed idea had not undergone great weakening in its strangulation, it remained active, frequently attempting to break through to consciousness. Finally, in somewhat of a compromise action, it was allowed to rise to the conscious surface, disguised so that it could assume another path, usually affecting a particular innervation. This was the cause of the symptom. In this way the repressed material was given expression; the psychic energy, formerly strangulated, was now *converted* into a physical disease process. If the patient could have given vent to her emotions at the time of their occurrence, the exclusion of the original idea might have taken a course other than the repression which ultimately led to her infirmity. Breuer's "talking cure" brought with it the complete obliteration of the symptoms by affording the patient the benefit of free expression of the idea, thus allowing its unhampered return to consciousness. The patient, having no fear of rebuke, worked off the pathogenic idea by re-living the experience, permitting free course to consciousness of the emotions which originally attended the traumatic material. To this cathartic phenomena they gave the name *abreaction*.

Soon after the appearance of *Studies in Hysteria* Breuer left Freud, retiring to his general practice. Breuer had some regrets that he had entered into collaboration with Freud. Following the presentation of their joint efforts an ugly storm of criticism raged upon the scientific horizon. Some of their readers, with angered indignation, threw away the book after perusing its introduction, for here the writers adduced that sexuality played the principal part in the pathogenesis of hysteria! While Freud seemed unaffected by the rantings of his critics, Breuer brooded over the insults, finally withdrawing from association with Freud. Nevertheless, Breuer's "talking cure" continued as the foundation for Freud's construction of the psychoanalytic theory.

The reader will remember that the earlier experiments of Breuer and Freud were conducted by means of hypnotic states. While Freud recognized hypnosis as a most efficient tool for broadening of consciousness in his investigative therapy, it offered many drawbacks which he could not reconcile, the most important being that not all of his patients made adequate response to his methods of induction. He also objected to the tyrannical qualities of suggestion. Much as he disliked discarding a practice that had had its advantages in the past, he, nevertheless, abandoned hypnosis. As the technique of hypnosis served to solder the gap between conscious and unconscious, another method had to be instituted in its stead. In a few of Bernheim's experiments Freud had witnessed a remarkable phenomenon. Bernheim had proven in these instances that it was possible, under insistent prompting, to facilitate the return of experiences obtained under hypnosis, although a suggestion of posthypnotic amnesia had been successfully demonstrated. These experiments were carried out in the waking state. Bernheim would ask a patient to recall the information which before he had been requested to forget. In so doing he would place his hand upon the patient's forehead. After much persistence, the forgotten experiences would be remembered, returning to consciousness with great lucidity.

From Bernheim's experiments he concluded that the patient's memories could likewise be made accessible to analysis although the patient remained in a waking state. The technique, more time-consuming and wearisome than hypnosis, brought satisfactory responses, but only after much coaxing and insisting on the part of Freud. Soon the "pressure on the forehead" technique was also discarded. The patient was asked to recline upon a couch; Freud assuming a position behind the head so that he could see his patient and in turn the patient could not see him unless he made an effort to do so by turning around.

Freud would ask his patient to let his mind wander, reporting all of the thoughts which occurred to him regardless of their importance. When the patient indulged in criticism of the thoughts, Freud would sternly admonish him for such practices, attempting to confine the patient's utterances to manifestations of the unconscious without the interception of conscious thoughts. At first, the spontaneous outpourings had little pertinence, but soon these *free associations* were properly led from flighty utterances to those of basic significance, finally, but not inevitably, locating the area of disturbance. Freud, delighted with his initial successes shortly afterwards had cause to revise his approach, for soon he realized that the thoughts of free association were not as *free* as he would have liked them to be; that their use was only justifiable in the light of analytical interpretation. Thus developed the method of psychoanalysis.

The methods of free association were obstructed by the patient's frequent resistance to the expression of the pathogenic material. Freud then inferred that the resistance that prohibited the venting of the material was due to its traumatic content, i.e., that its nature was either humiliating, grievous or oppressive to the well-being of the patient. Consequently, he could not harbor the conscious memory of it. Thus, it was apparent that the resurrection of the causative idea necessitated the previous conquest of the resistance. Now Freud could venture an explanation of the etiology of the neurotic symptom: a desire, which for some reason must be suppressed, makes its way into consciousness. Because of its nature it cannot coexist with a force already present. This results in the effort of the force totally to eject the new idea. In an attempt to overpower the intruder a psychic conflict takes place between the new idea and the resistance against it. At this moment the battle is ensuing on the field of consciousness, but soon the sum of energy (cathexis) of the impulse will be dissipated and it will retire from battle.

According to Freud this represented normal adjustment. The neurotic adjustment draws still another conclusion of the battle. The force of resistance (ego), soon after the battle begins, refuses further encounter with the impulse and retreats to an area of safety, thereby closing all possible entries to consciousness. The impulse, still maintaining its energy, becomes housed in a lower level, but nevertheless, persists. The painful idea has been repressed.

An example here will help to elucidate the nature of repression:

A male patient, 34 years of age, was brought to my attention by his family physician. For eight years he had been unable to lift either arm more than a few inches away from the shoulder girdle. While attempts at movement elicited no pain, a sharp contraction of the muscles would occur preventing further effort. Although various explanations for the symptom were in the offing as he consulted a number of physicians for his complaint, no satisfactory treatment had been given the patient. One physician, having knowledge of the patient's background, surmised that the origin of the complaint could well be psychogenic. The patient was then referred to me. After several consultations with the patient, the evidence which seemed most worthwhile was the fact that he demonstrated utter abhorrence for his sister-in-law. The usual methods of interrogation met with no success.

With the aid of hypnosis I was able to penetrate the patient's wall of resistance, and after much urging, laborious as it was, an old memory found its way to consciousness. The experience had occurred nine years previous to this day. The country was in the midst of its worst depression, employment being difficult to find. The patient, an automobile worker at the time, was desperate for help. He wrote to his brother who had established himself in California. Realizing his circumstances, the brother sent money for the fare and the patient left Detroit for California. While being supported he sought a job but with little luck. All of this time he felt badly for imposing upon his brother. There was probably little foundation for this feeling as his brother earned a large salary; the patient's presence in the household created no hardship. Besides, he received the best of care, especially from his brother's wife who would periodically engage him in long conversations.

Shortly thereafter, he began to build a fond affection for the girl, which seemed to be reciprocated. It was on one particular day that their eyes met as they had never met before. A kiss led to other responses. After the experience, a great many thoughts had entered his mind. He was faced with the most horrible of guilts. For weeks afterwards he indulged in self-condemnation. He felt that he had betrayed his brother by his despicable behavior. No rationalization could dissolve the contempt that he felt for himself. When he found, much to his regret, that however he tried to dispel these thoughts from his mind, they always reappeared, he decided upon the action of thinking them through. In one way or another, he discovered a means by which the guilt could be transferred, by a process of projection, to his sister-in-law. From this moment there arose such a strong hatred for her that to be alone with the girl for more than a few minutes at a time brought homicidal thoughts to his mind, and rapid retreat was necessary. "I had to get out of that house because I knew I'd kill her if I stayed there. I couldn't get it out of my head what she did to my brother, after he was so good to us both."

The patient left his brother's house with the explanation that he had obtained a job in another city. But the resentment toward his sister-in-law nevertheless continued. Moreover, in some of his fantasies he found himself torturing her: then quickly he would erase such thoughts from his consciousness, for he could visualize the great sorrow that would befall his brother if some misfortune had occurred to his wife.

After a year of such conflicts, his despondency left him. He gave less thought to the experience; but at this time he began to notice a peculiar sensation in both shoulder joints. A few days later he found himself unable to lift his arms. Until the present treatment he was incapacitated as far as gainful labor was concerned. His catharsis, under hypnosis, was quite dramatic. On several occasions, because of his behavior while living through the experiences, he had to be restrained.

When he returned to wakefulness he remembered all that had transpired during the hypnotic period. Remembrance of the experience left him somewhat unnerved. I took this opportunity to trace the symptom directly to its point of origin. The next few minutes were enlightening.

"By what means did you intend killing your sister-in-law?" I inquired.

"I wanted to choke her to death."

"What prevented you from doing so?"

"I didn't want to do any more harm to my brother," he answered. "He was good to me. I'm sure I would have gone back and killed her. I guess these arms stopped me."

"Then this condition prevented you from carrying out your intention. Could it be that it gave you good reason not to, because you realized that you were equally responsible for your brother's betrayal?"

"Maybe so," he sobbed, and after a pause, "That was it. I was guilty too. I guess if I killed her, I'd have to kill myself too."

After several of such sessions, the symptom gradually left the patient. It did not return.

The reader will note that it was not the repression of painful material which caused the symptomatic response, but the *failure* of the repression. After it had once become repressed, because of its traumatic nature, the force of resistance would hardly permit it to become conscious again, at least not without a struggle. If the repression had been complete, the patient's hatred for his sister-in-law might not have been so apparent. Therefore, we are aware of the fact that the pathogenic material remained active despite all efforts toward its destruction. If, on the other hand, the patient had accepted his experience and by rationalization of some sort succeeded in reconciling it, he would not have developed the symptom. His infirmity was the indirect manifestation of the failure of repression of the traumatic material. As such it represented a compromise between the primitive self (the id) and the ethical self (the ego).

In 1901, Freud added considerably to the knowledge of mental phenomena by publishing *The Psychopathology of Everyday Life*.* In it he maintained that the repressed idea frequently makes itself known to consciousness by slips of the tongue, everyday blunders and the thoughtless mislaying of objects. The usually wary censor has relaxed momentarily, and the rejected impulse struggles to higher levels in search of expression. A minister related to me what to him was his most mortifying experience in the pulpit, when during one of his sermons he said: "The meek shall *inhibit* the earth." Despite trickles of laughter the sermon was, nonetheless, enlightening. The minister, an apt student of the mind, devised an explanation for his quaint lingual misbehavior. On the day before, he appeared before a meeting of the trustees of his church. One of the trustees, an outspoken religionist,

* FREUD, S., *The Psychopathology of Everyday Life*, Macmillan, New York, 1914.

admonished him for his interjection of "modern examples" in his Bible interpretations. The other members of the board, usually *meek,* nodded their heads in approval of the stern reproof. The minister *did* feel inhibited.

It is easier to forget a debt that we owe than one that is owed us. It is more likely that we will know the date of a coming party than that of a particularly boring lecture that we must attend. Likewise if we appear at that party a week ahead of time our host has ample reason to feel flattered. Contrariwise, Mary, who is called "Jean" by her "date," feels unhappy.

At times these mechanisms of unconscious activities can be touched off by the chance remark of a friend. Thus teasing generally has its effect because it irritates a "sore spot" of which the victim may not have been aware. Likewise many of our prejudices are rooted in the unconscious due to ideas that have never been openly aired.

A. DREAM INTERPRETATION

Freud made an important contribution to our knowledge of unconscious mechanisms when he published *The Interpretation of Dreams.** In it he maintained that the dream, if analyzed far enough, was shown to embody the fulfillment of a wish that was either conscious or repressed. If the wish or impulse was of a traumatic nature it would appear in the dream in a disguised form, adequately distorted by symbols so that it could be more acceptable to consciousness. As such, the dream represented a phantasy picture which, in its true form, could not be accepted. The dream, as it is told by the patient, is referred to as the *manifest content.* As the patient indulges in free association his thoughts provide meaning to the content of the dream. The significance, in terms of mean-

* FREUD, S., *The Interpretation of Dreams,* Macmillan Co., New York, 1933.

ing, of these free associations represents the *latent content*. The psychoanalytic transformation of the *latent* to the *manifest content* is called the *dream-work*. The reason for the distortion of the impulse now becomes apparent. If the impulse, savage as it is, reaches consciousness, sleep is readily disturbed, either by nightmare or by sudden awakening. The force of distortion is therefore the protector of sleep.

Frequently, an impulse can be so distorted that its opposite alone is meaningful. A patient dreamed that she was carrying on divorce proceedings against her husband, while her husband pleaded with the judge to stop the action. In reality she did not want a divorce as she still loved him, but he insisted upon it. This also demonstrates how the dream represents a *wish fulfillment,* for as the patient has power over the continuation of the proceedings, she can stop it at any time. The dreamer is always the principal actor of the dream, but he can assume two roles if this is necessary for the distortion. In this manner a student who was destined for an examination the following morning and had a bit of apprehension about it dreamed that he was the professor examining a nondescript student who managed to pass with a high grade.

The extent of the distortion is always relative to the degree of inacceptability of the real wish, according to Freud. Serious conflicts in this way can be expressed with much lightness and even humor if greater distortion of them can be accomplished. Thus a patient who had lost large sums of money through unwise investments, fearing that his wife would discover his blunder, dreamed that she was throwing one hundred dollar bills into an open fire to keep warm. The dream not only softened the blow of reality, but also held his wife directly responsible for the loss, and, as such, he was immune to her critical judgment. The reader will remember a case described in this chapter where the patient projected his feelings so that the burden of guilt resulting from an experience with his brother's wife rested upon his sister-in-law instead. It is easy to note the similarity between conscious and unconscious distortions.

The chief patterns of distortion are displayed in the mechanisms of *symbolization, dramatization, condensation* and *displacement*.

Symbolization is the mental substitution of one thing for something else. A student who had anxiety about finances dreamed that a man named Riley was sharing his quarters. As he was not acquainted with anyone of that name, it could be assumed that the dreamer might have found prosperity in the Life of Riley. Likewise, a bed of roses might symbolize freedom from anxiety and the purchase of a baby crib might symbolize the hope for pregnancy. In everyday life a Hopalong Cassidy outfit puts a boy up there with the best of them, while a doll becomes a baby to a little girl. The interpretation of symbols is important, for it expresses the unconscious wish, leading to its recovery to consciousness. Moreover, it betokens a train of thought which gives expression to the deeper conflicts of personality. Symbols, therefore, represent complexes. A patient dreamed that she was playfully throwing dirt at her husband. The dream was easily explained when it came to light that she was in love with another man; her husband's demise supplying the best solution for her problem. The dirt thus symbolized his burial. Another patient dreamed that she had recovered a doll that she had played with as a child. This signified a wish to return to an age during which her wants were provided for, and anxieties were minimal. It symbolized a wish to withdraw from situations which oppress the adult. "If I could only be a kid again," is a common expression of everyday life. Dreaming will make it so!

The content of the dream occasionally seems alien to the dreamer, mainly due to its objectivity. As the patient is apart from his dream it becomes unnecessary for him to assume responsibility for his acts which to him seem base. Moreover, this process is of great service to the psychoanalyst for it permits the patient to "open up," thereby rendering information which he would normally keep to himself if he thought his baser nature would unfold in the exposition.

Dramatization provides animation to our thoughts, impulses and feelings. In our dreams people and places come to life. In this respect the dream has been compared to a motion picture. The phenomenon of time is distorted. When one has to travel from New York to California, the first scene shows him boarding the plane, the next, sitting comfortably in his seat, the third scene finds him leaving the plane and being greeted by his friends. The dreamer makes effortless journeys, appearing in distant places as easily as he can change his thoughts.

Condensation is an interesting mechanism to be found in some dreams. By this means two persons might fuse into one composite personality. One of my friends related a dream in which he was extolled along with the presentation of a medal for being a great physician, a celebrated automotive engineer and an outstanding musician. The dream had resulted from an argument that ensued just before bedtime. As a physician he had no business disassembling his car whenever the fancy struck him, or so his wife thought. The fact that he had also neglected his practice by devoting much too much time to the piano added further to the argument. His wife's final contention was that a person who dabbled in all three pursuits could only be one-third of a physician, one-third of a mechanic and one-third of a pianist. This was exactly what my friend had accomplished in his dream.

When it is convenient an opposite mechanism can manifest itself in the dream. The characteristics of the dreamer may become diffused in a Jekyll and Hyde manner. In this way, one tendency of the dreamer is dissociated from the remainder of the personality and occupies the form of a separate person in the dream; thus he exists apart from his animal tendencies, disclaiming responsibility for them.

Displacement is a common kind of behavior in everyday life. The irate husband who kicks the cat because he cannot kick his wife; the golfer who vents his anger on the caddy because the ball landed in the "rough," are examples of displacement. It is the transfer of tension from its perplexing bed to another place where it seems more innocent. A lawyer dreamed that he was defending a client who was on trial for embezzlement. Actually the lawyer was the culprit. He had juggled the finances of an estate left to his trust and could not replace the funds he had taken. As his client was, in reality, a prominent business man he was a fitting object for the transfer.

Thus dreams express our unknown impulses and lead to their discovery. Our actions, thoughts and biases spring from rejected tendencies which we attempted to disown at the time of their occurrence. These mingle with our memories of yesterday and the situations of today, and so govern our responses to changing scenes. The fact that many of our present opinions are based on infantile feelings of childhood leads us to suspect that our thoughts do not always follow logical sequence.

The methods of psychoanalysis have not only provided a vast array of important behavior conceptions, they have also produced a system of therapy which seeks to evoke the pathogenic material imbedded in the hidden strata of the unconscious, and in so doing, brings permanent relief to the emotionally sick.

B. TECHNIQUE

Psychoanalysis insists that its therapists must themselves undergo comprehensive analysis before being permitted to practice. As this must entail time, effort and money, few physicians care to make these sacrifices. If the novice should wish to pursue such a course he should place himself under the supervision of an analyst who is competent in such matters.

Before any type of psychoanalysis is embarked upon, the patient should be submitted to thorough physical examination to eliminate any possibility of an organic cause for the nervous symptoms. The diagnostician selected should be one with a background in psychosomatic medicine, for illnesses resulting from physical bases cannot be cleared up until the physical cause has been eliminated; as conversely, a physical ailment rooted in a psychogenic disorder cannot be cured until the patient has discovered its unconscious disposition.

In the technique of free association, the patient reclines upon a bed or couch in a darkened room, away from disturbances which might ordinarily affect him. The room is quiet so that the patient may feel as calm as possible. Some analysts prefer to place the patient in a chair facing them in order to note the varying facial expressions, while most of them assume a seated position beyond the view of the patient.

Then the patient is told to let his mind wander, to say anything that might enter his consciousness. At first, the outpourings have little pertinence, but if he is properly led from flighty thoughts to those of a basic significance, his response with information sheds light on the mechanisms of past behavior. The patient may speak of his feelings and impulses, he may tell of dreams or fantasies; no matter how foolish or irrelevant the material might appear to him, he is prompted to express it.

This is the method of free association, as it is employed in standard analytical procedure. It is based upon the theory that if the mind is permitted to wander from thought to thought, under guidance, of course, it will inevitably locate the area of disturbance; that the mind will eventually travel to trauma which is causing the distress. If a certain thought, impulse or desire seems to appear recurrently, the analyst guides the patient back to that point, and insists on iteration and reiteration, particularly if it seems to carry distress in its wake. The strategy is to attempt to probe beyond the censor's gate; to stimulate unconscious thoughts to rise to consciousness, where the patient himself is forced to recognize their presence and adjust himself to *himself* as he actually is; to accept that thought or feeling or act which was at one time repugnant enough to him to force him to repress it. Once he comes to terms with himself, symptoms automatically dissolve. He must learn to develop a tolerance for the material which was formerly repressed; his point of view must change; he is forced to grow. Through analysis of his dreams, and by the repeated sessions of free association which he undergoes, the patient develops an entirely new conception of his own personality. With the new understanding and integration the symptoms are banished.

Of course, the drawback to psychoanalysis is its expense. The analyst must have undergone many years of study and apprenticeship; must invest large sums of capital in his training. Likewise, the patient must generally make a large investment of both time and money as most analysts insist upon five or six sessions a week. Furthermore, no definite time limit can be established for the consummation of complete therapy. The conscientious therapist warns his patient that he may have to spend years at it, and even after this time, there is no absolute assurance that his difficulties will be entirely resolved. A patient who had been duly recommended to me by her analyst had undergone six years of persistent therapy.

C. HYPNO-ANALYSIS AND HYPNO-SYNTHESIS

Many innovations have been thrust into the psychotherapeutic field since the publication of the works of Breuer and Freud. Of these, the hypno-analytical approach provides considerable advantages, for not only does it shorten the time element involved in orthodox methods, but it also causes a more predictable contact with the unconscious. While it does not stray too far from the normal Freudian course, it offers the therapist greater and far more direct access to the pathogenic material that harasses his patient. Thus it enables him to bring about the desired integration within a shorter period of time. The usual analytic method must, of necessity, wade through the extraneous material before significant items appear in the free-association period. Many patients stall for weeks, talking around a point that they do not want to face. Their symptoms must become more painful than the fear of recognition before their "censors" will break down and admit that "the master could be capable of such thoughts."

Through the facilities of hypnosis such censorship is avoided, for in this state the "censor" may be dethroned, consequently promoting the dissolution of the inhibitions, thereby permitting the patient to remember what his former conflicts caused him to forget. The patient is brought back to the original experience that caused his trauma. He is prompted to recall the material with all the clarity of the original picture, plus the precise emotional reaction *of that time,* rather than a *rationalized* emotional reaction tacked onto it by twenty or thirty years of living. We can take him back, age by age, day by day, and, if necessary, back to experience by experience. We can cause him to dream under hypnosis, and we find that hypnotic dreams are less cluttered with protective symbolisms. We can even suggest that he will dream about a particular incident of his life, and we generally find that, with the aid of these dreams, he is able to recall the experience in its entirety.

The orthodox analyst, by free associations, brings his patient to recall various traumatic experiences which have affected him in the past and those pertinent experiences and thoughts which he once had and later forgot. When they begin to appear with sufficient intensity, the patient begins to cry profusely, or to tremble, or shake or scream with fear, as he relives the experience. He is encouraged to relate it to the analyst in detail, and then to repeat the story over and over again until the emotional expression dissipates, and he tells it as quietly as though he were discussing the weather. This constant reliving desensitizes him to the experience.

When abreaction occurs, the analyst gives his patient plenty of opportunity to indulge in any emotional play that might be associated with the experience while it is coming to the surface. Then he explains how the feeling affected his condition at that certain time, which procedure offers the patient insight into his personality disturbance. With the analyst's help, then, the patient is brought gradually and gently to a more mature attitude, and reaches the point of integration where he can solve his own problems upon an adult level of behavior.

The question arises, can hypnosis, our short-cut to the unconscious, be used to expedite this process; if so, how, and what benefits does it confer? The answer will evolve as we examine the technique of analysis as it is used in conjunction with hypnosis. There is, of course, a wide variety of techniques in the application of hypno-analysis, some of which will be mentioned in passing. Much important work has been done, and for the consideration of other approaches the reader is referred to the literature.

Before proceeding with an exposition of the methods in use, we must, for convenience and comprehension, divide our therapy into two separate stages of action. The first stage is the precise hypno-analysis. The word "analysis" implies the resolution of a compound into its parts or elements. As such it brings the patient to an adequate level of hypnotic response, in this way establishing contact with the repressed material and elevating it to the surface, thus stimulating its emotional revival proper to the original experience.

The second stage cannot properly be called hypno-analysis, as there is no further separation of the material into its basic elements, for this stage constitutes the moral, physical, mental and emotional adjustment to the material presented. Moreover, the second stage prepares the patient by suggestion during hypnosis to exert independence, self-reliance and serenity upon waking so that the transference which existed as a necessity between therapist and patient during therapy may be abandoned without undue conflict to the patient. Explanations to the patient of the connection between his symptoms and the material also aid in promoting and maintaining recovery.

As the second stage implies a combination of separate or subordinate parts into a new form, the term "hypno-analysis" is an apparent misnomer. The process of analysis keeps these elements separated. The word "synthesis," on the other hand, signifies the combination of separate elements into a whole, contrasted with analysis, which is from the whole to separate parts. Therefore, through *hypno-synthesis* the new personality, openly rejecting the pathogenic material, makes a suitable adjustment and is stimulated to grow. Thus the two states, hypno-analysis and later hypno-synthesis, are necessary for successful termination of the behavior disorder.

The first step in the process of hypno-analysis is to place the subject in Medium Sleep. He must demonstrate his ability to accept and react to simple and later fairly difficult suggestions. Then we proceed with a suggestion such as this:

"When I place the palm of my hand on the back of your neck, you will immediately think back to the occurrences which were responsible for your present difficulty. You will be able to visualize all of these experiences in full detail; you will be without any desire to hold back or to repress this information; you will be able to tell me everything that you feel about your condition, and the various causes of it as you recognize them. I will understand—you may depend upon it—I can and will help you."

The analyst then places his hand on the back of the patient's neck and waits until the patient develops a certain emotional reaction indicative of the emergence of the information. He must be steadily prompted by the analyst to give out as much information as he possibly can. It is necessary to retain complete control over the patient during this period, for he may develop fits of rage or quiver with emotion as he recounts his story. The analyst must be very tolerant and not interrupt the patient at any point of this procedure. If the patient should, however, at any time attempt to evade the subject, it is the analyst's duty to pull him back so that he will concentrate only on pertinences. When this method is satisfactory, the patient will unburden himself completely and describe vividly, in detail and with all the original emotion, the traumatic experiences.

During this abreaction, the analyst's calm must remain unbroken, for if he fails to display serenity, repose, and even a degree of apathy mingled with his interest, the patient senses the fact and takes alarm. The patient must never be rushed to end this session, for he might lose track of some experience or idea which will prove to be a key to the entire situation.

1. *Motion Picture Technique*

A method which I prefer to the one that has been described, however, is the one I call the "motion-picture technique." The patient, when in the desired hypnotic state, is given this suggestion:

"Soon I shall ask you to open your eyes. When you do, you will find that you are in a motion picture theatre. Ahead of you is the screen. On the screen you will see a movie. This motion picture is the story of your life. You will notice that all of the important details of your life have been successively woven into the story that you see before you on the screen. I want you to tell me about them, for I am unable to see the screen. Now I am going to ask you to open your eyes, and just ahead of you you will see the screen."

The patient opens his eyes and seems rather amazed at what he "sees" before him. He begins to recount everything that passes on his screen. As he watches, he occasionally laughs rather loudly, or grins sheepishly, or looks embarrassed, at times screaming with rage or anger. He describes the picture graphically, and it has been proven to me many times that what he is describing is actually a vivid account of experiences hitherto "forgotten." The session generally continues until the patient breaks down under the emotional stress caused by some condition which seems to have affected him at some time in his life. As he visualizes this, and as he recounts it, he enters suitable abreaction, for he recalls the very things which before were too painful for him to retain in conscious memory.

One case which I was fortunate enough to have recorded shows the various effects which can be caused by this method of hypno-analysis. The patient was given the suggestion that he would see everything upon the screen before him. The patient was a twenty-four-year-old boy who had finally been shipped back to the United States from a station hospital after breaking down completely under "battle fatigue." He had served an unusual number of missions without showing signs of strain, and then collapsed completely. His symptoms were those of tremendous anxiety and depression which were perpetually with him; he could not sleep, was greatly fatigued, and was totally unable to make any kind of adjustment either in his work or his personal life. He was so "torn to pieces" that he had been discharged almost immediately upon his return to the United States.

As soon as he was able to visualize the "screen" before him, he began to talk:

"I see the picture clearly now. I am in a plane with Red. . . . Red Stokes, that's his name. . . . Red's my gunner. . . . and there I'm looking over to Red to see how he's doing. . . . suddenly a couple of Jap Zeros are coming at us. . . . Red is getting ready to fire. . . . The Japs are firing at us. I can see Red has been hit. . . . a couple of bullets went right through the side. . . . out of the back of the plane a flame leaps out. I call to Red to jump. . . . I can't go on, I don't want to see it. It hurts like H. . . . I can't stand to look at it. . . ."

He broke off sobbing. I told him that for his own good he *must* look at it; it was his only chance of getting well. I made him look at the screen, and when finally, he brought himself to look up, he said:

"I can't stand to look at it. . . . I am calling to Red. . . . I am looking at him, calling to him, 'Jump, jump!' but he just doesn't look my way. He is holding his hand by his chest and it's full of blood. I know that he's a goner, but the plane is on fire; I must jump; I must take him with me; I must jump, this plane is a goner. I can't take him with me, I have to jump; I can't wait any longer—the plane is on fire. I open the door and I jump, without him. . . . and I left him."

At this point, the patient became most distraught and upset, screaming wildly, "I didn't kill Red—he was killed already. . . . I couldn't do anything for him. . . . I had to jump to save my life. . . ."

Right here, I interposed to assure him that of course he did the only thing he could possibly have done. His gunner was dead, and hampering himself with a dead body would only have destroyed his own chances of survival without helping Red.

In the next few sessions, I had him look at the "screen" to see the picture again and again, until he did become desensitized to it, at which time all of his symptoms cleared up completely.

I have used this method more frequently than any other, having found it to be very much the most satisfactory method of catharsis. The patient, in relating what he sees on the screen, becomes so objective about it that he makes very little attempt to repress either what he sees or his emotions concerning it.

In other cases, when I suspect that the condition was brought about at a certain period of a patient's life, I have employed the same motion picture technique, telling him that he will see himself at a certain age or in a certain experience. When I have instituted this suggestion, I have him open his eyes and look at the screen ahead; the blocks appear to dissolve and he relates precisely what he "sees" with no evasion at all, with ensuing therapeutic benefit.

In one case of impotency, where the patient was entirely unable to recall consciously any incident in his life responsible for his condition, I made him "see" a picture of his father on the screen. He opened his eyes and said immediately, "Look! that's me, over there in the corner, thumbing through a picture book. I can see the pictures very clearly now. Gee, I must be about four years old. Now, the picture is changing and I am in bed with my mother. The both of us are in bed together. Dad isn't in the room. I don't know where Dad is. I am lying in my mother's arms and she is doing something bad to me. At least I think it's bad; I seem to be enjoying myself. I know it's bad, and yet I am enjoying it tremendously. She is putting her hand on my penis and she is saying something. Now I know what she is saying. . . . Now I know. . . . She shouldn't have said that. She shouldn't have done it. Now I know exactly what happened. Now I know why I hate my mother. I could kill her for it. She made me think things that I wasn't supposed to think. Now I know exactly and I can't help myself. I must hate her for that."

When asked to tell what his mother said, he was very reluctant at first, but as his rage built up until he could not control himself, he said that his mother had murmured, while placing one hand on the organ, "When you are older, Ed, I'll tell you exactly what you're supposed to do with this. But until then, no one else is supposed to touch you there."

He became violent with rage; then the rage subsided and he became at first fearful and finally hysterical. He developed a panic reaction and begged not to have to look at the screen any more, for he was afraid of seeing something else. It would be better, he said, if he did not know it.

About this time, he was wakened, and during the next five sessions I repeated the demonstration to him; each time he added more to what had been said. Finally, he became so completely desensitized to the situation that he accepted the experience entirely with the thought that mother was only unfortunate in her ignorance, and should perhaps have been psychoanalyzed also.

As soon as he accepted this realization, the symptoms of impotence disappeared completely. The unconscious reaction from this experience had forced him to identify his wife with his mother and regress to the impotency of a four-year-old. The entire situation cleared up and he has been symptom-free ever since.

2. Hypnotic Dream Analysis

Occasionally we are confronted with a dream which defies interpretation because of the heavy symbolism which effectually disguises its content. In these cases I have found that under Medium Hypnosis the patient will interpret the dream for me. As an instance, one minister whom I had been treating dreamed that a tremendous tide had drifted in, completely enveloping a manuscript that he was writing. At first the content of the dream seemed vague to us both. Under hypnosis he gave me a complete interpretation. He said that the word "tide" in the dream should not be there at all, because "tide" spelled backward would be "edit," and that is exactly what the dream meant, for the Church had been "editing" the manuscript for him, and his whole being was in rebellion against that "editing." It was sweeping his manuscript away, "enveloping" it.

Again, the same patient dreamed that there was a little mouse; that the mouse was being chased by a lion, and finally the lion caught up with the mouse and devoured it. From this he awoke in a cold sweat and was unable to go back to sleep. Under hypnosis he said that he was the mouse and his father the lion; that he vividly recalled many times during his childhood when his father dominated him completely, sometimes chasing him to enforce that domination. He had always fantasied himself as a "wee mousie" and father, the lion.

The patient, 41 years of age at the time of treatment, was in charge of the largest church in his city. Being well liked by his congregation and commended many times by the church board of the state, he had little reason for his manifest feeling of insecurity. Nevertheless, it was there. He lived in fear that one day, because of some action that he could not control, he would be "thrown out" by the board. Such thoughts led to many depressing moments. While he "made good" at the church, his marital life seemed an unhappy one and "a flop." He had met his wife while a junior in college, marrying soon afterwards. As marriage brought with it his first sexual experience, it was on the wedding night that he discovered his inability to perform the sex act. This had caused him considerable anxiety. In the twenty-one-year period prior to his submission to treatment, he had remained impotent, without any sign of improvement.

In response to my request to "talk things out," he recalled an experience at the age of fourteen of having been ordered from the house by his father and told never to return. The patient could shed no further conscious light on the subject. At this time I utilized a particular method which had served me well in the past. After guiding the patient to Medium Sleep, he was told that soon the state of hypnosis would be converted into normal slumber, during which he would have a dream, that the dream would return him to the original experience, and he would recall it upon awakening twenty minutes later. Upon waking, he would write the full content of the dream on the paper lying on the desk before him.

Twenty minutes later he awakened, as if from a deep sleep, and after slight hesitation, he picked up the pencil from the desk and started to write. While he wrote he tried to restrain his tears, but to no avail. He began to sob, first quietly and then loudly. But he continued to write, stopping occasionally to wipe the tears from his eyes, or to dry the paper where they fell. After one hour and fifteen minutes his dream had been completely recorded. He presented me with the nineteen pages, and felt better for it.

Eventually we discovered, on the basis of the dream, that back of the "throwing out" scene lay a childish bit of investigation with his younger sister, which Father, a harsh, bigoted man, relentlessly "moral" in his own interpretation of the word, had chosen to regard as a particularly vicious bit of original sin. Once this reached the surface, one fact led easily to another and the cure was soon effected.

The patient was once again returned to the hypnotic state for hypno-synthetic therapy. He was asked to let his thoughts wander along certain paths, i.e., he was given something to think about. I asked him to concentrate upon any resemblance which might be apparent to him between his father and the church. At first, he repeated the fact that his father was a pious man who wanted his children to grow up within the religious fold, but soon he began to interpret the material which he had presented in his explanation of the hypnotically induced dream.

It seemed that the marriage license had little effect on the thoughts of morality that had been inflicted on him by his father, for even after he married, the marital act disturbed him because it stimulated the reappearance of the guilt that was connected with his incestuous advances in the original experience. The church was the symbol of his father; thus each time he attempted the sex act, though it was incomplete, he felt that the church would punish him for his indiscretions by "throwing him out." This mechanism was of course an unconscious one, and as such he had no knowledge of it, but it was responsible for his impotence and his insecurity. Both conditions left him almost immediately, and thereafter he was free of them.

If a patient cannot recall an experience by any of these methods—and in deeply rooted ones he may not be able to— he may be given the suggestion that he will dream of the experience which caused this condition, and furthermore (this is important) that upon wakening he will *remember the dream* and immediately write it down to submit to the analyst at the next session. This helps considerably. When the patient returns for the next visit, there is the dream in black and white, somewhat uncomplicated by symbolism and easy to interpret. When the patient brings the dream in, he is made aware of the previous suggestion, unless he first volunteers the information that there is a strong similarity between the dream and an incident in his life which he had forgotten. That is occasionally the case.

Mrs. A. G., age 42, complained of nervousness. Her physical condition seemed good, except for a persistent tachycardia, which at times made the pulse uncountable. Moreover, sharp pains would frequently shoot up and down the left arm, causing her no end of discomfort, occasionally preventing sleep. Careful examination of the chest by an able diagnostician failed to elicit a cardiac lesion or other pertinent signs of dysfunction. As many opinions were voiced in her journey from doctor to doctor, the patient received many treatments which proved of little benefit. It was on one of such visits that a physician noted a peculiar reaction in the patient. This had been occasioned by some workmen directly outside the office building banging away at metal pipes. The patient in response screamed, covered her ears in an attempt to exclude the sound and, as if to no avail, fainted dead away. The physician, discounting other opinions, detected some hysteria in his patient and thus had her seek psychiatric advice.

The patient's life had been somewhat rugged. Being brought up in Germany, and of a certain political disposition, she made open declarations of her discontents on the event of Hitler's assumption of power. As a result, she was arrested, and without benefit of trial interned in a camp with others who had made similar avowals. It was only after repeated efforts on the part of her friends and family that she was allowed her freedom to leave the camp and the country. Because of the severity of conditions in the concentration camp in which she was incarcerated, her final freedom, after two years, left her in a state of physical depletion and malnutrition, from which it took her some time to recover.

The patient, perhaps because of partial success in suppressing the memory of the horrors of that period, resisted all methods attempted. Nevertheless, she did respond to hypnosis, but only after we were able to overcome a certain amount of her initial recalcitrance. We finally brought forth greater achievement by placing a suggestion in her mind with regard to post-hypnotic dreaming:

"When you have gone to sleep tonight, a short time afterwards you will have a dream. The content of the dream will concern itself with the clanging sound of two metals hitting each other. After the dream you will awaken, write it down on paper with a pencil that you will keep close to your bed for this purpose. The dream will have no emotional effect on you. In fact, after completing the record of your dream, you will return to your bed and resume your sleep. You will bring your dream with you to your customary appointment with me tomorrow."

The patient carried out these suggestions to the letter, producing her dream the next day. Although few words were used to describe its content, the dream upon interpretation, furnished a solution to her case:

"I dreamt that I was in the concentration camp again. I was hungry and thirsty. Everybody else felt the same way. Sometimes the attendants would keep the food from us, especially when somebody made trouble. In the dream we lined up against the bars and made noises with our tin cups against the bars. Then everybody did the same thing until the noise was so loud it was deafening. Then the guards came. One of them, a woman, caught my arm—my left arm—and pulled it through the bars and tried to twist it against the bar. It hurt me. I screamed. I couldn't stand the pain. Afterwards I thought my arm was broken, but it wasn't. I could not move it for a few days—then it was all right."

Once I had examined the dream, I handed it to the patient, requesting her to read it again. As she perused the paper, she became overcome with emotion—her tears were profuse. My interrogation followed:

ANALYST: "What does the dream mean to you?"
PATIENT: "It's more than a dream. It's true. That is what happened."
ANALYST: "What happened?"
PATIENT: "As it was in the dream. That horrible noise . . . my arm. . . ."
ANALYST: "Is that why you fainted in the doctor's office, because you heard the same noise?"
PATIENT: "Yes. That was it. I can't stand that noise, so I faint to escape from it. I don't want to be reminded."
ANALYST: "Is it not your *left arm* that has been troubling you?"

PATIENT: "Yes. It hurts me right now—very much." (Patient massages her left arm.)

ANALYST: "Was it not the *same* left arm that was damaged by the woman attendant in the camp?"

PATIENT: (Pause) "That's right. It was that arm."

ANALYST: "Could it be possible that in attempting to wipe the memory of the incident from your mind, you allowed a few symptoms, such as the response to the clanging noise and a painful arm, to replace the memory?"

PATIENT: "That is what I have done."

ANALYST: "As the experience is over with, you should have no further reason to harbor such symptoms."

PATIENT: "I'm sure that they will disappear."

The symptoms did disappear, and with them went a good deal of the patient's nervous tension. The fast, persistent pulse, while it did not return to normal, showed marked improvement, probably as a result of the therapy.

It is sound procedure, in any event, whether using motion picture technique or that of placing one hand on the patient's neck, to tell him that the forthcoming night will bring a dream of an experience which he had forgotten but which the dream will recall, and which will contain within it the germ for his healing.

3. Word Association Tests

The word association tests developed by Jung and others seem to function differently under hypnosis from the manner in which they do in full consciousness. The words produced associatively in the hypnotic state apparently lie closer to the affective life and lead more directly to unconscious material. One of their advantages is that they can be an effective means for yielding information, in conjunction with other methods of analysis such as dream interpretation and free association. The efficiency of the word-association method is demonstrated readily in the following case:

Jack R., age 23, applied for psychoanalytic therapy, as

this was the course set forth by an understanding judge who released the patient on the provision that he would seek psychiatric attention.

A few weeks preceding the trial, Jack had parked his car several feet from the entrance of a school for girls, and, according to a later confession, waited until school was out, at which time he exposed his genitalia to some of the girls passing by. Soon after he started the engine and made for home, confident that his identity had not been discovered. This was not the case, for one of the girls had the presence of mind to record his license number. When she related the incident to her father, he, feeling that his daughter had been outraged by the scene she had witnessed, reported the story to the police. Within a few hours Jack was "booked" at the central station.

As soon as the police began their questioning, Jack made a clean breast of it. In tears he recounted the incident, just as the girl had described it. He could not understand what had provoked him to act as he did. He was convinced that his aggression against society had destroyed his life and had made him the subject for humiliation by his family and friends.

His wife, a rather quiet girl, could not understand her husband's act. Although the validity of his confession had been demonstrated to her, she refused to believe that he could become so involved, for his usual behavior seemed to nullify the act. Her husband had always been extremely modest in his habits. In innumerable instances she had inadvertently entered the room while he was dressing. He would rapidly make an effort to cover his body and show no end of embarrassment. Further conversation with her led to information which seemed paradoxical. For example, Jack would leave the room if she were undressing, on the pretense that he was going to the corner for a package of cigarettes. Instead she noticed with particular confusion that he would leave the house, stand at her window, and peer into the room through an opening in the shade. While his actions in this regard were incomprehensible to her, she had never before discussed them with anyone. On one occasion, a friend of her husband's had returned from overseas on a furlough. As he had no family and few friends in the city, he was invited to make his home with them for the short duration of his stay. On the second day of his friend's visit, an interesting conversation took place between the patient and his wife. As Eddie, the temporary boarder, had been away for a long time, he needed to be entertained by the opposite sex. Jack thought that his wife should assume this duty. This demand resulted in a bitter quarrel, for she objected to being "prostituted" by her husband. The matter was henceforth dropped.

The first consultation with Jack was given to a discussion of the incident which led to his trial. He was completely at a loss for an explanation of the event. Although it was the first time he had submitted to the impulse to expose himself, it had existed for many years. He could not remember the first incidence of the urge, but he was confident that it had occurred before puberty.

As a routine procedure, I submit a number of words to the patient for his associative response. He is asked to give each association as quickly as possible after the stimulus word is heard. Following through with the association method in consciousness, I hypnotize the patient and repeat the identical stimulus words. The word associations are generally most informative during Medium Sleep. On this occasion ten words were chosen from my standard list. The patient's responses to them in the conscious period were:

STIMULUS WORD	ASSOCIATION
1. dark	— light
2. sickness	— health
3. mountain	— river
4. woman	— man
5. cold	— quite cold

STIMULUS WORD	ASSOCIATION
6. beautiful	— ugly
7. smooth	— round
8. command	— order
9. slow	— fast
10. courage	— cowardice

His conscious responses were by no means atypical, and there-fore, could throw little light on his behavior patterns. The following were his associations to the same stimulus words under hypnosis, in the same analytical session:

STIMULUS WORD	ASSOCIATION
1. dark	— hell
2. sickness	— me
3. mountain	— breast
4. woman	— my mother, the only woman
5. cold	— the way she treats me
6. beautiful	— my wife; she reminds me of Mom
7. smooth	— a woman's body
8. command	— my father ruled me
9. slow	— I'm too fast with my wife
10. courage	— courage to die

The patient was then asked to speak whatever thoughts entered his mind after he had responded to the words I had given him. As he had not been returned to the waking state, the associations he had offered were fresh in his memory, and as such, they led to a provocative explanation.

When Jack had reached his tenth birthday his mother celebrated the occasion by inviting a few friends to the house. Cake and wine were served. It was the first time that Jack had tasted wine; he liked its effect on him. His mother, being too occupied with her guests, failed to notice that Jack had taken excessive amounts of the liquid. In the beginning he was gripped by a most disturbing nausea, but soon he felt good. It was only after the party had broken up that his mother noticed that her son was slightly inebriated, and insisted that he be put to bed immediately. She helped him to undress, and it was then that the thought occurred to her that a cold bath might help to sober him. In preparation for this, and in order to keep from getting wet in the process, she removed her blouse, partially exposing her chest. The patient's words follow:

"Christ, I don't know what came over me then. I did something terrible. Mom was leaning over the tub and I grabbed her breast. She was screaming—trying to get me off. Then she got me by the hair and hit me over and over again across the face. Pop came up when he heard the screaming and did the job up right. After that, Mom didn't talk to me much.

"After that, I used to get funny feelings—like dreams. The first one came on the day after. I started thinking about what happened in the bathroom. It got me all excited. But what really did it was when I tried to feel and imagine Mom hitting me. It was a hell of a feeling. I wanted her to do it again, but I didn't have the nerve."

Jack had identified sexual experience with humiliation, and, as other qualities of this nature made themselves manifest in his personality, he discovered that acts promoting degradation were, in some ways, enjoyable even if they did result in mortification. Thus Jack wanted to be "caught" and humiliated. But he did find other means by which he could be debased. When he had suggested to his wife that she submit to his friend, he was doing so with this apparent purpose. When he exposed his person to the young girls in front of the school, he might have been "confident" that he could make a "getaway," but inwardly his act had satisfied a desire for double humiliation—one in the exposure, the other in the capture that followed, and the consequent confession.

We elicited the following information during an analytical session several months later:

"When I was kid I used to look in people's windows. I

was a 'peeping Tom' or something. Once I got caught. I got a good beating for it; I didn't mind. Some gal was undressing. Her husband was coming home from work. It was at night. He caught me looking in the window. After that I used to do it whenever I could, even if I knew I could get killed for it. I even looked through the window at my wife. It gave me the same feeling."

On another occasion:

"I'm smaller than the average man. I've always felt lousy about it. Never wanted anyone to see me. When I was in the Navy, I'd get the idea that the kids were laughing at me. One time I wanted to jump over the side, but I didn't have the 'guts.'

"The guys used to talk about the time it took them. I used to be ashamed because I was so quick. I'm glad my wife never paid any attention—anyway she never said anything about it. I always keep myself covered when she's around. I hate to have her see me. That's one humiliation I've never wanted."

The patient had, by this time, gained sufficient insight into his behavior, many of its expressions having disappeared, but it took six months of persistent effort to neutralize the pathogenic material and draw a happy conclusion from the case.

4. *Suggestion in Analysis*

After the patient has once abreacted to a given situation recalled under hypnosis, the ordeal can be eased if the session is augmented by counselling which the analyst gives while the patient is still in hypnosis. Now our method of hypno-synthesis must come into play. This must be designed with a view toward helping the individual to accept the experience which he has just produced and adjusting his life accordingly. The hypnotist should also impress upon the patient's mind the various associations and connotations of his illness, and how they conform to this particular experience which he has relived. He must show where all the symptoms are actually related to the symptom connected with this particular experience. It will not be necessary for the patient to receive specific suggestions for the amelioration of the symptom, for if the analysis of the experience is a true analysis, the symptoms will vanish without suggestion; if the analysis be untrue or incomplete, it is better to keep "digging" now than to banish a symptom only to have it pop out at a later date in a more virulent form. Frequently a case is complicated enough to require a number of abreactions and the reliving of many experiences before the analysis may be considered complete. Beware the too hasty conclusion.

Despite the many methods in hypno-analysis, it is still necessary to coax the patient into giving more and more information. This coaxing must never be done in a way to offend the patient under treatment. He must be made continuously aware of the fact that the information is only desired in order to effect his complete rehabilitation. After the first session of hypno-analysis, the patient may be nervous upon awakening unless given suggestions which will waken him calm and serene. This must be taken into consideration, for if the patient is unduly upset and transference incomplete, he will leave the analyst's office not to return, and in worse shape than ever because new fears have been added to the load he is already carrying.

It would appear that the implementation of psychoanalysis with hypnosis is the most effective way we have at present for the clarification of certain types of neuroses and the release of neurotic symptoms. It is the quickest method known to alleviate causative conditions and to bring the patient to a contented integration both within himself and with his environment.

If the reader should be interested in pursuing further works of hypno-analytic technique, he is referred particularly to Wolberg's *Hypnoanalysis* and Lindner's *Rebel Without a Cause,* both of which provide abundant information on pathological behavior and its cure through the use of hypnosis. In the first work, Wolberg discusses the successful analysis of a psychotic, Johan R., and shows how, by masterful handling of hypnotic techniques, a schizophrenic was able to return to the reality from which he had escaped.

Lindner's book should be of interest to the sociologist, the criminologist and the therapist, for it relates the case of a psychopathic personality, whose maladjustment to life and society had made him a criminal. By means of hypnosis and psychoanalysis, Dr. Lindner was able to make known the repressed memories of his patient, Harold; as he adjusted himself to them, remarkable personality alterations followed. Harold was no longer a "rebel." He was able to assume a place in a society that he had despised since childhood.

When unconscious resistances on the part of the patient prevent adequate induction of hypnosis, depressant drugs are sometimes resorted to, which are presumed to produce the same effect. It is my opinion that they are less successful; the end result is narcosis, not hypnosis. There are various drugs which have been used from time to time for this purpose, the most popular being sodium amytal, phenobarbitol and sodium pentathol.

While there have been certain instances in which the drugs have been useful, they should not be used save as a last resort, and then only by those persons who are qualified to handle them.

"Bis dat qui cito dat"—"He gives twice who gives it quickly." My own conclusions are that ingenious "surprise attack" will accomplish anything the drug might, and, should

that fail, it is not hypnosis that has failed, but the ingenuity of the hypnotist.

REFERENCES

ADLER, D. L., *The Experimental Production of Repression,* Proceedings of the 8th Annual Meeting of Topological Psychologists, 27–36, 1940.
ALEXANDER, F. AND WILSON, G. W., "Quantitative Dream Studies," *Psychoanalytic Quarterly,* 4, 371–407, 1935.
BERGLER, M. D., *Battle of the Conscience,* Washington Institute of Medicine, Washington, 1948.
BREUER, J., AND FREUD, S., *Studies in Hysteria,* translated by A. A. Brill, Nervous and Mental Disease Publishing Co., New York, 1936.
BRILL, A. A., *Freud's Contribution to Psychiatry,* W. W. Norton Co., Inc., New York, 1944.
BRILL, A. A., *Psychoanalysis, Its Theories and Practical Application,* W. B. Saunders Co., Philadelphia, 1913.
ERICKSON, M. H., *The Successful Treatment of a Case of Acute Hysterical Depression by a Return Under Hypnosis to a Critical Phase of Childhood,* 24, 95–133, 1941.
ERICKSON, M. H., *The Applications of Hypnosis to Psychiatry,* Medical Record, 150, 60–65, 1939.
FARBER, L. H. and Fischer, G., "An Experimental Approach to Dream Psychology Through the Use of Hypnosis," *Psychoanalytic Quarterly,* 12, 202–216, 1943.
FENICHEL, O., *The Psychoanalytical Theory of Neurosis,* W. W. Norton Co., New York, 1945.
FERENCZI, S., *Theory and Technique of Psychoanalysis,* Boni & Liveright Co., New York, 1927.
FREUD, S., *The Psychopathology of Everyday Life,* Macmillan Co., New York, 1914.
FREUD, S., *An Autobiographical Study,* Hogarth Press, London, 1948.
FREUD, S., *The Ego And The Id,* Hogarth Press, London, 1947.
FREUD, S., *The Interpretation of Dreams,* Macmillan Co., New York, 1933.
FREUD, S., *Group Psychology and the Analysis of the Ego,* International Psychoanalytical Press, London, 1922.

HADFIELD, J. A., "The Reliability of Infant Memories," *British Journal of Medical Psychology*, 13, 87–111, 1928.

HART, B., *The Psychology of Insanity*, Cambridge University Press, 1921.

HORSLEY, J. S., *Narco-Analysis*, Oxford University Press, New York and London, 1943.

JONES, E., "The Action of Suggestion in Psychotherapy," *Journal of Abnormal Psychology*, 5, 217–254, 1910.

KANZER, M. G., "The Therapeutic Use of Dreams Induced by Hypnotic Suggestion," *Psychoanalytic Quarterly*, 14, 313, 1945.

KARNOSH, L. J., and Zucker, E. M., *Handbook of Psychiatry*, C. V. Mosby Co., St. Louis, 1945.

KEMPFF, E. J., *Psychopathology*, C. V. Mosby Co., St. Louis, 1921.

LINDNER, R. M., *Rebel Without A Cause*, Grune & Stratton, New York, 1944.

MASLOW, A. H. and Mittleman, B., *Principles of Abnormal Psychology and the Dynamics of Psychic Illness*, Harper & Brothers, New York, 1941.

MASSERMAN, J. H., *Principles of Dynamic Psychiatry*, W. B. Saunders Co., Philadelphia, 1946.

MULLAHY, PATRICK, *Oedipus—Myth and Complex*, Hermitage House, Inc., New York, 1948.

NEUSTETTER, W. L., *Early Treatment of Nervous and Mental Disorders*, Churchill, London, 1940.

PRINCE, M., *The Unconscious*, Macmillan Co., New York, 1929.

RAPAPORT, D., *Emotions And Memory*, Williams & Wilkins, Baltimore, 1942.

REIK, THEODORE, *Listening With The Third Ear*, Farrar, Straus & Co., New York, 1948.

ROGERSON, C. H., "Narcoanalysis with Nitrous Oxide," *British Medical Journal*, 1, 811–812, June 17, 1944.

SPEYER, N. AND STROKVIS, B., "The Psychoanalytic Factor in Hypnosis," *British Journal of Medical Psychology*, 17, 217–222, 1938.

STEKEL, W., *The Interpretation of Dreams*, translated by E. & C. Paul, Liveright Co., New York, 1943.

STEKEL, W., *Psychoanalysis and Suggestion Therapy*, Kegan Paul, London, 1923.

STRECKER, E., Ebaugh F. and Ewalt, J. R., *Practical Clinical Psychiatry*, Blakiston Co., Philadelphia, 1947.

248

TAYLOR, W. S., "Behaviour Under Hypnoanalysis and the Mechanism of Neurosis," *Journal of Abnormal Psychology*, 18, 109–124, 1923.

THOMPSON, C. AND MULLAHY, P., *Psychoanalysis: Evolution and Development*, Hermitage House, Inc., New York, 1950.

WOLBERG, L. R., *Hypnoanalysis*, Grune & Stratton, New York, 1945.

Appendix

The patient, under hypnosis, was brought back, year by year in his life, the analyst watching his facial expressions closely.

Mr. H. C., thirty-two years old, suffered frequent periods of anxiety and depression, which appeared without external provocation. He feared crowds, becoming so panicky that his wife was forced to accompany him to the office. He suffered acute claustrophobia in any church, fearing he would "pass out"; he avoided small rooms, elevators, and coat closets. These fears were interfering with his position as an engineer in a ship-building concern, where it frequently became necessary for him to crawl into narrow openings in ships for construction purposes. He was forced by the phobia to leave one job after another.

Orthodox analytic procedure met with slight success. He was cooperative in every way, but there were large gaps in his memory that prevented the "digging out" of relevant material.

In an attempt to fill in the missing parts, I induced a Medium Stage of hypnosis and instituted the following series of suggestions:

"I shall bring you back, year by year, over your entire life.

249

As you return to the past, you will be able to recall all the experiences which you have forgotten. They will appear to you very vividly, and you will relive the experiences with all the emotions which originally attended them.

"Now, you are thirty-one; now you are thirty; now, twenty-nine, twenty-eight, twenty-seven, twenty-six; twenty-five, twenty-four, twenty-three, twenty-two, twenty-one, twenty. How old are you?" Patient: "Twenty." I continued. "Now you are nineteen, eighteen, seventeen, sixteen, fifteen, fourteen, thirteen, twelve, eleven, ten. How old are you?" Patient: "Ten years old, sir."

My suggestions went on; "Now you are nine, now you are eight. . . ." I was about to go back to six when I noticed that he was sweating profusely, and broke out into tears. The following was recorded on a tape recorder and transcribed.

ANALYST: "Certain thoughts are in your mind. What are they? Don't hold anything back."

PATIENT: "My sister is dead. Irene is gone. I'll never see her again." (During the previous sessions there had been no mention of a sister; he had apparently believed himself an only child.)

ANALYST: "When did she die?"

PATIENT: "On Wednesday. We went to church this morning. They buried her. I'll never see her again." (He broke out into tears, burying his head in his hands. It is interesting to note that these were "little boy's tears," not those of an adult male.)

ANALYST: "Did you love your sister, Harry?"

PATIENT: "I loved her better than anybody. She brought me presents all the time."

ANALYST: "How old was she?"

PATIENT: "I don't know; she was married. Now nobody cares about me." (He continued sobbing.) "Irene is dead—she'll never come back."

ANALYST: "What happened at the church this morning?" (The word "church" had always presented a block during word-association tests.)

PATIENT: (By now he was crying very loudly.) "I'm ashamed; I can't tell you. Please don't make me tell you."

ANALYST: "You must tell me everything. What happened at the church?"

PATIENT: "The whole town turned out. Everybody was watching us. All the seats were taken. (Sobs.) We walked down the aisle. We walked behind the casket. I felt very dizzy, as if I was going to faint. I wanted to run out. There were a lot of people walking in back of me—the pews on the side were filled and in front was the casket. I felt so weak I could hardly walk. I wanted to run, but my legs felt stiff. I thought I was going to faint, but I didn't. It seemed like a long time—then it was over and my mother and father took me home. All this time I tried not to cry, but when we got home I ran up to my bedroom and fell on the bed and I must have passed out. I woke up in—I don't know how long. I could hear a lot of people downstairs. I opened the door. I could hear they were talking about Irene. I couldn't help it. I cried out loud. I must have screamed. Dad came up—I hate him! I hate him!" (Sobbed hysterically.)

ANALYST: "What about Dad? What happened then?"

PATIENT: "He asked me what I was doing up in the room. He was mad that I *wasn't* downstairs. I told him that I don't want to see those people, because they came over to the house to make believe that they cared about Irene. They don't care about Irene. They always talked bad about her, I said to him. He hit me in the face and he said, 'What makes you think that you were the only one who cared about your sister?' I cried all day. I can't stop crying. I hate Dad! If I had a gun, I'd kill him! I'd kill him! He should have died instead of Irene!"

When I was certain that no further information was forthcoming during this period, I suggested to him that he would recall the experience upon awakening. I brought him back to his present age—this is essential!—by suggesting: "Now you are nine, now you are ten, eleven, twelve, etc."

Before rousing him, I suggested that he would feel very well upon awakening and that he would be able to associate the experience he would remember with his symptoms and thus be able to understand his condition fully in the light of the recalled experience.

Upon waking, Mr. C. showed truly marvellous insight. The first thing he said upon opening his eyes was, "That's funny; I forgot all about my sister. I forgot that I had one. I can understand a lot of things now. Now I know why I feel panicky in crowds. I was associating the crowds with the people who were jamming the church. I had a 'closed-in' feeling. I got the 'clausters' then, just as I get them now when I'm in a place where it's hard to get out.

"I've always hated my father without knowing why. Now I know, but it's silly. He must have been under a lot of strain at the time. I'm sure he never meant to slap me. I guess I owe him an apology.

"I just thought of something. It's a little startling to me. When you took me 'back,' I kept seeing a picture of my sister. She was so much like my wife, it threw me for a while. Funny, isn't it?—maybe that's why my wife attracted me. I guess I was looking for someone like Irene."

Needless to say, the symptoms quickly disappeared and have not returned.

CASE HISTORY OF ALICE K.: UNDERGOING HYPNO-ANALYSIS AND HYPNO-SYNTHESIS BY FREE ASSOCIATION

Appended here, in essence, is the case history of Alice, which was recorded on tape in its entirety. A short introduction will suffice to see Alice as she was the day she presented herself for treatment.

One might immediately accuse her of purposeful neglect, for from all indications, it was obvious that Alice, age 31, had gone out of her way to defy the natural and esthetic traditions of her sex, and in consequence had succeeded in deforming certain physical attributes which might have held the envy of other girls. Her mode of dress—drab and unbecoming; her spectacles—monstrously large with black rims; her hair—loosely pinned with a few precarious strands falling disturbingly over the nape of her neck; her weight—excessive; her posture—almost ape-like—these and other characteristics would indicate that she had taken great pains to disfigure herself. But such an accusation would have been offensive to her and would have prompted indignant denial. If she were really ugly, she contended, it was because fate had intended her to be so, and no effort on her part would remedy the situation.

Nevertheless, the reason for her visit seemed quite apart from a desire to change her appearance. She had read in some popular medical literature that myopia could result from a desire not to rewitness a traumatic event. With amazing acumen she reasoned that some disturbance of the past, of which she was not cognizant, had never been properly understood, and as no adjustment was forthcoming she had relinquished a part of her vision to avoid repetition of the sight of the experience. Alice felt that she was presently victimized by some horrifying episode of her childhood of which she had no recollection. What led her to confirm this observation was the fact that when she attempted to administer conscious thought to this "blanked out" period, she received retribution in return, taking the form of a sick headache that continued for days, eventually being replaced by lengthy periods of moroseness and general malaise. Because of these symptoms, she would frequently beg off treatment in the midst of an analytical session and cancel subsequent appointments.

Day by day, it became increasingly apparent that a more rapid form of therapy was indicated if the patient was to obtain relief. Hypnosis provided a solution to the problem of overcoming the disguised negativity, but during the initial sessions the methods that are normally employed for regression had little evident effect upon her. Free association, on the other hand, yielded almost immediate results. This of necessity became the method of choice. Earlier I had used a standard word-association test, and those over which she had faltered were added to another test. Those words, which were finally put aside as significant for future observation were: ugly, clothes, sex, sleep, headache, mother, father. To these words, conscious association revealed nothing.

In a semi-deep state of hypnosis, Alice was able to associate freely, for the barriers which normally had obstructed her thought pathways were removed by a hypnotic suggestion that she would be able to examine the facts of her case with impersonality.

It will be noted that the course of hypno-analysis does not call for absolute imperium on the part of the therapist, for while he resolutely insists upon compliance he does so with leniency. The word "please," as it precedes a command provides reassurance to the patient once the preliminaries of hypnotic induction are dispensed with.

Portions of the recording of the most significant session follow:

ANALYST: "I wish you to think of your mother and father. You will think aloud, saying everything that enters your mind.

These thoughts as they appear will cause you no distress. Instead, you will be like a detective probing a case—accepting each clue, every fact that you arrive upon with a minimum of personal emotion—as if they concerned someone else. Now tell me what you remember of your mother and father."

PATIENT: "As I remember her—she's dead now—Mom was a very pretty woman. She never changed. She was always very well dressed—made her own clothes—cut pictures of well-dressed women out of fashion magazines and made patterns of the designs of their clothing. She would look forward to the church parties in town, and here she would be in her glory. Pop was the opposite. He was much older. He made his living shoeing horses. When horses went out, he took a job in the mill. Pop was different from Mom. He never cared about his personal appearance. She would always fight with him about it—especially about bathing. A bath always came after a terrific fight. I can remember a time when Mom was really irritable. Pop had been laid off at the plant. As he had never bothered to put anything away for a rainy day, Mom had to skimp on bare necessities." (Pause)

ANALYST: "Please go on—about Mom and Pop."

PATIENT: "It's very vivid. It frightens me. I feel as if I were there —seeing everything all over again."

ANALYST: "Tell me about it."

PATIENT: "How it came about, I don't know. I think it was the minister who recommended him—but anyway, we had a boarder in the house. Mom was fascinated by him. I don't know if I mentioned it before—we lived in a little town. Mr. Brennan was of the big city—New York or some place. He had traveled all over the world—had even written a book about Australia or something. He was a spellbinder. He could tell stories of his travels by the hour. Mom would have a funny gleam in her eyes when he came into the room. Pop hated him. He'd say nasty things when Mr. Brennan wasn't around. Maybe Pop hated him because Mom looked interested—or maybe because Pop believed in hard-working men. Maybe it was just jealousy. I think he tolerated Mr. Brennan because he helped pay the household expenses. I think it was about that time that Mom and Pop began to grow further and further away from each other. I was only about eight when. . . ." (Pause)

ANALYST: "Please go on. What thoughts are entering your mind at this moment?"

PATIENT: (Pause) "My mind seems to go blank. I—I. . . ."

ANALYST: "What happened when you were eight? Tell me about it."

PATIENT: "Something really horrible. It doesn't seem true, and yet—I know it *is* true. There seems to be a film around it —like a fog. . . ."

ANALYST: "As you tell it to me, the film will disappear and you will remember everything."

PATIENT: "I feel a horrible pain in my temples. I've never felt it so badly. It's as if my head was falling apart."

ANALYST: "I am going to count from one to ten. I am now placing my hands upon your temples. When I reach ten, the ache will be gone completely—you will be able to continue. One—two—three—four—five—six—seven—eight—nine— ten. (Pause) How do you feel?"

PATIENT: (Pause) "The ache is gone—just a hollowness."

ANALYST: "Continue, please."

PATIENT: "It happened one night. I must have been eight. Yes, I was eight years old. It happened a few days after my birthday. I had gone to sleep without my doll. I always took her to bed with me. I woke up, I think, in the middle of the night—Sarah wasn't with me. I remembered leaving her in the parlor on the sofa. It was downstairs. I remember getting out of bed. To get to the stairs I had to pass their room—Mom's and Pop's. I tried to make as little noise as possible. When I got to their room, I realized that they were not asleep. Mom was moaning and sobbing— She was saying, 'You're hurting me—Stop—You're hurting me. I can't stand it.' I was afraid. I didn't know what he was doing to Mom. I thought he was killing her. (Pause) It's hard for me to go on."

ANALYST: "You must continue. It is the only way I can help you."

PATIENT: "I'll try."

ANALYST: "What was happening in the room?"

PATIENT: "At that time, I didn't know. I was too young. But I know now. I was afraid. I didn't know what he was doing to Mom. It seemed so awful. I thought he was killing her. I looked into the room to see what he was doing to her. (Pause) They were lying in bed together and he was on top of her. I was frightened. I ran back to my bed—closed the door—and put my head under the cover. After a while, I could hear Mom getting up and going to the bathroom. The water ran for a few minutes—then she went back to bed. Then I heard an argument. After a few minutes it was over. Then everything was all right. I felt relieved, but it was a long time before I got off to sleep. I forgot all about Sarah. The next morning a strange thing happened. Now I remember." (Pause)

ANALYST: "What happened?"

PATIENT: (Pause) "I know now why I can't see. It happened the next day. It's fantastic. Now I remember. I could hardly see enough to walk down the stairs. Before this, I could see perfectly. (Pause) My head ached. That didn't happen until I saw Pop at the breakfast table. My emotions were all mixed up when we came face to face. On one hand, for some reason, I felt guilty. On the other hand, I hated him for torturing my mother. I tried my best to convince myself that this was all just a dream—that he didn't really abuse her. I think I managed to convince myself, finally—but after that, I began to notice his faults." (Pause)

ANALYST: "You say that you had a mixture of emotions when you met the next morning at the breakfast table. One was hatred, the other, guilt. Why did you feel guilty?"

PATIENT: "I don't know. Maybe because I hated him for the first time. I had looked up to him before. Maybe I didn't know what to think of him. He had always been very good to me, and good to Mom. I guess she was just frigid. But I didn't understand those things as a child. I think I felt guilty because I hated him."

ANALYST: "Now, you noticed your vision failing you. Did you tell your mother about it?"

PATIENT: "Yes, I told her after Pop had gone off to work. She kept me home from school that day. She called in old Doctor Parkson. He was a kindly old man, but he knew very little. He told Mom that my headache was due to eye-strain. He took the examination for the fitting himself and ordered the glasses by mail. It was a week before they came. With the glasses, I could see very well. (Pause) My head is beginning to pound again—like mad."

ANALYST: "I want you to count from one to ten silently. When you have arrived at 'ten' the ache will be gone and you will feel well." (Pause)

PATIENT: "I feel all right now. It was because I remembered something. Something else happened a few months later. It was a terrible shock—also like a dream—but it wasn't, because I was wide awake, and it happened in the afternoon. About three o'clock. I had just come home from school. The back door was open as usual. I had just gotten my report card. I was anxious to show Mom my grades. They were pretty good. I was a pretty good student up until that time —after that I couldn't concentrate too well. Anyway, as soon as I got in the door, I called to Mom. I called a number of times. Finally she answered. She said she would be down in a minute. She was answering from the bedroom. I guess I couldn't wait for her to come down. I ran upstairs and opened the bedroom door. Mr. Brennan was with Mom in bed. Neither of them were wearing clothing. He was doing the same thing that Pop had done. This time Mom wasn't moaning. I had a horrible sensation. I wished that I had not seen it. Both of them knew that I had seen them doing it. She talked to me about it afterwards. I remember feeling very embarrassed while she was talking to me. I think she felt guilty. She told me to make out as if I had not seen anything. She said that I would understand when I got older. (Pause) Now I see the whole thing."

ANALYST: "What do you see?"

PATIENT: "Why my eyes are the way they are. For about five or six hours afterwards, I couldn't see anything, even with my glasses. (Pause) We never talked about it again. For days after, I remember hoping that I would never be like Mom. (Pause) No man would ever do anything like that to me. I hated Pop. I hated Mr. Brennan. I hated all men. They were all alike. I hate them today. I can't stand to have a man put his hands on me. Now I know why—it's because I was going to be the exact opposite of Mom—in every way —then I would be too repulsive to touch. I tried not to smile because Mom was always smiling. I would make myself ugly because Mom was beautiful. I really succeeded. (Pause) I've always hated my appearance, but I got satisfaction out of it. I can see all the reasons now—why I've stuffed myself with candy, just to be overweight—why I've dressed the way I have. I became a mess because I wanted to! It's crazy."

Alice's progress was surprisingly rapid. Within a month she had regained her normal vision. Many changes came about in time—a thorough metamorphosis in appearance, spirit and personality.

CASE HISTORY OF CARMEN R: A STUDY IN HYPNO-SYNTHESIS

Mrs. Carmen R., twenty-seven years of age, of Italian extraction, might have been called a "war bride." Her marriage had occurred on the spur of the moment as her fiancé had been destined to leave for overseas the following morning. As might have been expected, their "honeymoon" lasted but a few hours, and, except for an infrequent letter, she had periodic cause to wonder whether her husband was alive or dead. "I was a good girl all the time he was gone," was her comment to me. Raised in a religious family, Carmen had been carefully indoctrinated in the ways of the Bible, and in this trying period she sought and found comfort in her church. While some women in like circumstances amused themselves in the company of other men, Carmen looked upon such deeds with disgust, for she had been brought up to regard the sanctity of marriage and home as inviolable.

Only on one occasion did she deviate from this course, and while the following incident seemed harmless at the time she lived to regret it, for later it shook her entire life and almost made her a chronic mental invalid. A friend had invited her to a birthday party. While she would usually turn down such invitations, she accepted this one for several reasons: for two years she had had no excitement; although she had always loved to dance, she had refrained from doing so; moreover, she felt particularly oppressed and lonely at the time, for a few months had elapsed during which her husband had not written. The party was a joyous occasion. She danced, had a few drinks and spontaneously entered into the gaiety of the affair. Someone had suggested "spin the bottle," and it was then that the moral conflict took hold. As she expressed herself later: "I wanted to get into the game, even if just to be a good sport, but something inside of me said 'No,' and so I took a chair next to the group. They were sitting on the floor. As I did not participate in the game, I had to be a little away from them—but I was close enough so that I could see what was going on."

When the game had gotten underway, one "spin" brought the bottle to rest between Carmen, who had remained seated in her chair, and a young man who was "in the game." It was then that the unexpected happened, for in the spirit of fun the fellow arose from the floor, went to Carmen's chair and made an attempt to kiss her. She struggled against it, drawing herself back in the chair; he was persistent, and finally he succeeded. For some reason, which later was inexplicable to her, she was overcome with emotion. She relaxed her guard, allowing herself to be kissed. The onlookers playfully chided her for her "indiscretion," much to her consternation. When opportunity presented itself she took leave of the party, returning home. That night she tossed in bed. Sleep never came. She tried to visualize the experience and the same emotions took effect. Soon these were replaced by a strong feeling of guilt, as she could not imagine a married woman, on one hand, expressing undying love for her husband, and on the other, being stirred by another man. In spite of her efforts to suppress the conflict, she could not release it from her mind.

A week later she was pleasantly surprised, for without warning her husband returned home. For a while the experience that she had at the party was forgotten. Her husband's presence seemed to cloud everything of the past. Within a month after his return she discovered that she was pregnant. She looked forward, and happily, to the birth of her child. In the months that followed she knitted all sorts of things in preparation for its arrival.

When Carmen first saw her child it was difficult for her to believe that she was not living through some horrible dream. Despite orders a nurse committed the unforgivable sin and brought the child to his mother for her inspection. Its face and body were distorted in typical mongoloid fashion. Of the three-fourths of one percent of anomalous embryos that come to term, this one had survived. Of those anomalous infants, some die very shortly thereafter because of the nature and extent of their structural defects. But Carmen's child continued to live. She recovered from her shock, but some of its effects remained with her.

Carmen indulged in much self-examination. She made every

effort to recall the experiences of her life, for she felt that in those experiences God had found justification to punish her. Soon all of her thoughts seemed to embrace her experience at the "kissing game." God had therefore punished her for those emotions. Her baby was thus born malformed because she had succumbed to that moment of ecstasy. Absolution by her priest failed to dissolve her guilt. She became morose and nervous. She could not stand to be alone for even a moment, and, paradoxically, did not want people around her. The baby was a constant reminder of her "sin."

The discerning student will discriminate between this case and others he has encountered in this work. The principal difference which keeps it apart from the analytical cases we have examined is the fact that the patient, though she might have tried, did not succeed in repressing the material. Thus psychoanalysis did not prove the method of course. Rather, it was necessary to assist the patient, in whatever way feasible, to a practicable acceptance of her situation. Psychological counselling appeared to offer the best hope for successful therapy. Several psychologists had made the effort in this regard, one of whom was recommended by her church. The various modes of therapy proved of little avail— in fact the patient grew worse. As time went on, she became so convinced that her explanation of the situation was true that she refused to accept any explanation which did not consider the wrath of God as the cause.

It was evident that a force of greater intensity was necessary to overcome the patient's resistance. Hypno-synthesis provided the method. It will be rememberd that hypno-synthesis implies the open rejection of the pathogenic material and enables the patient to make a suitable adjustment—morally, physically, mentally and emotionally. As this method utilizes hypnosis, the patient's resistance to a new idea is eliminated, and thus he is able to accept it with a minimum of struggle. The patient is led to the acceptance of the idea in the form of a hypnotic suggestion, as such, it encounters less of the barrier than would normally be set up by logic.

The first few consultations were devoted to the patient's impressions of her illness. On her fourth visit I asked her to accompany me to the offices of a downtown newspaper, for, as I explained, there was something going on at that building which would be of benefit to her. As Carmen had in the past paid little attention to linotype machines and printing presses, she expressed greater and greater interest as she watched the operations of the various machines. As we walked from the building into the street, she said, "The whole thing is so perfect. It can do everything but bake a cake." I agreed with her. As we rode back to the office she talked on about the wondrous phenomena of printing.

Upon our return to the office I proceeded to hypnotize her. Her response was immediate. When I was convinced that she had reached a Medium Sleep, I asked her to repeat in detail what she had witnessed at the newspaper plant; she did so with little effort. The following conversation ensued between us:

ANALYST: "You still have the impression that God punished you by producing an abnormal child?"

PATIENT: "Yes."

ANALYST: "What would cause Him to do that?"

PATIENT: "The experience I had at the party. The way I felt when the man kissed me."

ANALYST: "In your religious beliefs, do you hold to the idea that God is omnipotent; that He is all-powerful; that He could do anything He wanted to do?"

PATIENT: "That is true."

ANALYST: "Therefore, if He did not want you to have such a feeling, He could have prevented it."

PATIENT: "He could have if He wanted to. I never thought of it before in that way."

ANALYST: "Your belief also holds that God is all-loving and all-understanding. If this is so, what would lead you to believe that God would vent His wrath upon a child, who was born innocent of all sin, just to punish its mother? Does that sound like the action of an omnipotent, all-loving, all-understanding God? You are only a mortal being, Carmen. As this is true, your power, your love and your understanding are limited. But although they *are* limited, would you inflict such a life upon an innocent baby because, for some reason you wanted to get back at its mother?"

PATIENT: "Everything you say is logical (Pause), but why did He do this to me? Why was *my* baby born sick?"

ANALYST: "I had a special purpose in mind in taking you to the newspaper office this afternoon. I wanted you to observe the mechanism of printing. You said that the 'whole thing was so perfect.' Did you mean what you said?"

PATIENT: "It *was* perfect."

ANALYST: "I wonder if you noticed that occasionally there was a mistake in the manner in which a paper was printed."

PATIENT: "Yes. The man would take it out of the tray and throw it away. It didn't happen very often."

ANALYST: "Then the machine was not really perfect, was it? Would you blame the inventor or the maker of the machine because an imperfection occurred, from time to time, in its workings?"

PATIENT: (No answer)

ANALYST: "If God had produced man, and later set a continuous process in motion, would you blame Him for an occasional error which took place in the process?"

PATIENT: (Hesitation and finally) "No."

ANALYST: "Then from every standpoint you have no reason to feel as you do."

PATIENT: (Crying) "That's right. I have no reason. It's all a big mistake. I felt so guilty—I wanted to be punished for it."

About a year after the above consultation I received a Christmas card from Carmen. On the back of it she had written a short note to tell me that everything was well with her. In the meantime, her baby had died—but it had not come as a shock; instead its death had brought with it genuine relief for mother and father. It was as if a curtain had been brought down after a truly pathetic scene. As far as they were concerned, the play had a happy ending.

A PERSONAL WORD FROM MELVIN POWERS, PUBLISHER, WILSHIRE BOOK COMPANY

My goal is to publish interesting, informative, and inspirational books. You can help me to accomplish this by sending me your answers to the following questions:

Did you enjoy reading this book? Why?

What ideas in the book impressed you most? Have you applied them to your daily life? How?

Is there a chapter that could serve as a theme for an entire book? Explain.

Would you like to read similar books? What additional information would you like them to contain?

If you have an idea for a book, I would welcome discussing it with you. If you have a manuscript in progress, write or call me concerning possible publication.

Melvin Powers
12015 Sherman Road
North Hollywood, California 91605

(818) 765-8579

MELVIN POWERS SELF-IMPROVEMENT LIBRARY

ASTROLOGY

BRIDGE

BUSINESS, STUDY & REFERENCE

CALLIGRAPHY

CHESS & CHECKERS

____ CHESS TACTICS FOR BEGINNERS Edited by Fred Reinfeld 7.00
____ HOW TO WIN AT CHECKERS Fred Reinfeld 5.00
____ 1001 BRILLIANT WAYS TO CHECKMATE Fred Reinfeld 10.00
____ 1001 WINNING CHESS SACRIFICES & COMBINATIONS Fred Reinfeld 10.00

COOKERY & HERBS
____ CULPEPER'S HERBAL REMEDIES Dr. Nicholas Culpeper 5.00
____ FAST GOURMET COOKBOOK Poppy Cannon 2.50
____ HEALING POWER OF HERBS May Bethel 5.00
____ HEALING POWER OF NATURAL FOODS May Bethel 7.00
____ HERBS FOR HEALTH—HOW TO GROW & USE THEM Louise Evans Doole 7.00
____ HOME GARDEN COOKBOOK—DELICIOUS NATURAL FOOD RECIPES Ken Kraft 3.00
____ MEATLESS MEAL GUIDE Tomi Ryan & James H. Ryan, M.D. 4.00
____ VEGETABLE GARDENING FOR BEGINNERS Hugh Wilberg 2.00
____ VEGETABLES FOR TODAY'S GARDENS R. Milton Carleton 2.00
____ VEGETARIAN COOKERY Janet Walker 10.00
____ VEGETARIAN COOKING MADE EASY & DELECTABLE Veronica Vezza 3.00

GAMBLING & POKER
____ HOW TO WIN AT POKER Terence Reese & Anthony T. Watkins 7.00
____ SCARNE ON DICE John Scarne 15.00
____ WINNING AT CRAPS Dr. Lloyd T. Commins 5.00
____ WINNING AT GIN Chester Wander & Cy Rice 3.00
____ WINNING AT POKER—AN EXPERT'S GUIDE John Archer 10.00
____ WINNING AT 21—AN EXPERT'S GUIDE John Archer 10.00

HEALTH
____ BEE POLLEN Lynda Lyngheim & Jack Scagnetti 5.00
____ COPING WITH ALZHEIMER'S Rose Oliver, Ph.D. & Francis Bock, Ph.D. 10.00
____ DR. LINDNER'S POINT SYSTEM FOOD PROGRAM Peter G Lindner, M.D. 2.00
____ HELP YOURSELF TO BETTER SIGHT Margaret Darst Corbett 7.00
____ HOW YOU CAN STOP SMOKING PERMANENTLY Ernest Caldwell 5.00
____ MIND OVER PLATTER Peter G Lindner, M.D. 5.00
____ NATURE'S WAY TO NUTRITION & VIBRANT HEALTH Robert J. Scrutton 3.00
____ NEW CARBOHYDRATE DIET COUNTER Patti Lopez-Pereira 2.00
____ REFLEXOLOGY Dr. Maybelle Segal 5.00
____ REFLEXOLOGY FOR GOOD HEALTH Anna Kaye & Don C. Matchan 7.00
____ 30 DAYS TO BEAUTIFUL LEGS Dr. Marc Selner 3.00
____ WONDER WITHIN Thomas S. Coyle, M.D. 10.00
____ YOU CAN LEARN TO RELAX Dr. Samuel Gutwirth 5.00

HOBBIES
____ BEACHCOMBING FOR BEGINNERS Norman Hickin 2.00
____ BLACKSTONE'S MODERN CARD TRICKS Harry Blackstone 7.00
____ BLACKSTONE'S SECRETS OF MAGIC Harry Blackstone 7.00
____ COIN COLLECTING FOR BEGINNERS Burton Hobson & Fred Reinfeld 7.00
____ ENTERTAINING WITH ESP Tony 'Doc' Shiels 2.00
____ 400 FASCINATING MAGIC TRICKS YOU CAN DO Howard Thurston 7.00
____ HOW I TURN JUNK INTO FUN AND PROFIT Sari 3.00
____ HOW TO WRITE A HIT SONG AND SELL IT Tommy Boyce 10.00
____ MAGIC FOR ALL AGES Walter Gibson 7.00
____ STAMP COLLECTING FOR BEGINNERS Burton Hobson 3.00

HORSE PLAYER'S WINNING GUIDES
____ BETTING HORSES TO WIN Les Conklin 7.00
____ ELIMINATE THE LOSERS Bob McKnight 5.00
____ HOW TO PICK WINNING HORSES Bob McKnight 5.00
____ HOW TO WIN AT THE RACES Sam (The Genius) Lewin 5.00
____ HOW YOU CAN BEAT THE RACES Jack Kavanagh 5.00

_____ MAKING MONEY AT THE RACES David Barr 7.00
_____ PAYDAY AT THE RACES Les Conklin 7.00
_____ SMART HANDICAPPING MADE EASY William Bauman 5.00
_____ SUCCESS AT THE HARNESS RACES Barry Meadow 7.00

HUMOR

_____ HOW TO FLATTEN YOUR TUSH Coach Marge Reardon 2.00
_____ JOKE TELLER'S HANDBOOK Bob Orben 7.00
_____ JOKES FOR ALL OCCASIONS Al Schock 7.00
_____ 2,000 NEW LAUGHS FOR SPEAKERS Bob Orben 7.00
_____ 2,400 JOKES TO BRIGHTEN YOUR SPEECHES Robert Orben 7.00
_____ 2,500 JOKES TO START'EM LAUGHING Bob Orben 10.00

HYPNOTISM

_____ CHILDBIRTH WITH HYPNOSIS William S. Kroger, M.D. 5.00
_____ HOW TO SOLVE YOUR SEX PROBLEMS WITH SELF-HYPNOSIS Frank Caprio, M.D. . . 5.00
_____ HOW YOU CAN BOWL BETTER USING SELF-HYPNOSIS Jack Heise 7.00
_____ HOW YOU CAN PLAY BETTER GOLF USING SELF-HYPNOSIS Jack Heise 3.00
_____ HYPNOSIS AND SELF-HYPNOSIS Bernard Hollander, M.D. 7.00
_____ HYPNOTISM (Originally published 1893) Carl Sextus 5.00
_____ HYPNOTISM MADE EASY Dr. Ralph Winn 7.00
_____ HYPNOTISM MADE PRACTICAL Louis Orton 5.00
_____ HYPNOTISM REVEALED Melvin Powers 3.00
_____ HYPNOTISM TODAY Leslie LeCron & Jean Bordeaux, Ph.D. 5.00
_____ MODERN HYPNOSIS Lesley Kuhn & Salvatore Russo, Ph.D. 5.00
_____ NEW CONCEPTS OF HYPNOSIS Bernard C. Gindes, M.D. 10.00
_____ NEW SELF-HYPNOSIS Paul Adams 10.00
_____ POST-HYPNOTIC INSTRUCTIONS—SUGGESTIONS FOR THERAPY Arnold Furst . . . 10.00
_____ PRACTICAL GUIDE TO SELF-HYPNOSIS Melvin Powers 5.00
_____ PRACTICAL HYPNOTISM Philip Magonet, M.D. 3.00
_____ SECRETS OF HYPNOTISM S.J. Van Pelt, M.D. 5.00
_____ SELF-HYPNOSIS—A CONDITIONED-RESPONSE TECHNIQUE Laurence Sparks 7.00
_____ SELF-HYPNOSIS—ITS THEORY, TECHNIQUE & APPLICATION Melvin Powers 7.00
_____ THERAPY THROUGH HYPNOSIS Edited by Raphael H. Rhodes 5.00

JUDAICA

_____ SERVICE OF THE HEART Evelyn Garfiel, Ph.D. 10.00
_____ STORY OF ISRAEL IN COINS Jean & Maurice Gould 2.00
_____ STORY OF ISRAEL IN STAMPS Maxim & Gabriel Shamir 1.00
_____ TONGUE OF THE PROPHETS Robert St. John 10.00

JUST FOR WOMEN

_____ COSMOPOLITAN'S GUIDE TO MARVELOUS MEN Foreword by Helen Gurley Brown . . 3.00
_____ COSMOPOLITAN'S HANG-UP HANDBOOK Foreword by Helen Gurley Brown 4.00
_____ COSMOPOLITAN'S LOVE BOOK—A GUIDE TO ECSTASY IN BED 7.00
_____ COSMOPOLITAN'S NEW ETIQUETTE GUIDE Foreword by Helen Gurley Brown 4.00
_____ I AM A COMPLEAT WOMAN Doris Hagopian & Karen O'Connor Sweeney 3.00
_____ JUST FOR WOMEN—A GUIDE TO THE FEMALE BODY Richard E. Sand M.D. 5.00
_____ NEW APPROACHES TO SEX IN MARRIAGE John E. Eichenlaub, M.D. 3.00
_____ SEXUALLY ADEQUATE FEMALE Frank S. Caprio, M.D. 3.00
_____ SEXUALLY FULFILLED WOMAN Dr. Rachel Copelan 5.00

MARRIAGE, SEX & PARENTHOOD

_____ ABILITY TO LOVE Dr. Allan Fromme 7.00
_____ GUIDE TO SUCCESSFUL MARRIAGE Drs. Albert Ellis & Robert Harper 7.00
_____ HOW TO RAISE AN EMOTIONALLY HEALTHY, HAPPY CHILD Albert Ellis, Ph.D. .. 10.00
_____ PARENT SURVIVAL TRAINING Marvin Silverman, Ed.D. & David Lustig, Ph.D. 10.00
_____ SEX WITHOUT GUILT Albert Ellis, Ph.D. 7.00
_____ SEXUALLY ADEQUATE MALE Frank S. Caprio, M.D. 3.00

_____ SEXUALLY FULFILLED MAN Dr. Rachel Copelan 5.00
_____ STAYING IN LOVE Dr. Norton F. Kristy 7.00

MELVIN POWERS'S MAIL ORDER LIBRARY
_____ HOW TO GET RICH IN MAIL ORDER Melvin Powers 20.00
_____ HOW TO SELF-PUBLISH YOUR BOOK Melvin Powers 20.00
_____ HOW TO WRITE A GOOD ADVERTISEMENT Victor O. Schwab 20.00
_____ MAIL ORDER MADE EASY J. Frank Brumbaugh 20.00
_____ MAKING MONEY WITH CLASSIFIED ADS Melvin Powers 20.00

METAPHYSICS & OCCULT
_____ CONCENTRATION—A GUIDE TO MENTAL MASTERY Mouni Sadhu 7.00
_____ EXTRA-TERRESTRIAL INTELLIGENCE—THE FIRST ENCOUNTER 6.00
_____ FORTUNE TELLING WITH CARDS P. Foli 5.00
_____ HOW TO INTERPRET DREAMS, OMENS & FORTUNE TELLING SIGNS Gettings 5.00
_____ HOW TO UNDERSTAND YOUR DREAMS Geoffrey A. Dudley 7.00
_____ MAGICIAN—HIS TRAINING AND WORK W.E. Butler 7.00
_____ MEDITATION Mouni Sadhu 10.00
_____ MODERN NUMEROLOGY Morris C. Goodman 5.00
_____ NUMEROLOGY—ITS FACTS AND SECRETS Ariel Yvon Taylor 5.00
_____ NUMEROLOGY MADE EASY W. Mykian 5.00
_____ PALMISTRY MADE EASY Fred Gettings 5.00
_____ PALMISTRY MADE PRACTICAL Elizabeth Daniels Squire 7.00
_____ PROPHECY IN OUR TIME Martin Ebon 2.50
_____ SUPERSTITION—ARE YOU SUPERSTITIOUS? Eric Maple 2.00
_____ TAROT Mouni Sadhu 10.00
_____ TAROT OF THE BOHEMIANS Papus 10.00
_____ WAYS TO SELF-REALIZATION Mouni Sadhu 7.00
_____ WITCHCRAFT, MAGIC & OCCULTISM—A FASCINATING HISTORY W.B. Crow 10.00
_____ WITCHCRAFT—THE SIXTH SENSE Justine Glass 7.00

RECOVERY
_____ KNIGHT IN RUSTY ARMOR Robert Fisher 5.00
_____ KNIGHT IN RUSTY ARMOR (Hard cover edition) Robert Fisher 10.00
_____ KNIGHTS WITHOUT ARMOR (Hard cover edition) Aaron R. Kipnis, Ph.D. 10.00
_____ PRINCESS WHO BELIEVED IN FAIRY TALES Marcia Grad 10.00

SELF-HELP & INSPIRATIONAL
_____ CHARISMA—HOW TO GET "THAT SPECIAL MAGIC" Marcia Grad 10.00
_____ DAILY POWER FOR JOYFUL LIVING Dr. Donald Curtis 7.00
_____ DYNAMIC THINKING Melvin Powers 5.00
_____ GREATEST POWER IN THE UNIVERSE U.S. Andersen 10.00
_____ GROW RICH WHILE YOU SLEEP Ben Sweetland 10.00
_____ GROW RICH WITH YOUR MILLION DOLLAR MIND Brian Adams 7.00
_____ GROWTH THROUGH REASON Albert Ellis, Ph.D. 10.00
_____ GUIDE TO PERSONAL HAPPINESS Albert Ellis, Ph.D. & Irving Becker, Ed.D. ... 10.00
_____ HANDWRITING ANALYSIS MADE EASY John Marley 10.00
_____ HANDWRITING TELLS Nadya Olyanova 7.00
_____ HOW TO ATTRACT GOOD LUCK A.H.Z. Carr 7.00
_____ HOW TO DEVELOP A WINNING PERSONALITY Martin Panzer 7.00
_____ HOW TO DEVELOP AN EXCEPTIONAL MEMORY Young & Gibson 10.00
_____ HOW TO LIVE WITH A NEUROTIC Albert Ellis, Ph.D. 10.00
_____ HOW TO OVERCOME YOUR FEARS M.P. Leahy, M.D. 3.00
_____ HOW TO SUCCEED Brian Adams 7.00
_____ HUMAN PROBLEMS & HOW TO SOLVE THEM Dr. Donald Curtis 5.00
_____ I CAN Ben Sweetland 8.00
_____ I WILL Ben Sweetland 10.00
_____ KNIGHT IN RUSTY ARMOR Robert Fisher 5.00
_____ KNIGHT IN RUSTY ARMOR (Hard Cover) Robert Fisher 10.00

_____ LEFT-HANDED PEOPLE Michael Barsley 5.00
_____ MAGIC IN YOUR MIND U.S. Andersen 10.00
_____ MAGIC OF THINKING SUCCESS Dr. David J. Schwartz 8.00
_____ MAGIC POWER OF YOUR MIND Walter M. Germain 10.00
_____ MENTAL POWER THROUGH SLEEP SUGGESTION Melvin Powers 3.00
_____ NEVER UNDERESTIMATE THE SELLING POWER OF A WOMAN Dottie Walters 7.00
_____ NEW GUIDE TO RATIONAL LIVING Albert Ellis, Ph.D. & R. Harper, Ph.D. 10.00
_____ PRINCESS WHO BELIEVED IN FAIRY TALES Marcia Grad 10.00
_____ PSYCHO-CYBERNETICS Maxwell Maltz, M.D. 10.00
_____ PSYCHOLOGY OF HANDWRITING Nadya Olyanova 7.00
_____ SALES CYBERNETICS Brian Adams 10.00
_____ SCIENCE OF MIND IN DAILY LIVING Dr. Donald Curtis 7.00
_____ SECRET OF SECRETS U.S. Andersen 7.00
_____ SECRET POWER OF THE PYRAMIDS U.S. Andersen 7.00
_____ SELF-THERAPY FOR THE STUTTERER Malcolm Frazer 3.00
_____ SUCCESS CYBERNETICS U.S. Andersen 7.00
_____ 10 DAYS TO A GREAT NEW LIFE William E. Edwards 3.00
_____ THINK AND GROW RICH Napoleon Hill 10.00
_____ THINK LIKE A WINNER Walter Doyle Staples, Ph.D. 10.00
_____ THREE MAGIC WORDS U.S. Andersen 10.00
_____ TREASURY OF COMFORT Edited by Rabbi Sidney Greenberg 10.00
_____ TREASURY OF THE ART OF LIVING Sidney S. Greenberg 10.00
_____ WHAT YOUR HANDWRITING REVEALS Albert E. Hughes 4.00
_____ WONDER WITHIN Thomas F. Coyle, M.D. 10.00
_____ YOUR SUBCONSCIOUS POWER Charles M. Simmons 7.00
_____ YOUR THOUGHTS CAN CHANGE YOUR LIFE Dr. Donald Curtis 7.00

SPORTS
_____ BILLIARDS—POCKET • CAROM • THREE CUSHION Clive Cottingham, Jr. 7.00
_____ COMPLETE GUIDE TO FISHING Vlad Evanoff 2.00
_____ HOW TO IMPROVE YOUR RACQUETBALL Lubarsky, Kaufman & Scagnetti 5.00
_____ HOW TO WIN AT POCKET BILLIARDS Edward D. Knuchell 10.00
_____ JOY OF WALKING Jack Scagnetti 3.00
_____ LEARNING & TEACHING SOCCER SKILLS Eric Worthington 3.00
_____ RACQUETBALL FOR WOMEN Toni Hudson, Jack Scagnetti & Vince Rondone 3.00
_____ SECRET OF BOWLING STRIKES Dawson Taylor 5.00
_____ SOCCER—THE GAME & HOW TO PLAY IT Gary Rosenthal 7.00
_____ STARTING SOCCER Edward F Dolan, Jr. 5.00

TENNIS LOVER'S LIBRARY
_____ HOW TO BEAT BETTER TENNIS PLAYERS Loring Fiske 4.00
_____ PSYCH YOURSELF TO BETTER TENNIS Dr. Walter A. Luszki 2.00
_____ TENNIS FOR BEGINNERS Dr. H.A. Murray 2.00
_____ TENNIS MADE EASY Joel Brecheen 5.00
_____ WEEKEND TENNIS—HOW TO HAVE FUN & WIN AT THE SAME TIME Bill Talbert ... 3.00

WILSHIRE PET LIBRARY
_____ DOG TRAINING MADE EASY & FUN John W. Kellogg 5.00
_____ HOW TO BRING UP YOUR PET DOG Kurt Unkelbach 2.00
_____ HOW TO RAISE & TRAIN YOUR PUPPY Jeff Griffen 5.00

The books listed above can be obtained from your book dealer or directly from Melvin Powers.
When ordering, please remit $2.00 postage for the first book and $1.00 for each additional book.

Melvin Powers
12015 Sherman Road, No. Hollywood, California 91605

WILSHIRE HORSE LOVERS' LIBRARY

The books listed above can be obtained from your book dealer or directly from Melvin Powers. When ordering, please remit $2.00 postage for the first book and $1.00 for each additional book.

Melvin Powers
12015 Sherman Road, No. Hollywood, California 91605

Notes